METAPHYSICS AND AESTHETICS
IN THE WORKS
OF EDUARDO BARRIOS

JOHN WALKER

METAPHYSICS AND AESTHETICS
IN THE WORKS
OF EDUARDO BARRIOS

TAMESIS BOOKS LIMITED
LONDON

Colección Támesis
SERIE A - MONOGRAFIAS, XCV

© Copyright by Tamesis Books Limited
London, 1983
ISBN 0 7293 0160 5

Depósito legal: M. 40856-1983

Printed in Spain by Talleres Gráficos de SELECCIONES GRÁFICAS
Carretera de Irún, km. 11,500 - Madrid-34

for
TAMESIS BOOKS LIMITED
LONDON

To

James and Clare and John

CONTENTS

This book has been published with the help of a grant from the Canadian Federation for the Humanities, using funds provided by the Social Sciences and Humanities Research Council of Canada.

PREFACE

I have not attempted in this study to write a critical biography nor a Life and Works *of Eduardo Barrios. Biographical data on Barrios can be found in the various general studies on the writer listed in the Bibliography. I have, of course, had cause to make reference to his life throughout this study in so far as it is connected with the topics under discussion. Nor have I undertaken a socio-economic or political analysis of Chile in the twentieth century. Since, however, any work of art is somehow a manifestation of the vital sensibility of the people in that area at that time, Barrios' work will reflect something of the social, economic and political conditions in Chile during that period. They are subservient, of course, to the real concerns of Barrios, metaphysics and aesthetics, the treatment of which is the aim of this particular study.*

Now revised and expanded, some of the material contained in several chapters of this work originally appeared as part of individual articles in the following journals: The Romanic Review, International Fiction Review, Revista Canadiense de Estudios Hispánicos, Ibero-Amerikanisches Archiv, Revista de Estudios Hispánicos, Bulletin of Hispanic Studies, Mosaic, The American Hispanist. *I am grateful to the editors of these journals for their kind permission to use and reproduce this material.*

For his initial inspiration and long-standing influence, I am also grateful to Professor Donald Shaw, now University of Edinburgh, who first revealed to me many years ago in Glasgow the «joys» of angustia, *both in its Romantic and Modernist guise, and who introduced me to the heart-centred world of Eduardo Barrios, peopled by* locos, abúlicos *and* perdidos—*and much more, as I shall demonstrate.*

For her valuable secretarial help in the preparation of this manuscript, I am indebted to Eleanor Smith. I should also like to thank my wife Irene for her patient and careful reading of manuscript and proofs, and for her constant support.

J. W.

Queen's University,
Kingston,
Canada.

REFERENCES

Throughout this work page references to Barrios' works are to the two-volume *Obras completas* (Santiago: Zig-Zag, 1962), unless otherwise stated. Whenever convenient and/or necessary, I have used in references the following abbreviations of the titles listed below:

OC	*Obras completas*
DL	*Del natural*
TL	«Tirana ley»
EN	*El niño que enloqueció de amor*
UP	*Un perdido*
HA	*El hermano asno*
PAG	*Páginas de un pobre diablo*
También	«También algo de mí»
TAM	*Tamarugal*
GS	*Gran señor y rajadiablos*
HH	*Los hombres del hombre*

Thus a typical reference to a novel under discussion might be I, 181; to an unnamed novel it might be GS II, 843.

CHAPTER 1

THE LITERARY SITUATION

Eduardo Barrios, one of the neglected masters of Chilean and Latin American fiction, is generally defined as a «psychological» novelist. Following the lead of the older generation of traditional critics like Torres-Ríoseco, Jefferson Rea Spell and Raúl Silva Castro, more recent scholars like Ned Davison and Vázquez-Bigi have concentrated on the «psychological values» and «psychological truth» in Barrios' work.[1] In fact, Vázquez-Bigi's findings are so medically oriented that his thesis would have much merit in the field of psychiatry. In the light of the doctoral research of both these critics perhaps the word that best comes to mind to describe this aspect of Barrios' work is «analytical».[2] Milton Rossel, a Chilean scholar and friend of Barrios, uses Ortega y Gasset's definition to characterise the novels of Barrios—«el imperativo de la novela es la autopsia». According to Rossel, «la peculiaridad más distintiva de Barrios es la disección que hace en sus novelas del alma humana».[3]

This aspect of Barrios' work is an important part of his literary development and I accept its validity in the framework of the research of the critics cited above. Eduardo Barrios was undoubtedly an analytical writer who, with penetrating studies, has revealed the mysteries of the different passions in men's souls. He was equally adept at portraying the character

[1] See the doctoral thesis titles of both scholars: NED J. DAVISON, «Psychological Values in the Works of Eduardo Barrios», University of California, Los Angeles, 1957; ANGEL MANUEL VÁZQUEZ-BIGI, «La verdad sicológica en Eduardo Barrios», University of Minnesota, 1962.

[2] Both Davison and Vázquez-Bigi justify their use of the term «psychological», Davison basing his usage on the generally accepted vague notion of what constitutes a «psychological novel»: «the characteristic oneness of Barrios' protagonists is undoubtedly the result of his interior rather than exterior search for human reality» (Thesis, pp. 11-12). Vázquez-Bigi, whilst admitting that the meaning of the term «psychological», like that of any other concept of literary criticism, depends upon the user, tends to agree with Anderson Imbert's definition of Barrios' literary technique as «subjective» rather than «psychological» (Thesis, p. 23).

[3] In his introduction «Eduardo Barrios, el hombre y su obra», to *Obras completas de Eduardo Barrios*, 2 vols. (Santiago: Ed. Zig-Zag, 1962), p. 9. It is interesting, to say the least, that Rossel leans rather heavily on the theories of the German scholar Ernst Kretschmer, especially his *Constitución y carácter*, which are central to Vázquez-Bigi's thesis.

1

of his literary creations and showing the link between their behaviour, their physical constitution, their environment, and heredity. However, in their eagerness to highlight this aspect of Barrios' work, many critics have paid less attention to other praiseworthy facets of his literary achievement.[4]

The value of Barrios as a writer is not just restricted to his portrayal of abnormal types—madmen, abulics, pariahs, alcoholics and the sexually repressed. Literature, furthermore, is based on more than defective genes, the class struggle and the law of evolution. Manuel Gálvez, a novelist in his own right, described it accurately: «Yo creo que lo esencial en un novelista es su visión de la vida.» It is highly appropriate that the remark was made in the prologue to Barrios' *Un perdido*.[5] I should like to stress, therefore, that below the surface of the apparent themes of Barrios' novels—sexual repression, excessive sentimentality, childish abnormality, etc.—lies the more important philosophical commentary. Beyond the apparent *novela de la ciudad (Un perdido)*, beyond the apparent *novela de la tierra (Gran señor y rajadiablos)*, beyond the apparent *novela minera (Tamarugal)* and so on, is something more important that transcends regional and national frontiers—Barrios' view of the world, a changing view that is manifested in the progression of his novels. What I shall stress in this study, rather than the valid and proven psychological values, are the metaphysical truths that emerge from the underlying philosophical commentary.

Related to the metaphysics of Barrios' fiction, and inextricably bound up with it, is the question of aesthetics. So much attention has been paid to the analytical qualities of Barrios' prose that many critics have underestimated Barrios' aesthetic achievements—apart from token references to Barrios as a stylist. This is all the more surprising given Barrios' own preoccupation with defining his art, the role of the artist, and his own position vis-à-vis aesthetic movements and organisations—without taking into account his grave concern for style, language and form. I shall also demonstrate that this metaphysical preoccupation, rather than vitiating the artistic side, accentuates the role of aesthetics. In fact, I shall go as far as to state that

---

[4] Two of the exceptions are Ned J. Davison and Joel C. Hancock. Throughout this work I shall be referring to Davison's articles of the 1960s which, along with his dissertation, provide the basis of the material incorporated in his *Eduardo Barrios* (New York: Twayne, 1970). Despite the known intent and format of the Twayne series (popular orientation, for uninitiated readers), Davison, given the limitation of the series, has many useful comments to make on matters philosophical and stylistic.

Stylistics, especially as applied to Barrios' last novel, *Los hombres del hombre*, is also the concern of JOEL C. HANCOCK in «Compositional Modes of Eduardo Barrios' *Los hombres del hombre* with an Appended Bibliography of his Uncollected Prose», unpublished doctoral dissertation, University of New Mexico, 1970. Reference to this thesis and to Hancock's articles on Barrios' prose style will be made throughout this work.

[5] Madrid: Espasa-Calpe, 1926, 2 vols, pp. 9-13, and reproduced in Zig-Zag edition (Santiago, 1965), pp. 7-9.

2

metaphysics and aesthetics are closely bound up in a complementary way; that art has a role to play in Barrios' work and his view of the world; and conversely that forces like emotion and religion help to mould his philosophy. In other words, it is difficult to divide the fiction of Barrios into content and form, since both interact and influence each other. The very qualities that he uses as a force in his metaphysical view of the world constitute the vehicle by which he produces these forces, e.g. emotion, religion and art.

It is in this sense that one can say that Eduardo Barrios, long regarded as a master in the field of the psychological novel, is also worthy of praise for his metaphysical novels which have been written with a demonstrable concern for aesthetics.

AN ARTISTIC PARADOX

Barrios, it has been generally admitted, has not received just recognition in literary circles.[6] In spite of having written exceptional individual novels like «El niño que enloqueció de amor», *El hermano asno* and *Gran señor y rajadiablos,* which were all well received, Barrios has never achieved the fame of lesser contemporaries. The only full-length studies in recent times have been produced in North America—the solid «psychological» disserta-tions of Vázquez-Bigi and Davison (precursor of his Twayne *Eduardo Barrios*), and the Hancock dissertation already mentioned. Other critics, who have devoted their time and energy to his work, have written either superficial biographical studies, reiterating the oft-quoted platitudes on Eduardo Barrios as a psychological writer, or concentrating on the auto-biographical elements in the works of Eduardo Barrios.[7] Even Chilean scholars like Torres-Ríoseco, Silva Castro, and Milton Rossel, have never done Barrios complete justice, underestimating the universal qualities in his work.[8] In spite of a powerful early trilogy like *El niño que enloqueció de*

[6] Vázquez-Bigi, in his thesis, postulates various theories for the neglect of Barrios. The general ignorance (in other continents) about things Latin American militated against Barrios. A non-Latin American, looking for refined, psychological literature, did not expect to find it in the barbaric continent of the South. On the other hand, those in search of the exotic and the erotic, will find little to their taste in Barrios' works. Also, there is the general feeling that great literature (of universal application) cannot come from small countries like Chile — in spite of the example of Pablo Neruda and, even more striking from the point of view of size, Rubén Darío from Nicaragua and Miguel Angel Asturias from Guatemala.

[7] e.g. JOSÉ ANTONIO GALAOS, «Eduardo Barrios. Novelista autobiográfico», *Cuadernos Hispanoamericanos,* LVI, No. 166 (octubre, 1963), 160-74.

[8] Torres-Ríoseco, although he did a great deal of pioneer critical work not only on Barrios but on Latin American literature in general (for which we are indebted to him), does not always grasp the total significance of Barrios' novels, e.g. *Un perdido* (whose American qualities he stresses) and *Gran señor y rajadiablos* (see my treatment in Chapter 3). Without belitting the efforts of the older school of critics, one should

amor, Un perdido and *El hermano asno,* Barrios is perhaps the most neglected of the so-called «traditional» novelists.[9] Apart from the reasons offered by Vázquez-Bigi (see note 6) for the poor reception of Barrios, a few others spring to mind.

One of the reasons for his lack of esteem is that Barrios, who is so difficult to label, can hardly be identified with any of the so-called regional or *indigenista* novelists of the 1920s and 1930s, nor does he appear to fit any of the conventional patterns. This accounts partly for the difficulty in assessing his worth as a writer in comparative terms. By a dubious piece of deductive work on the part of some critics, if Barrios cannot be slotted into the novel of the land, then by reverse logic his fiction must belong to the other main category, simplistically labelled the novel of the city, merely by default. On the strength of the diaphanous «El niño que enloqueció de amor» and *El hermano asno* Barrios could hardly be classified as a novelist of the city. *Un perdido,* however, by analogy with Manuel Gálvez' *El mal metafísico* (1916), another analytical novel, dealing with the metaphysical problems of an unhappy protagonist living amongst a bohemian group in Buenos Aires, might well deserve the label. The question that has now to be posed is: which city? Barrios' novels, in spite of the efforts of critics to fit them into the *criollo* stream, tend to be more universal than American, or even Chilean. Notwithstanding the claims of Torres-Ríoseco, in his categorisation of «traditional» fiction, *El niño que enloqueció de amor* and *El hermano asno* have little that is typically Chilean or Latin American about them. This perhaps accounts for their lack of total acceptance at a time when regionalism was such an important criterion for success. Barrios does not have the same popularist appeal as his fellow-Chilean, Manuel Rojas who, although moving out of *criollismo* towards cosmopolitanism in his fiction, never leaves his proletarian background too far behind in his characterisation and portrayal of atmosphere. Nor does Barrios try to appeal to the masses by vitiating language to obtain effects of local colour. Compared to the bad grammar and coarse language of Icaza in Ecuador, for example, Eduardo Barrios maintains a pure attitude to prose that is almost Castilian in its essence. Praising the «castizas sonoridades y clásica

be aware that Torres-Ríoseco, Spell and others, who made valuable contributions to the field of narrative, plot and characterisation, did not always appear to see the deeper meaning and the hidden implications below the surface of the novel. Torres-Ríoseco is further handicapped by his tendency to see *lo americano* in everything Barrios does. See his *Grandes novelistas de la América Hispana,* Vol. II (Berkeley: University of California Press, 1949), p. 57.

[9] The year 1939 marks the publication of JUAN CARLOS ONETTI's *El pozo,* perhaps a valid point of departure. This division, which is purely arbitrary, is one of convenience and is not meant to be totally binding. There are obvious exceptions that transcend the boundaries of time and genre. It is interesting that Ciro Alegría did not publish his prize-winning *indigenista* novel *El mundo es ancho y ajeno* till 1941 — an obvious anachronism, but justified by the prevailing conditions in Peru and the social and political motives which prompted the writing of the novel.

limpieza»[10] of Spanish peninsular writers, he lamented the depths to which Chilean prose had fallen: «Suele faltar en nuestras prosas esa nobleza lingüística.»[11] Barrios was opposed to all abuses of language whether it be in «las adaptaciones francesas» or «el pauperismo indiano». He had little patience with young writers because of their disregard for the Spanish dictionary and grammar. In general, Barrios was not prepared to court cheap popularity by distorting the language, nor did he jump on the regionalist band-waggon. In fact, he almost seemed to be going against the current by following the European type of novel when all around were abandoning it. This attitude probably did not endear him to the Latin American reading public nor to the critics who seemed to be unaware that they had a rarity in their presence—a Latin American writer who treated lasting, universal themes, who dealt with problems that beset man, not just American man.

The great pity, then, and one of the reasons for his lack of popularity, is that Eduardo Barrios was not fully understood in his time because he did not fit into the mould of those around him. As Vázquez-Bigi in particular has pointed out, Barrios was formulating intuitively as early as 1907 in «Tirana Ley», but especially in the first trilogy of 1915-22, ideas that were to be the stuff of later novels based on Freudian analysis—at a time when Freud's theories were not generally widespread, and certainly not in Latin America. In this sense Barrios was ahead of his time and not appreciated by those who still viewed literature in terms of traditional criteria. This helps to account for the misunderstanding of El hermano asno and the furore it caused when published in 1922. Most people saw it simply as an attack on conventional religion, orthodox Catholicism and the Franciscan order.

Paradoxically, Barrios, who seemed ahead of his time with the first great trilogy, did not hesitate to go against the stream and write occasionally what appeared to be anachronisms. In 1944 he published Tamarugal, ostensibly a novela minera, and in 1948 Gran señor y rajadiablos, at first glance a rural novel of nineteenth-century Chile. On its superficial level Gran señor y rajadiablos would have been a resounding success if it had appeared in the 1920s contemporaneous with Don Segundo Sombra, La vorágine and Doña Bárbara, and Barrios would have been accepted as yet another novelist of the land. Ironically, it was a huge popular success (as a novela criolla written out of its time), which highlights the lack of understanding. Though American, it was much more, as I shall demonstrate in Chapter 3. So too with Tamarugal, which looks so much like the Zolaesque novel of the first decade of the century, superficially similar to

---

[10] Review «Balmaceda: político romántico por Luis Enrique Delano», Las Ultimas Noticias, XXXV (7 de julio, 1937), 5.
[11] Review «El hombre en la montaña por Edgardo Garrido Merino», Las Ultimas Noticias, XXXII (23 de mayo, 1934), 12.

the short stories of Baldomero Lillo's *Sub terra,* which portrayed the miserable life of the exploited, abused Chilean miners. *Tamarugal* did not achieve the same success partly because it was poorly written and also because there is nothing romantic or escapist about underground slavery. *Tamarugal,* however, is important for other reasons that we shall see also in Chapter 3.

Another reason for the lack of appreciation of the fiction of Eduardo Barrios is that Latin Americans have so often read their novels as documents of social protest and political abuse that they have neglected the philosophical content and ignored the aesthetic level of these works. José Antonio Portuondo has expressed it thus: «El carácter dominante en la tradición novelística hispanoamericana [es] la preocupación social, la actitud criticista que manifiestan las obras, su función instrumental en el proceso histórico de las naciones respectivas... Grave consecuencia del sentido instrumental, pragmático, dominante... en la mayor parte de las novelas hispanoamericanas, es que la crítica se ha acostumbrado a tratarlas como documentos y no como obras de arte, desdeñando lo estético para destacar sólo lo sociológico en ellas.»[12]

Given the concern expressed in the 1920s and 1930s for the land, indigenous problems, and social protest, the modern reader can only agree with Barrios' own assessment that he was out of tune with the times. The prevailing outlook could be significant in helping to explain his twenty-year silence during these very decades. Critics have sought to see in his quiet period many reasons for his non-production—lack of inspiration, the completion of his literary mission, the need to gather more material, to gain more experience, to philosophise more about life. One critic applies to Barrios the words of the protagonist of his last novel, *Los hombres del hombre* (1950), to explain his silence: «Ha de haber por la tierra no pocos escritores como yo, que por muchos años no escriben y, de buenas a primeras, lo necesitan y lo hacen.»[13]

No one has suggested literary or political disillusionment, with its concomitant disengagement. However, although Barrios wrote *Tamarugal* about the life of the nitrate miners, he in no way intended it to be *literatura comprometida.* Barrios had little sympathy with the plight of the workers and no intention to write a work of social protest. A noted conservative, even reactionary, Barrios was openly anti-communist, anti-Russian and pro-U.S.A. He had scant respect for Chilean communist writers who, he felt, were using communism for their own ends.[14] When he did break the

---

[12] «El rasgo predominante en la novela hispanoamericana», *La novela iberoamericana* (Albuquerque: University of New Mexico Press, 1952), pp. 84-85.

[13] DONALD FOGELQUIST, «Eduardo Barrios, en su etapa actual», *Revista Iberoamericana,* XVIII, No. 35 (1952), 13-26. See OC II, 990.

[14] BERNARD DULSEY, «A Visit with Eduardo Barrios», *Modern Language Journal,* XLIII (November, 1959), 349.

silence it was to write a *novela minera* in reverse. Whatever the reason for his previous silence, he chose to turn again to writing in the 1940s when the atmosphere, with the passing of the traditional novel of the land and the Indian novel of social protest, was more conducive to his approach. Paradoxically, in the rarefied atmosphere of the first days of composition of the new novel, he reverted to a format and genre typical of the turn of the century. As always, the novel was accepted at its face value. However, as I shall demonstrate in Chapter 3, this regional plane constitutes only one level of the work. Choosing material, background and an era that he knew well, he was able to make a philosophical comment about life that was not immediately obvious to the reading public. Also, since it was anachronistic, there was no political backlash or involvement. Unfortunately, being poorly written, the novel had little impact either on the public or the critics. Once again, as in the 1920s, Barrios, apparently out of step, was misunderstood. Though *Gran señor y rajadiablos,* written four years later (1948) was a best-seller, it too was not fully appreciated, being in the style of two decades earlier. The appearance of *Los hombres del hombre* two years later (1950) did little to increase his popularity, since it was a difficult novel, containing something of the analytical qualities of the early trilogy, and yet not quite in the mainstream of the new novels of the late 1940s and early 1950s. However, as we shall see in the Conclusion of this study, Barrios was, in this last novel, in advance of his era, using techniques and ideas that prefigured the new novelists of the next two decades.

Apart from his anomalous position in time as a writer in Latin America, i.e. sometimes anachronistic, sometimes advanced, Barrios also stands out as a rarity because of the kind of writer he was. Latin America has always been short of philosophical writers,[15] and therein lies one of the tragedies not only for the continent but also for writers like Barrios who, apart from Mallea, stood almost alone. *Pensadores* they have had, but this breed of journalist-cum-essayist has been more concerned with Latin America and its future than with metaphysical problems. Rodó, Vasconcelos, Reyes, Martínez Estrada suffered more from a continental or national identity crisis than from metaphysical *angst.* Even Mallea is different from Barrios in that he shows a strain of *argentinidad* that starts with *Historia de una pasión argentina* (1935) and is developed through *La bahía de silencio* (1940). Running parallel with his «universal» works of metaphysical concern (from *Cuentos para una inglesa desesperada* [1926] through *Todo verdor perecerá* [1941]), the national concern is manifest. These two strands, however, do

---

15 The same criticism can be made of Spain. Apart from Ortega y Gasset and Unamuno, for example, the '98 Generation writers were more thinkers preoccupied with the particular problems of Spain at the turn of the century than with the human condition. Unamuno, however, shows the same kind of double concern (national and universal) that we find in Mallea—hence *En torno al casticismo* as well as *Del sentimiento trágico de la vida.*

not exist in Barrios' work. Although the setting of several of his novels is obviously Chile, there is no great revelation of, nor concern with, *chilenidad*. His only real Chilean novel of the land was *Gran señor y rajadiablos*, which was a great commercial success on account of the rural element and the evocation of the values of a past epoch. The real point of the novel, as I shall demonstrate in Chapter 3, is that Barrios used the American scene to work out a more general view of the world and a philosophy of life. The tragedy for Barrios, then, is that often his work has been lauded for the wrong reasons, whilst his unique position as a Latin American novelist with a metaphysical view of life has often gone unnoticed.

Herein lies another paradox in the life of this unusual man. In spite of his wide tastes in literature and philosophy—nineteenth-century French Romanticism, Spanish mysticism, Generation of '98, the atheistic philosophers of nineteenth-century Germany—and his European, especially Germanic background, this cosmopolitan thinker never travelled outside of Latin America, and never beyond Chile after his youthful trips to neighbouring countries. Yet, despite the lack of personal contact, he was able to treat in profound fashion the universal problems of man's place in the world, how he evolves, matures and changes. The aim of this study is to show this other side of Eduardo Barrios—apart from the psychological, social and costumbrist values for which he has been duly praised—that is, his metaphysical vision of life that stems from the philosophical commentary and the aesthetic preoccupations, all of which together make the artist.

LITERARY SITUATION

Barrios, as we have seen, has never allowed himself to be bound by the -isms or literary movements, although he has made use of them to comment on life. Whilst reflecting the changes, he has never followed them slavishly to be in fashion. Often, rather, he has given the impression of going against the stream, which makes certain novels so obviously out of date that they must be deliberately anachronistic, e.g. *Tamarugal* and *Gran señor y rajadiablos*. Writing throughout the whole of the first half of the twentieth century, Barrios was exposed to all literary movements from Romanticism up to the sophisticated innovations of the new novel, during which time he used the vehicle that best suited his philosophical mood.

As Barrios evolved his philosophy of life, the literary manifestation of these ideas changed too. Open to all influences and trends, Barrios was a kind of weathervane, albeit an erratic one. To say that Barrios changed does not indicate a lack of mental or emotional stability but rather an evolving approach to the problems of life. Since man is not a static animal, the human being's outlook matures as he grows older, and as times change man changes with them. Obviously the Barrios of the 1950s cannot be the same young Barrios of the turn of the century, nor can his literature remain stagnant. Not to have changed from *Del natural* (1907) to *Los hombres del hombre* (1950) would render Barrios a kind of automaton, unthinking, unfeeling and insensitive to flux and fusion. One looks for evolution in the maturing writer, without necessarily a betrayal of principles. The Barrios of *Los hombres del hombre* still emphasises some early basic themes and ideas, but tempered with the maturity of age and experience. Themes that had their beginnings in *Del natural* run like a leitmotif throughout his work and still appear in his last novel—the role of emotion, the heart, sentiment, the position of children, the function of art, the theme of jealousy, especially between the sexes, etc.—but all modified by his new view of the world which has been formed and moulded by fifty years of life, suffering and experience.

One finds the same evolution in his language. The strong, coarse, sexual imagery of *Del natural*, reflecting the youthful Barrios' protest against the false bourgeois morality, censorship of the artist's natural freedom, and the opposition of the church and organized religion to the authentic portrayal of sexual matters, contrasts with the diaphanous, pristine prose of *El hermano asno*, culminating in what one critic has called the purification of Eduardo Barrios' sensorial prose in *Los hombres del hombre*.[16]

ROMANTICISM AND ITS REACTIONS

Given the evolution of Barrios' novels, there has to be a point of departure. The roots of Barrios' view of life and his fiction lie in Romanticism, and his themes are essentially nineteenth-century themes reflecting the Romantic sensibility—love, madness, fate, destiny, sentimental education. Some would say that his responses are also nineteenth-century, i.e. the role of emotion, the displacement of reason by sentiment, the heart's ruling the head. It is in this sense that Barrios is regarded as a *novelista del corazón*. Barrios' treatment, however, of what he would consider essential themes is twentieth-century and universal, i.e. he touches on metaphysical problems that confront all men in all times and in all places—things of the heart, sentiment and passion. Some aspects of his work may seem dated, e.g. the role of destiny, fate and heredity in *Un perdido*. What could be more modern, however, than the themes of alienation, the outsider, the existentialist unhappiness, the absurd, all so relevant to our time and treated in masterly fashion by Barrios in his novels? Though rooted in Romanticism, then, Barrios' fiction (and his sensibility), emerging out of his philosophical

16 In the article thus entitled, JOEL C. HANCOCK, *Hispania*, LVI, No. 1 (March, 1973), 51-59.

insight, develops themes and ideas which are universal in their application and transcend the particular circumstances of the nineteenth century which caused the shift in the vital outlook which was at the root of the literary movement.

One has to bear in mind that Romanticism, like all other literary movements, came late to the New World.[17] Like all Latin American literature, it is derivative and tends to lag behind its European inspiration or source. Also, after the Wars of Independence against the mother country, Spain was anathema to Latin America in the nineteenth century and influenced little in the literary development of the continent.[18] It is significant that the Colombian novel *María,* the Romantic novel *par excellence* (in any language?), did not appear till 1867, whereas the Romantic movement in Spain was generally regarded as dead by the 1850s.[19] If one considers that *María* is an example of «primitive» Romanticism in the fashion of *Paul et Virginie* or Chateaubriand's *Atala, René, Les Natchez,* then one is not really surprised that Romanticism survives right into the twentieth century «sobre todo en Hispanoamérica donde el *sentimental,* en el sentido que yo creo Barrios quiso darle a este vocablo, abunda hoy día».[20] Many of the so-called precursors of Modernism could be more easily and more correctly classified as late Romantics. It is not surprising, then, that Barrios has been labelled a twentieth-century Romantic: «Barrios es pues un hombre sentimental, vale decir un romántico del 1800 y como tal hay que aceptarle. Como a Rousseau, Chateaubriand, Musset, le gusta abrir su corazón a sus lectores, entregarse entero a la confesión íntima, para justificar ciertos actos morales que acaso fueron erróneamente interpretados.»[21] As we have noted, works like *El niño que enloqueció de amor* and *Un perdido* are the stuff of the previous century's novels. Barrios' spiritual fathers he unashamedly confesses to have been mostly of the nineteenth-century, mostly French in

[17] This phenomenon of delayed transmission of literary trends is seen as early as Gongorism, and is partly explained by the Spanish crown's desire to keep the colonies in a suspended state of ignorance for fear of political and religious corruption. Though the number of printing presses and universities during the colonial period in Spanish America was surprisingly high, all instruments of disseminating information and culture were used expressly for the maintenance of Spanish rule rather than the propagation of literature.

[18] The irony is that in the twentieth century it is Latin America that tends to influence Spain in the literary field. As well as Modernism, which was accepted by Spanish poets, especially the generation of 1927, the new novel, which has been emerging from Latin America for the last several decades, is making its presence felt on the contemporary Peninsular novel.

[19] Valera, for example, was of the opinion that Spanish Romanticism, if it can be said to begin in the early 1830s, was dead as a movement by the mid-1850s. In fact, it has been said that even in the early period of the movement eclecticism was more the rule.

[20] CARLOS LOZANO, «Paralelismos entre Flaubert y Eduardo Barrios», *Revista Iberoamericana,* XXIV, No. 47 (enero-junio, 1959), 116.

[21] ARTURO TORRES-RÍOSECO, *Grandes novelistas de la América Hispana,* Tomo II (Berkeley: University of California Press, 1949), p. 22.

literature and German in thought, though one ought not to make distinctions between such interdependent disciplines, especially in Barrios' case. In the field of letters Balzac, Hugo, Constant and especially Flaubert have demonstrably influenced Barrios,[22] whilst in the field of philosophy, as I shall show in Chapter 2, he owes much to Schopenhauer and Nietzsche. Manuel Gálvez, whose protagonist Carlos Riga in *El mal metafísico* has affinities with Luis Bernales of *Un perdido,* sees Luis as a spiritual descendant of Fédéric Moreau, Flaubert's hero and a victim of *l'éducation sentimentale.*[23] Both Riga and Luis are descended from *Adolphe, Werther* and *René,* and have their distant roots in Rousseau. Gálvez sums it all up in a brief phrase: «Todo eso es, pues, romanticismo»—a Romanticism that is an integral part of the Latin American mentality, as compared to the practical, industrious outlook of North America whose people, according to at least one thinker, lack the romantic spirit and who have even suppressed from their lives all sentiment.[24] Barrios' German background also inculcated in him a feeling for German Romanticism, with Heine, Schiller and Goethe bringing influence to bear on papá Juan, Luis' grandfather (I, 224), who is drawn from Barrios' own grandfather. If Barrios' heroes and heroines have their sensibilities rooted in Romanticism, and are products of *la educación sentimental,* with the difficulties that stem from their overprotective environment and over-stimulated emotions, like Emma Bovary and Fédéric Moreau, they have to confront the same problems and atone for their illusions, their dreams and their inability to cope with everyday living. When *el niño* goes mad with love, Luis ends up a moral and physical degenerate on the road to perdition, and Olga a neurotic through sexual frustration, Barrios portrays their romantic decline in realistic, credible fashion within the framework of the artistic entity of the novel. There is little clash between art and reality, since Barrios generally depicts their tragedy with a constant fidelity to the mood of the novel, though obviously subservient to the novelist's view of life. His protagonists may try the conventional means of escape into the *paradis artificiels* of sex, alcohol,

[22] As well as the Lozano and Torres-Ríoseco works cited above, see ANGEL MANUEL VÁZQUEZ-BIGI, «El tipo sicológico en Eduardo Barrios y correspondencias en las letras europeas», *Revista Iberoamericana,* XXIV, No. 48 (julio-diciembre, 1959), 265-96.

[23] In his article «The *Perdido* as a Type in some Spanish-American Novels», *PMLA,* LXX, No. 1 (March, 1955), 19-36, ARNOLD CHAPMAN takes Manuel Gálvez to task for his semantic misinterpretation of this term «éducation sentimentale». Gálvez's understanding of it as «education (upbringing) that is excessively sentimental» seems to indicate a clash with the Flaubertian sense of the phrase—«the education of the sentiments». The Mexican writer Jaime Torres Bodet would seem to favour Flaubert's point of view in his novel significantly, if not imaginatively, entitled *La educación sentimental* (1929).

[24] This is, in essence, part of the argument of RODÓ in *Ariel,* where he highlights the spiritual, ethereal qualities of Latin Americans as personified by Ariel, compared to the energetic, practical, materialistic Caliban, who symbolised for his readers, given the political situation of the time (1900), the North Americans.

11

drugs, etc. in order to free themselves from their metaphysical problems, but in true Romantic fashion there is no evasion from adverse destiny or the blows of fate. It is significant that Barrios should adopt this ambivalent attitude to God/Destiny that one finds in the early Latin American Romantics like Echeverría, who in *La Cautiva* finds nothing contradictory in the evocation by turn of God and Destiny.[25]

Though Romantic in his analysis of this type of sensibility, Barrios does not belong to the escapist, exotic side of the movement that would evade the harsh world of reality by fleeing, to use the Baudelairean phrase, «anywhere out of this world», geographically and temporally. As a writer, Barrios was aware that the spiritual ills of his characters were a result of the times and the background, and the metaphysical malaise a product of the sociological and moral problems of the century and the setting. Barrios does not provide local colour for its own sake but rather as a means to portray better the emotional difficulties of his tormented characters. In this sense, Barrios cannot be accused of picturesqueness, escapism, exoticism or mere *costumbrismo*. Like Flaubert, he is not afraid to depict reality as it is, understanding that Realism is the other side of the coin, the complement of Romanticism. It is this Flaubertian alternation between Romanticism and Realism that maintains Barrios' verisimilitude and credibility, and keeps his fiction within the frame of metaphysics, thus preventing it from being mere story-telling and painting of customs. His description of the stages of the rapid degradation of Luis in *Un perdido* is surpassed in realistic terms only by the analogous portrayal of the dreams, deceit, infidelity and final suicide of Emma Bovary.

In this depiction of the downfall of Luis, as he travels through the seamier side of Santiago and other Chilean cities—bohemian quarter, cheap boarding houses, brothels and back streets—Barrios' Realism merges into Naturalism which was very much in vogue at the turn of the century. This «exaggerated Realism», or the portraying of reality blacker than it is, is a literary extension of European thought movements of the late nineteenth-century transferred to Latin America, especially through the novels of Zola. Under the influence of thinkers like Comte, Spencer, Saint-Simon and Bentham, Positivism and Utilitarianism, coming in the wake of the Industrial Revolution in Europe, were supposed to raise the level of life for the working class and help them to escape from the stranglehold of the church. The social sciences were to replace metaphysics and theology, the heritage of three centuries of Spanish political and ecclesiastical control. The new

---

[25] Echeverría, in Argentina, is a good example of the young Latin American writer who, imbued with the new ideas of European Romanticism, returned to his own continent not only to write Romantic/Realist literature about America, but also to participate in the political struggle (cf. «El matadero»).

José Hernández uses this double-edged technique too in order to explain away the woes of the world in *Martín Fierro*.

ideas, coupled with the growing industrial wealth in the hands of the magnates, ably supported by the progressive young *científicos,* were to provide the greatest possible happiness for the greatest number of people. This was particularly true of Chile whose rich mines and natural resources attracted a huge proletariat not only from Latin America but also from Europe. Positivist thinkers like Bilbao and Lastarria propagated new concepts and doctrines that were readily received in a country where new notions of socialism, Marxism, and Trade Unionism had more than normal significance. These doctrines which constituted the social side of Romanticism—perfectibility of man, the inevitability of progress, earthly paradise, etc.—were avidly swallowed by the new, politically-conscious, twentieth-century man. However, the Utopias and the new Jerusalems of the Positivists were not to be within the grasp of the masses. The «progress and order» message of the new thinkers produced a state of affairs that militated against the people, producing wealth for a few industrialists but bringing misery to the masses who toiled in mines and factories. Although life was no more than a vale of tears, out of the suffering came hope. New ideas on the rights of man, brotherhood, solidarity and Trade Unionism provided the people with the weapons they needed to defend themselves against the abuses of their masters.

Barrios, it is interesting to note, although he depicted the sordid details of city life in *Un perdido,* and actually worked in the mines at the turn of the century, does not associate himself with the new radical ideas nor does he even portray them in a sympathetic light. Though he describes the industrial accidents, the underground suicides and the degrading conditions of the mines in *Tamarugal,* he does so without social commentary —more with artistic objectivity and political dispassionateness.

His descriptive Naturalism is perhaps best displayed in *Un perdido,* which most critics have labelled creole Realism. No doubt the accidents of fate, the unhappy experiences, the degradations that are described, do take place in life. Where Barrios seems to fail, however, is in his exaggeration and multiplication of the horrors as they beset one person—the weak protagonist. To do this so consistently, so often, and so severely is excessive. The alcoholism, poverty, abulia, total physical and mental incapacity of the hero overwhelm him—and us—especially in a novel written in 1918, long after the period of such literary excesses. This is more in keeping with the Naturalistic novel of Eugenio Cambaceres, *Sin rumbo,* written as early as 1885.[26] However, as we shall see, it served his

[26] Argentina has produced other such novels like *La bolsa* (1891) by JULIÁN MARTEL [José Miró], another sordid example of Naturalistic fiction—this time against the background of the stock exchange. More in tune with *Un perdido,* however, is JOAQUÍN EDWARDS BELLO's *El roto* (1920), which Barrios' compatriot has called «un reflejo del sadismo y de la crueldad nacionales» (*Recuerdos de un cuarto de siglo,* Ed. Zig-Zag, 1966, pp. 85-89).

philosophical purpose, and although anachronistic to some degree, it constitutes a link in his metaphysical development.

One must not assume that Barrios was unaware of trends, topicality and times. Much more in keeping with the general mood of Naturalism was his first collection *Del natural,* poor aesthetically [27] but interesting for the basic themes and the social, ethical and moral opinions expressed in the prologue. His views on morality and sexual freedom reflect the views of his aforementioned compatriots Bilbao and Lastarria, as well as the Argentinian Ingenieros' *Hacia un moral sin dogma.* Apart from the plea for sexual freedom, one finds illuminating Barrios' comments on censorship, the freedom of the artist, and his right to pursue true art, since these views anticipate his aesthetic concerns and the role of art and the artist, which I shall develop in Chapter 4. Barrios' hope is that the Naturalistic views expressed here, coupled with the advent of modern psychology, are going to break down the barriers of hypocrisy and conventional morality erected by narrow-minded and bigoted authorities, ecclesiastical and political. This explains his association with the Naturalists as an attempt to give free rein to his own youthful rebellion in matters social, sexual and religious. Barrios developed these social-ethical-moral views in his plays, *Mercaderes en el templo* (1910), *Por el decoro* (1913), *Lo que niega la vida* (1913), *Vivir* (1916), the last two dealing more specifically with the role of women in society and the restrictions imposed upon their freedom. In this sense Barrios is in the Ibsen/Shaw tradition of feminists. Barrios makes no attempt to disguise his affiliation nor to deny his models. The Mexican Naturalist Federico Gamboa had already published a collection of short stories entitled *Del natural* (1888) and a novel *Suprema ley* (1896), from which Barrios had drawn his own parallel title «Tirana ley» for the novel in *his* collection also called *Del natural.* The common denominator in both novels is sexual attraction, though the attitude of the authors is diametrically opposed. Gamboa sees it as destructive, whilst Barrios views it as a cohesive force which unites the physical and the spiritual. This idealisation of sex corresponds to the exaltation of the flesh by the early Modernists and marks the point at which Barrios departs from the Naturalists.

An off-shoot of Barrios' dabbling with Naturalism is his interest in the *fin de siècle* Sensualists and the Decadents, denoting the influence of Oscar Wilde and D'Annunzio. This is seen specifically in the character of Carlos Romero (in the story «Amistad de solteras»): «The Byronic mystery, the satanical attraction of a sinful past, and the imposing sexual tone of the

---

[27] This collection of three short stories and a short novel was an embarrassment to Barrios who later tried to discourage its circulation because of its artistic inadequacies.

characterisation place Romero in the tradition of the "Fatal man".»[28] Apart from the popularity of the gothic novel in Chile, one finds traces of Decadentism even in Modernists like Casal in «Neurosis» whose sensual heroine, «Noemi, la pálida pecadora», was wont to «beber en copa de ónix labrado / la roja sangre de un tigre real». This same kind of *homme fatal* and sense of sexual mystery is repeated in the sumptuous brothel scene of «Lo que ellos creen y lo que ellos son» and in «Celos bienhechores».

It is no wonder that the mature Barrios put little store by the early efforts of *Del natural*.[29] However, what Barrios failed to recognise was that in his youthful labours he had laid the foundations of his later novels in his treatment of themes and types. It is an essential point of departure, the cornerstone, on which he built his more mature work.

«MODERNISMO» AND ITS AFTERMATH

Though written in the Naturalistic vein, *Del natural* reflects a difference in the attitude of Barrios to sex as compared to the Naturalists. This exaltation of sex, as well as his preoccupation with art, even in his first published work, pushes Barrios more into the ranks of the Modernists. Even by temperament Barrios would have been drawn to an élitist movement like Modernism. Unlike his compatriot Lillo, he had no wish to be involved with the proletariat nor to dirty his hands by social compromise. It is significant that Barrios participated in government only under the aegis of the dictator Ibáñez, upon whose fall Barrios withdrew from public life. Also, even in his first work, *Del natural*, it is noteworthy that in the short novel «Tirana ley» he has his protagonist Gastón Labarca, who is forced to choose between art and love, go off to Paris to study painting, abandoning his Romantic ideal woman.

It is well known that, although Darío published *Azul*, his breviary of Modernism, in Chile, he had no disciples there and little interest was shown in his work. One can assume that Barrios must have known the work of Darío and other Modernists, like the Chileans Magallanes Moure and Diego Dublé Urrutia, through the many readings and tertulias which were

[28] NED J. DAVISON, «The Significance of *Del natural* in the Fiction of Eduardo Barrios», *Hispania*, XLIV, No. 1 (March, 1961), 28. See also DAVISON's *Eduardo Barrios*, pp. 19-27, for a useful treatment of this collection.

[29] Torres-Ríoseco rightly points out that at this stage the youthful Barrios had not yet learned to discriminate, when he cites as his influence in the depiction of explicit sex both Galdós and Zamacois whom he admired for their courage and nobility: «Como Galdós es uno de los grandes novelistas de España y Zamacois un audaz representante de la más tonta pornografía, se echa de ver que Barrios no ha digerido bien sus lecturas» (*Grandes novelistas*, p. 24).

a feature of that period. The date of the publication of *Del natural,* 1907, may seem rather late for any Modernist influence. However, a few well-chosen dates would indicate that Barrios must have been aware of the movement. Without pinpointing the exact date of the death of Modernism,[30] it is to be noted that Pedro Prado published his *Flores de cardo* in 1908, a date which some critics would regard as marking the aesthetic death of the movement in Chile. However, González Martínez did not publish his famous sonnet «Tuércele el cuello al cisne» till 1911, and Darío did not die till 1916, both of which dates have been suggested to mark the definitive end of Modernism. Also, Modernism in Chile is rather confused and behind the times because of the revolution of 1891. One cannot assume that there the writers of Realistic or Naturalistic fiction are, by definition, barred from the movement. In fact, one of the features of Chilean Modernism is the co-existence of various streams within the movement—in many cases within the same writer who produces, without aesthetic or emotional conflict, creole, social and decadent poetry, as in the case of Carlos Pezoa Véliz, Pedro Antonio González and Antonio Bórquez Solar. This kind of anomaly was possible in the Chilean movement, which could not boast of a leader or a famous protagonist.

Del natural (1907), we have seen, had several traits—the sensual elegance of the characters, the luxury of background and accessories (furniture, jewels, etc. of, for example, «Como hermanas», I, 35, 39), the role of art and artists («Tirana ley»)—which were the stuff of the early Modernists. In 1912 Barrios was contributing to the Modernist journal *Pluma y lápiz,* in which Armando Donoso was expressing the feeling that «*Modernismo* was not yet a completely settled historical issue».[31] In the last number of *Pluma y lápiz,* dated 13 September 1912, appeared an article anticipating the arrival of Darío (which, in fact, was never to take place). It is significant that this article, recalling Darío's early career and literary successes in Chile, was much more enthusiastic about Modernism than earlier pieces. Barrios, writing for *Pluma y lápiz* at this period, must have been cognizant and appreciative of the efforts of the master.

Max Henríquez Ureña, in his celebrated *Breve historia del modernismo,* states categorically Barrios' connection with the movement «por lo que toca al estilo, a la forma de expresión, libre de clisés y de frases hechas».[32] Some of these links were achieved through the influence of Naturalism and Impressionism which the Modernists extended and spread. Many Chilean writers, although they flourished at the time of Modernism and adjusted

---

[30] For discussion of this see D. L. SHAW, «*Modernismo:* A Contribution to the Debate», *Bulletin of Hispanic Studies,* XLIV, No. 3 (July, 1967), 195-202.

[31] Quoted by JOHN M. FEIN, *Modernismo in Chilean Literature: The Second Period* (Durham, North Carolina: Duke University Press, 1965), p. 88.

[32] México: Fondo de Cultura Económica, 1954, p. 362.

their first creative steps towards the aesthetic tendencies of that movement, survived its demise and went on to other things, without ever losing the unmistakable, indelible mark of the Modernist. Such is the case with Barrios: «Hasta ahí [1915] no cabe duda de que Barrios siguió la corriente modernista. Después su orientación cambia, aunque todavía hay dejos de modernismo en no pocas páginas de su celebrada novela psicológica *El hermano asno*» (Henríquez Ureña, p. 362). It seems obvious, then, that Barrios was familiar with, and came under the spell of, Modernism, especially in its later stages. He was impressed by the quietist poetry and the «mysticism» of Amado Nervo whose verses of terrestrial harmony mark a transition from the voices of the *modernistas angustiados*. I cannot agree with Henríquez Ureña that *El niño que enloqueció de amor* is more Modernist than *El hermano asno* which he claims to show mere traces. Though preceding *El hermano asno* chronologically, *El niño que enloqueció de amor* belongs more to the «neo-Romantic» reaction epitomised by writers like Gabriela Mistral who thought that Modernism had gone far enough in its élitist, difficult verse and demanded a return to the field of human communication. It is significant that Mistral, whose poetry reflects something of her frustrated maternal instincts, composed a sonnet in memory of *el niño*. Though there are traces of the Modernist language in *El niño que enloqueció de amor, El hermano asno,* with its concern for colourism and musicality, is closer to the Modernist style. Though not a poet in the sense that he wrote formal verse, Barrios is closer to the Modernist movement than most critics would allow. *El niño que enloqueció de amor,* especially *El hermano asno,* passages from as late as *Gran señor y raja-diablos* and *Los hombres del hombre,* are poetry in prose. If *El hermano asno,* by force of date, has to be labelled a post-Modernist novel, it is so in the sense that Güiraldes' highly idealised and aesthetically conceived *Don Segundo Sombra* is a post-Modernist novel. If *Don Segundo Sombra* is more than a regional novel, *El hermano asno* is more than a novel of sexual frustration in a religious setting.

If post-Modernism is to be used as a label to describe the literary situation after the demise of the great movement in the second decade of this century, then one has to distinguish between the two tendencies, one of which is anathema to Barrios. If the Modernists sought verse that was concerned with beauty, art and poetry for poetry's sake, then after the peak of the movement certain writers felt that the movement had not gone far enough and wanted to carry Modernism to its vanguardist extreme, e. g. Huidobro and the middle Neruda. Opposed to *vanguardismo,* the other reaction was a natural tendency, a return to Romanticism and a poetry of human emotions, as represented by Gabriela Mistral, the later Nervo and González Martínez.

17

Though Barrios was not technically nor formally a poet, there can be no doubt about his position in the post-Modernist movement: «Barrios consciously sought to write poetically. It was his belief poetry was the most direct—as well as the most charming—means of communication.»[33] As a metaphysical writer, concerned with the human condition, a self-confessed sentimentalist by temperament and by definition, with his roots in nineteenth-century Romanticism, he followed the path of the neo-Romantics. The hermetic poetry of Neruda and the complex style of Huidobro's *creacionismo* had little appeal for him. With his strong views on simplicity, correctness and purity of language, to take the road of the Vanguardists towards the abstruse jungles of Surrealism was not to his taste.

It is an interesting coincidence that many of the key figures in the development of literature in these decades were Chilean—Mistral (neo-Romantic), Neruda (Vanguardist), Huidobro *(creacionista).* This is not to say that Chile was immune to the growing awareness of *criollismo.* Regionalism had early shown its two faces—interest in both city and country, as long as they were American. If the novel of the land described best the rural form, Barrios, especially in *Un perdido,* has tended to be seen as a novelist of the city, because of his detailed descriptions, apt settings and lively backdrops of Chilean cities against which his abulic hero, Luis Bernales, played out the farce of life. In spite of the vivid portrayal of types and places, the pace and diversity of the novel, the striking evocation of Chilean life which he achieves by altering the geographical background of his protagonist and by moving him up and down the social scale (middle class, military, bohemian, gutter), the novel is significant for other reasons. Although he makes use of *criollismo* like Manuel Rojas, in a sense he prefigures the great master who is generally credited with moving Chile out of its regionalist fixation into the field of cosmopolitanism. What has been said of Manuel Rojas could easily (and earlier) have been applied to Barrios: «Tiene el mérito de haber iniciado la reacción contra el costumbrismo tradicional en Chile, abriendo la tendencia hacia el trascendentalismo sin abandonar el fondo local de sus relatos..., usando el caudal de su experiencia vital que tiene como escenario

---

[33] JOEL C. HANCOCK, «The Purification of Eduardo Barrios' Sensorial Prose», *Hispania,* LVI, No. 1 (March, 1973), p. 52. Barrios also identified with the poets of the group *Los diez* and with the many poets who composed sonnets to commemorate *El niño que enloqueció de amor,* especially Gabriela Mistral who always wrote appreciatively of Barrios' novels, as we shall see throughout this work. For an interesting view of the personal and literary friendship between Barrios and Gabriela Mistral, see two recent «epistolary» articles by JOSÉ ANADÓN, «Una carta de Gabriela Mistral sobre *Desolación»,* *Hispamérica,* No. 19 (abril, 1978), 27-42, and «Epistolario entre Gabriela Mistral y Eduardo Barrios», *Cuadernos Americanos,* CCX, No. 2 (marzo-abril, 1977), 228-35.

la realidad de Chile.»[34] Using these criteria, the partisans of *criollismo* could claim Eduardo Barrios as one of their own on the basis of *Un perdido*[35] in the early trilogy, and especially in the later *Tamarugal* and *Gran señor y rajadiablos* which were much more apparently Chilean and American, if one were to take regional or rural *costumbrismo* as the criterion. However, these supporters of regionalism do Barrios a great disservice by trying to confine him within his own frontiers.

What one critic has said about Canadian literature is an extremely apt description of the Latin American scene:

> A warm emotion for one's own *petit pays* can lead to a very charming art... In the end, however, regionalist art will fail because it stresses the superficial at the expense, at least, if not to the exclusion, of the fundamental and universal. The advent of regionalism may be welcomed with reservations as a stage through which it may be well for us to pass, as a discipline and a purgation. But if we are to pass through it, the coming of great books will be delayed beyond the lifetime of anyone now living.[36]

Of course, *Un perdido* could be regarded as a valuable contribution to regionalist literature, if one were to judge it as a document, a brochure of customs and mores of Chilean city life. What could be more rural than *Gran señor y rajadiablos,* ostensibly a sociological-historical-fictional series of tableaux, depicting the life of a nineteenth-century Chilean landowner. Beneath the regional level and beyond the rural setting, however, is to be found the real function of the novel—the portrayal of Barrios' view of life, as revealed through the philosophical commentary.

Thus, it is clear that Barrios was aware of, and susceptible to, all literary movements, some of which he borrowed from and identified with, as long as they were compatible with his metaphysical development. Barrios, however, had scant respect for barriers, whether they be literary, geographical or philosophical. Fiction was his way of working out a philosophy of life which would give some kind of meaning to this existence. Although his principal aim was to get his metaphysical perspective in focus, the artist in him demanded that it be done in an aesthetic manner. It is significant that as his literature developed, Barrios shed the influence of those movements that were marginal and of no lasting importance in his fiction—Naturalism, Decadentism, regionalism. What survive in Barrios'

---

[34] ORLANDO GÓMEZ GIL, *Historia crítica de la literatura hispanoamericana* (New York: Holt, Rinehart and Winston, 1968), pp. 683-84.

[35] It is rather odd that ARNOLD CHAPMAN in his «Perspectiva de la novela de la ciudad en Chile», *La novela iberoamericana* (Albuquerque: University of New Mexico Press, 1952) should have only one fleeting reference to *Un perdido* (on p. 198).

[36] E. K. BROWN, «The Problem of a Canadian Literature», published originally in *On Canadian Poetry* (Toronto: Ryerson, 1943) and reprinted in *Masks of Fiction* (Toronto: McClelland and Stewart, 1961), p. 52.

work are Romanticism, whose pessimistic spirit pervades his novels and vital outlook from first to last, and Modernism, in its preoccupation with aesthetics and its underlying *angustia* [37] which is at the root of the human condition. Both movements, which denote a shift in sensibility, were instrumental in shaping Eduardo Barrios' philosophy of life.

[37] Barrios' affinity and identification with the Generation of '98 in Spain, via Schopenhauer, Nietzsche and others, will be treated in Chapter 2. Without becoming embroiled in the discussion as to how far one should link Modernism and the '98 Generation, which some critics would like to consider a European counterpart of the Latin American movement, Barrios' debt to both is patently illustrated.

THE PHILOSOPHICAL FORMATION

THE ROLE OF PHILOSOPHY

In Chapter 1 I undertook the difficult task of trying to situate Eduardo Barrios from the literary standpoint, and to show the influences the various movements brought to bear upon his literary formation. To classify him *only* as a «psychological» writer avoids the difficulty and contributes little to our notion of his literary and philosophical position in Latin American letters. I use the terms «literary» and «philosophical» advisedly, since the point I am trying to stress about Barrios is that one cannot separate literature from life, hence his fiction from his philosophy. His novels are the creative manifestation of his vital outlook which is moulded by his own experiences and based on philosophical insight.

Much has been written about Barrios as a psychologist, and his importance as an intuitive psychologist should continually be borne in mind: that is to say, his sensitivity to certain psychological phenomena which he expressed in an articulate, literary manner in his novels, long before they were formulated and processed in scientific terms. What Barrios had to say about Alfonso Hernández Catá, the Cuban writer, is eminently, and significantly, applicable to himself: «Posee este gran artista una erudición científica excepcional, que se adivina, que él ha transformado de conocimiento en cultura, de alimento en fuerza...; no me sorprende el haber leído en Gregorio Marañón, hombre de ciencia y arte a la vez, la afirmación de que Catá asombra por su profundo conocimiento de la psiquiatría y de las neurosis.»[1] This precociousness is particularly true with regard to some of the claims of Freud whose theories Barrios anticipated in fictional form in *El niño que enloqueció de amor* and *Un perdido*.[2] Thus it seems

---

[1] «Prólogo de Eduardo Barrios», in ALFONSO HERNÁNDEZ CATÁ, *Sus mejores cuentos* (Santiago de Chile: Ed. Nascimento, 1936), p. 9.

[2] Although it is not the aim of this study to highlight the value of Eduardo Barrios as a psychologist, it would be remiss of me were I not to underline Barrios' success in anticipating the ideas of Freud. Ned Davison and Vázquez-Bigi (especially in the aforementioned theses) and Milton Rossel («El hombre y su psique en las novelas de Eduardo Barrios»», *Atenea*, CXXXIX, No. 389 [julio-septiembre, 1960],

clear that the psychological truths and values of his work were a result of his deep, philosophical thought on the human condition, that his capacity for psychological intuition stemmed from his profound vision in the metaphysical field. In other words, the philosopher prefigured the psychologist.

Because of the intuitive qualities of the man, one must not think of Barrios as a primitive in the field of philosophy, despite his inherent modesty about his own scientific, specialist knowledge. Barrios may have been an amateur psychologist, but in the field of life he was a professional. In the other concern of this study, the field of aesthetics, he was very much the conscious artist, holding literature and the creative process to be almost a religion, as I shall demonstrate in Chapter 4. It is rather ironical that in the field where he attained most prominence, psychology, he was least sure of his prowess.[3] In spite of the impression that Barrios gives of himself, he was a thinking, well-read man who did not always parade his ventures into the philosophical world to the many scholars who visited him in his study at Santiago. He did not have to. His view of life, moulded by his experiences and his readings, is to be found in his novels where, to mention but a few, names like Kant, Fénélon, Nietzsche and Schopenhauer appear.

BARRIOS AND THE GERMAN TRADITION

Though most critics have tended to stress the affinities between Barrios and French writers, Barrios has a special link with German literature and things Germanic. His maternal grandfather, Hudtwalcker, who is a model for papá Juan in *Un perdido,* exerted a great influence on him. Barrios, who took great pains in «También algo de mí» (I, 26) to deny the auto-

---

182-207, reprinted in *Cien años de la novela chilena* [Santiago: Universitaria, 1961], especially p. 190) have treated at length this aspect of Barrios' work. This has also been looked at more recently by James W. Brown who also adds, for good measure, Barrios' relationship with Darwin, whom Barrios places in conflict with medieval innocence, and Pasteur («*El hermano asno* from *Fioretti* through Freud», *Symposium,* XXV, No. 4 [Winter, 1971], 326-27).

Because of his basic modesty, Barrios appears overwhelmed that his scientific views should be so highly esteemed. In a letter to Vázquez-Bigi (reproduced as an Appendix in the latter's thesis, pp. 342-43), he states: «su estudio logra una de las mayores calidades, la que no había yo merecido al parecer antes: la científica... Me alumbra con la ciencia lo que yo he realizado tan sólo por conocimiento de la humanidad y por incursión en la multitud de personalidades que hay dentro de mí...».

[3] See note 2 above. In one of several published interviews, «Eduardo Barrios Talks About His Novels», *Hispania,* XLV, No. 2 (1962), DONALD M. DECKER, discussing «El niño que enloqueció de amor», states: «The point which Barrios seemed to wish to make by telling me this true anecdote, which was exemplary of several other incidents, was that this had been an experience about which he was afraid of writing—thinking people would not be able to accept it as plausible—and now readers were affirming that they too had had exactly the same experience when they were young» (p. 255).

biographical quality of *Un perdido,* readily admitted: «Sólo hay allí un tipo totalmente exacto a su modelo: papá Juan. Aun cuando la mayoría de sus episodios son equivalentes y no históricos, es él mi abuelo materno, el alemán, con sus pensamientos, con su alma, con su corazón, y hasta con sus palabras. El influyó como nadie en mi conformación anímica; de su espíritu me reconozco descendiente genuino» (I, 26-27). As Barrios' grandfather had influenced him, so too did papá Juan mould Luis: «él formó su corazón, acogiendo y fomentando sus innatas fuerzas de ternura y docilidad» (I, 223), whilst papá Juan himself was being influenced in turn by his readings of the great German Romantic masters, Schiller, Goethe and Heine (I, 224).

It is significant that the only German-born character in the novel is Major Von Büllow who, beneath the stern surface of the military college teacher, reveals a sentimental trait. In fact, he is one of the few characters in the whole depressing novel who is kind to Luis—because the boy knew a German folk song learned from his grandfather (I, 395). Barrios' mother had been educated in Hamburg till the age of sixteen when she came to Peru, where Barrios attended a German high school in Lima. It is not surprising, then, that Barrios had a special affinity for, and pride in, things Germanic.[4]

Appreciative of German values, by bent attracted to Romantic literature, and by temperament timid, sentimental and melancholy, Barrios could not hope to escape the influence of Schopenhauer and Nietzsche whose ideas pervaded Europe before spreading to Latin America in turn. As Europe had been the cultural mecca of all educated young Latin Americans at the turn of the century, given the circumstances of the period (political and philosophical), Schopenhauer and Nietzsche were studied carefully by many thoughtful young men, who had the opportunity to read in Spanish the quotable (and often distorted) dicta of both thinkers.

One must not look for a systematic pattern of Schopenhauerian and Nietzschean ideas throughout Barrios' novels. In fact, Schopenhauer and Nietzsche were not always consistent either in their own doctrines, as H. D. Aiken has pointed out: «But this inconsistency is not serious, if we

---

[4] Without my labouring the point, one would have to be insensitive not to observe the spiritual and artistic parallels between Barrios and several of his German contemporaries in the field of fiction, like Thomas Mann, whose theme of the artist striving to conform to the pattern of everyday existence in *Tonio Kröger* (1903) is close to Barrios' heart. *Kinderseele* (1920) of Hermann Hesse, as Vázquez-Bigi has also noted, shows a striking similarity to *El niño que enloqueció de amor* (1915) in its analysis of childhood in psychological terms (Thesis, pp. 110-13). The Franciscan simplicity of *Peter Camezind* (1904) and the first person narrative of the hypersensitive Emil Sinclair in *Damien* (1919) parallel not only *El hermano asno* but the whole tenor of *El niño que enloqueció de amor* and *Un perdido*. *Steppenwolf* (1927) with its basic idea of two beings (man-wolf, cf. Mario-Lázaro of *El hermano asno*) extending to the «doctrine of the thousand souls» has been paralleled by the multiple personality of BARRIOS' *Los hombres del hombre.*

view Schopenhauer's metaphysics, not as an essay in logical construction, but as a personal *Weltanschauung* which is his answer to the "objective" ideologies of his predecessors.» It is less important, in Schopenhauer's case, that the life of contemplation gets rid of the will than that, as in the case of Barrios' aesthetic metaphysics, it «provides an adequate solution to the spiritual problems of anxiety and disillusionment, self-estrangement and isolation»[5] which are the features of contemporary life.

Barrios' tastes were catholic, as indicated by his interest in writers and thinkers as varied as Kant, Fénélon, Thomas à Kempis, Saint Francis, Balzac, Hugo, Flaubert, amongst others, all of whose view of the world provided grist for his philosophic mill. One is conscious of the danger of simplifying the philosophies of Schopenhauer and Nietzsche, both eminently quotable because of the aphoristic nature of their work,[6] writers who have been more misunderstood and put to the service of so many contradictory causes and groups than almost any other philosophers in history. Thus they are subject to simplistic, if not erroneous, interpretations. I do not suggest that Barrios analysed the views of these thinkers with the perspicacity of a modern Kaufmann, Copleston or Gardiner. Rather, given the availability of the work in both German and Spanish, Barrios would have read and been easily familiar with the principal conceptions of both thinkers—superman, eternal recurrence, will to power, will to live—and put them to his own use. Apart from assimilating the key ideas of both thinkers, he absorbed their general view of the world, aesthetics, religion, etc. and identified with the general mood and ambience characterised in their work. That he read the writings is obvious from the sympathetic rendering of their point of view (especially in *Un perdido*) and his references to their work.

BARRIOS AND SCHOPENHAUER: THE WILL TO LIVE

Given Barrios' view of life, it is not surprising that the Schopenhauerian philosophical current which permeates Latin American literature of the period, especially in the characterisation of *perdido* types like Carlos Riga of *El mal metafísico* and Luis Bernales of *Un perdido,* should run through his novels. As early as 1885 in *Sin rumbo* Cambaceres explores «the dilemma of the man who has lost traditional faith and who rides the tide of Schopenhauerian pessimism».[7] Andrés, the protagonist, rails against the

---

[5] *The Age of Ideology: The Nineteenth Century Philosophers* (New York: Mentor Books, 1956), p. 103.

[6] See, for example, *Essays and Aphorisms* [of Schopenhauer] (Harmondsworth: Penguin, 1970), intro. R. J. Hollingdale, and NIETZSCHE's *Twilight of the Idols* in, for example, *The Portable Nietzsche* (New York: Viking Press, 1966), intro. Walter Kaufmann.

[7] JEAN FRANCO, *An Introduction to Spanish American Literature* (Cambridge: Cambridge University Press, 1969), p. 117.

24

vanity of life and the pointlessness of existence: «Dios no es nadie; la ciencia un cáncer para el alma. Saber es sufrir; ignorar, comer, dormir y no pensar, la solución exacta del problema, la única dicha de vivir.»[8] With the death of his daughter, who had provided fleeting moments of relief from the *angustia* of life, he is left with the conviction that everything —science, prayer, love, «todo el arsenal humano»—is in vain. Gálvez, in his novel, actually designates the root cause of *el mal metafísico* as «el pesimismo schopenhauriano de Riga». Although the German philosophers are cited only a few times in Barrios' novels, it is done in such an explicit and succinct way that he summarises the implicit influence felt throughout his work: «Leyó a Nietzsche y lo abandonó sin comprenderlo bien. Siguió con Schopenhauer: era muy posible que el placer fuera sólo la ausencia del dolor» (I, 388).[9] These two sentences succinctly express the extent of Barrios' debt to the two philosophers. Overt references like this, however, are rare. Nevertheless, as early as *Del natural* (1907), the artist hero, Gastón Labarca, concludes the novel with a plea to live for the moment and follow the advice of the master Schopenhauer: «Pero por ahora no nos aflijamos por el porvenir. Sigamos el consejo de Schopenhauer, que dice: "Es muy cuerdo gozar lo más posible del presente, el solo momento de que se tiene seguridad, puesto que la vida toda no es más que un gran pedazo de presente y, lo mismo que él, pasajera"» («Tirana ley», I, 142).

One must not assume that Barrios, or the other writers of the period, followed to the letter of the law the Schopenhauerian or Nietzschean doctrines. In Barrios' case it was more an absorption of the basic principles as laid down, the general attitude to life,[10] and the metaphysical atmosphere created by the propagation of ideas—with the escape clause, when necessary. Nor would one expect to find a logical pursuit of Schopenhauerian thought in the portrayal of characters. As we shall see in Chapter 3, Barrios' view of life was worked out over his own lifetime. Thus the final meaning of *Un perdido* does not become clear till the appearance of the second trilogy, especially *Gran señor y rajadiablos*, thirty years later, with the development of the character of Valverde. Luis by himself does not follow totally the Schopenhauerian direction in that he finds no escape from the rigours of life through the contemplation of art, though Charlie, in *Los hombres del hombre*, appears to have been endowed with this gift/outlet.

To go back to first principles: Schopenhauer, in his theory of knowledge,

---

[8] (Buenos Aires: Plus Ultra, 1968), p. 74.

[9] Hence his appreciation of and sympathy with Hernández Catá in the previously cited prologue to the latter's short stories: «había un dulce gozarse en el sufrir... Por inclinación o por sistema, el placer estético predominante de este artista es el placer del dolor» (p. 10). One is reminded of SCHOPENHAUER'S «The joy of grief» («The World as Will», p. 322).

[10] «His pessimism is authentic. Nor is it peculiar to himself; like the Italian poet Leopardi, Schopenhauer represents the world-weariness and loneliness which are implicit in so much of the Romantic movement...» (AIKEN, p. 98).

accepts the distinction between the *phenomenon* (appearance of the thing to the perceiving mind) and *noumenon* (thing as it is itself). It is this theory of knowledge, which is at the root of his metaphysics, that Barrios seems to have identified with—a metaphysics which has a genuine function, i. e. to resolve certain fundamental problems which, though beyond the scope of science, seem naturally to arise. Given his definition, then, the world for each individual is his idea of it. Reality cannot be found in that «will as idea», since reality in the ordinary sense is unknowable, since what is knowledge is only the «order of appearances». The whole external world is simply a construction of the intellect, and «the intellect is simply the instrument that arises in the service of that inner reality which each of us experiences as the desire which he is aware of in his own body, in his physical tensions, in his unconscious strivings, in his will».[11] External behaviour is merely an expression of the metaphysical will, which is blind, an insatiable force without conscious purpose or direction. The intellect has merely an auxiliary function, to assist the will to achieve its goal: «Schopenhauer understands the precariousness of reason and the futility of opposing the will with mere "ideas"» (Aiken, p. 104). Although an irrationalist like Barrios, Schopenhauer never glorified irrationality. His grasp of the sub-rational prefigures, like Barrios' intuitive conclusions, much of the material of contemporary Freudian scholars. Barrios, long considered a *novelista del sentimiento,* accepts the label, if «es uno sentimental por estar convencido de que la idea, la verdadera idea, no brota en el cerebro como una callampana, sino que nace de nuestras emociones» (GS II, 933). Barrios, like Schopenhauer, realises that the intellect has a role to play, but «los grandes pensamientos... han sido presentidos primero... El cerebro los ha ordenado después... Como instrumento concretador, tiene su función» (GS II, 933). Whereas Kant, with whom Barrios was also acquainted (TAM II, 780), had found reality in an unknowable that was posited as an act of practical reason or faith, for Schopenhauer the unknowable reality is that will, which provides a non-intellectual access to reality, in the interests of which knowledge arises. Although, according to Schopenhauer, will is the basic metaphysical category, the root of all that we regard as real, and it is only in our acts of will that we realise ourselves as existing beings, it is also a blind striving in whose service the slavish intellect constructs a practical and illusory world. Since the blind striving will is the inner reality of nature and the essence of life, Schopenhauer's philosophy is perforce doomed to privation since its very striving indicates nonfulfilment. Even when it does find fulfilment it proves to be an illusion,

[11] *The Philosophy of Schopenhauer,* ed. IRWIN EDMAN (New York: Modern Library, 1956), Intro. p. ix. The findings of this chapter are firmly based on *The World as Will and Idea* (1833), the cornerstone of Schopenhauer's philosophy. My great debt to Edman, Aiken and Gardiner here and throughout this section is also acknowledged.

since our ideas provide no access to a world beyond our sense perceptions. Although Schopenhauer tends to personify will, he also «regards it as a malignant force which at every turn frustrates the spiritual life of man» (Aiken, p. 100).

In this description of the human condition Schopenhauer clothes in philosophical terms the fictional world of *Un perdido*. Luis, the supreme example of the malignant force of emotion, buffeted by fate, struggles against the disadvantages of an unhappy childhood (his sentimental temperament moulded by heredity and environment), and fails miserably in the business of living. From the rigours of the military college, the library, and the bohemian life Luis seeks escape in the world of sex and alcohol, which, as in Schopenhauer, prove deceptive. Without attaining fulfilment in the struggle for life, and finding the artificial paradises as unreal as Schopenhauer had predicted, Luis succumbs before the twin forces of frustration and boredom. Schopenhauer and Barrios come together in this manifestation of romantic irony which expresses a «romantic disgust over a world that does not meet the needs of the assertive will, and the irony of that will which finds the emptiness of what it thought it needed» (Edman, p. xi).

Schopenhauer, however, is not just a «satanic metaphysician», subverting the reality which other philosophers deem «rational» and «real». Like Barrios, who was also an anti-rationalist (though Barrios saw the function of reason as a concretiser of what the heart had already pre-felt), Schopenhauer too was something of a Naturalist whose views on the conscious life of man as a by-product of will obviously prefigure Freud, whose ideas Barrios also intuited. Vázquez-Bigi, in his scientific studies of Barrios, has proved the value of the novels from the psychiatric point of view (Thesis, Part II). Schopenhauer too, by his use of empirical, biological data, also illustrates his theories that the will to live is the basic law of life.[12]. Barrios, especially in his use of foils in the first trilogy (Anselmo, Rojitas, Blanco in *Un perdido*) and by means of contrasts in the second trilogy (Morales in *Tamarugal*, Valverde in *Gran señor y rajadiablos*), as illustrated in Chapter 3, demonstrates his affinity with, if not dependence on, Schopenhauer's philosophy of will and his acute psychological insight.

In the relation between the metaphysical and the aesthetic, Barrios and Schopenhauer also come close. One of the aims of this study is to prove the value of Barrios' metaphysical assertions and the role of aesthetics in this view of life, not just as a vehicle for rendering in artistic terms the philosophical conclusions arrived at by Barrios, but also as a force to combat the tragic view of the universe and to help man to escape by giving

---

[12] «Again and again in his writings one finds an amazing grasp of the subrational and unconscious volitional life which the followers of Freud have dramatised for our own age» (AIKEN, p. 104).

meaning to life. In this sense, Schopenhauer's theory of art is fundamental to Barrios' philosophical vision.

Since happiness is impossible, man is compelled to try to escape from his angst and find some kind of redemption. In the world of Schopenhauer (and Barrios), this is possible, if only fleetingly, through the medium of art: «Schopenhauer's pessimistic description of the world, his reflections on the emptiness and worthlessness of life, his denigratory account of the ends and purposes human beings pursue, and his exposure of the manner in which they tend to justify their activities, both in their own eyes and in the eyes of others—all these prepare the way for his theory of art and of the place of the aesthetic consciousness in the realm of experience.»[13] The idea of contemplation or quietism is a key concept in the understanding of life, since through artistic achievement the human will recognises those eternal grades of the will, its «changeless essences which outlive the vicissitudes of change itself» (Edman, p. xi). They are archetypes in which the will can escape the vagaries of time and change, of suffering and disillusion. This therapeutic, even existentialist, role of art, which I shall develop in Chapters 3 and 4, is fundamental to an understanding of Barrios.

Luis, despite the advice of papá Juan, does not find this consolation in the path of art and thus seeks fulfilment in other fields which lead only to disillusion. The stirrings which one finds in Adolfo (*Páginas de un pobre diablo*) are taken up by Valverde whose flights into the realms of the Latin classics bring some relief from strife. The final word is, appropriately, with the last novel, *Los hombres del hombre,* where young Charlie, under the guidance of his sensitive father, at least partly finds a key to the meaning of life in his poetry and his aesthetic sensibility. Barrios, gradually working out his formula for living, gets to the essence of things through these archetypal ideas, trying to communicate in fictional guise what Schopenhauer calls «the permanent essential forms of the world and all its phenomena». It is this concern with the permanent and the universal that raises Barrios above the level of the regionalist. Though Barrios chose to express his ideas in fictional terms he was well acquainted with the media of painting and poetry, which manifestations of art he used in «Tirana ley» and *Los hombres del hombre* respectively. Even in the realm of the novel he sought to achieve the effect of music (*También* I, 28), which has a very special place in Schopenhauer's philosophy: «We must attribute to music a far more serious and deep significance, connected with the inmost nature of the world and our own self» («The World as Idea»).[14] By experiencing universal types and by identifying with

[13] Patrick Gardiner, *Schopenhauer* (Harmondsworth: Penguin, 1963), p. 187.
[14] *The Philosophy of Schopenhauer*, p. 199. For treatment of the function of music see sections 52-53 of «The World as Idea», pp. 199-214. One also remembers Schopenhauer's influence on Wagner.

permanent emotions, one can escape from the pain and frustration of one's ephemeral troubles. Art, then, as papá Juan continually advised Luis, can provide brief moments of respite from the world of illusion, and escape into what Edman calls «the timeless and will-less perception of artistic contemplation» (p. xii). Thus, by means of art one can evade the world of illusion which is the world of knowledge, and the world of pain and disillusion which is the world as will. This, surely, is the route of José Pedro Valverde who, by means of his beloved Horace and Ovid, lifts himself above the barbarism that surrounds him. Poetry, which represents for Barrios all the arts, signifies for the protagonist of *Los hombres del hombre* (along with love of his son) the only meaningful prop in an otherwise absurd world.

Since art provides merely a temporary escape, in Schopenhauer's view there has to be a more permanent way of escape which transcends the aesthetic, i. e. the ascetic—the eternal escape of the ascete. For Schopenhauer this is achieved through a radical denial of the world which is destroyed by a denial of the will. By means of the discovery of Buddha one learns through one's insight that one's sufferings are part of a universal suffering which produces a sympathy which leads on to saintliness. Like Schopenhauer, whose debt to Buddha and the Hindu mystics has been noted (Aiken, p. 103), Barrios, probably via the post-Modernist «mystics», demonstrates a familiarity with the teachings of Buddha: «El Buda fue un maestro que enseñó a su pueblo una metafísica y una ética admirables; según algunos, más admirables que las cristianas, aunque muy parecidas» (UP I, 392). *El hermano asno,* coming immediately after *Un perdido* which had highlighted the need of even a momentary escape along the path of art and the desirability of the more permanent way of the mystic, demonstrates the affinity of Barrios with Amado Nervo, who best represents the quietist redemption and escape through asceticism which are the keynotes in Barrios' evolving view of the world. It was *The Little Flowers of St Francis,* along with Thomas à Kempis, and the Spanish mystics of the Golden Age, which inspired the novel. Fray Lázaro, the protagonist, highly intelligent and analytical, the man of reason and science, a product of the world, tries to achieve saintliness by turning his back on the world of illusion. Only at the end of the novel, by an act of abnegation and selfless love, does he experience the first intimations of the peace that he has sought—and failed to find in the world of illusion, i. e. the world of knowledge.

It is significant that suicide, which might seem an easier and more immediate way of escape,[15] is never used by Schopenhauer nor by his disciple, Barrios. Schopenhauer rejects suicide as the ultimate, most desperate act of the will. In any case, it does not destroy will itself, only the phenome-

---

[15] «If volition is evil, then the cure should be its extinction» (AIKEN, p. 102).

nal body—hence his choice of «will-less contemplation». Not one of Barrios' anguished characters resorts to the ultimate action of self-destruction. *El niño*, Luis, Mario, José, Olga, of the earlier protagonists, suffer till their final tragedy. Although there are no suicides amongst Barrios' heroes, there are no saints either. Thus, those of his protagonists who make any effort to avoid the tragedy, suffering and disillusion of this world, tend to do so through the more transient way of art, especially literature—Adolfo (a transitional figure, hints at it), Valverde, Charlie and *el hombre*. Since *El hermano asno* is open-ended, we cannot be sure of Lázaro's fate. However, by the first charitable act in his life—accepting the blame for a crime he did not commit—he demonstrates his humility, and appears to be on the path to, if not sainthood, at least salvation.

If the object of art is one of the key concepts in «The World as Idea» that influences Barrios,[16] Schopenhauer's deterministic theory of human action and motivation (from «The World as Will») is at the basis of Barrios' view of life, especially as it is reflected in *Un perdido*. However man behaves and whatever form his action takes is an expression of his inner will, which is fixed and unchangeable. This is the whole basis of Blanco's theory of the world, as he describes it to Luis: «Nadie ha podido elegir sus taras, ni el ambiente de su niñez, ni la tonificación de sus órganos. Ahí está la cuestión. Llegamos a la vida como efectos de causas en las cuales no se dio participación a nuestra individualidad. Nacemos con nuestra suerte echada.»[17] As a *perdido,* Luis finds it a comforting excuse for his own lack of energy and will power: «Me encuentro como preso, y sin voluntad» (I, 379). Schopenhauer expresses it thus: «A man cannot resolve to be this or that, nor can he become other than he is; but he *is* once and for all, and he knows in the course of his experience *what* he is.»[18] Free will, then, is obviously an illusion, since free choice is no more than the external manifestation of an internal, unalterable character.

It is in his use of the will as a primary factor in the destiny of his *perdido* protagonists that one sees close parallels between Barrios and Schopenhauer. To possess qualities of will power or to be *un tipo sin voluntad* constitutes the difference between strength and weakness, success or failure, between an Anselmo or a Luis, between a *fuerte* and an *abúlico*, in '98 Generation terms, or a slave as opposed to a master, in the terms of the philosophy of Nietzsche, whom Schopenhauer also influenced.

---

[16] «For Schopenhauer, release from volition comes through aesthetic contemplation, and in particular through the contemplation of art. In the response to great art, and particularly to music, there is for the nonce, a characteristic disinterestedness, a suspension of belief and disbelief, of hope and despair, which leaves us free to contemplate the forms of things without concern and even the manifestations of will itself without personal involvement or care» (AIKEN, p. 103).

[17] UP I, 365-66. See pp. 365-67 for a full novelesque exposition of Schopenhauer's deterministic theories.

[18] «The World as Will», Fourth Book, p. 234.

In fact, this Schopenhauerian influence on Barrios can better be appreciated by taking into account the complementary Nietzschean philosophy. It is in the synthesis of both that we achieve the complete metaphysical picture. It was Schopenhauer's insight into the metaphysical urge, and especially his doctrine of the will, that prefigured new thought categories that emerged with progress in fields like psychology. The contribution that Schopenhauer's philosophy made to the formation of Barrios, the intuitive psychologist, is not to be ignored. Schopenhauer's general dissatisfaction with science is seen partly as a dissatisfaction with the seventeenth- and eighteenth-century obsession with physics which had been extended to try and include all facets of life and human experience. The important discussion between Morales, the Positivist, and the sentimental young seminarian, Javier, in Chapter XVI of *Tamarugal,* reflects this Schopenhauerian concern. In this doctrine of science/faith, Barrios is even closer to Pascal, who was anathema to the other great German philosophical influence on Barrios' life and literature, Friedrich Nietzsche.

BARRIOS AND NIETZSCHE: THE WILL TO POWER

As Schopenhauer had influenced Nietzsche, who in turn praised the former for his philosophy of will, Barrios, both by extension and directly, came under the Nietzschean aegis. It is not insignificant that Mann and Hesse, with whom Barrios had strong affinities, and Freud, whose ideas Barrios had early intuited, should also have come under the influence of Nietzsche.

The Nietzschean is a stock figure in the Latin American novel of the early years of this century, especially in the *perdido*-centred novels such as *El mal metafísico,* and Barrios' *Un perdido* in which the abulic protagonist, like Luis Bernales and Carlos Riga, appears in opposition to his Nietzschean counterpart. The significant title of one of the novels chosen by Arnold Chapman in an interesting article,[19] *El hombre de hierro* (1907) by Rufino Blanco Fombona, is an unsubtle way of contrasting the strong man of will power and energy, in the superman tradition, with the weak *perdido* who is an extension of Nietzsche's slave type. Crispín, the weak hero, confesses not to have read Nietzsche because «es autor prohibido. Creo que está en el Indice». His brother Joaquín, set opposite him as «un bello espécimen de hombre», by contrast obviously belongs to the master class. By Nietzsche's standards too, Carlos Riga in *El mal metafísico,* with his modest ambition, simple tastes and lack of glory, falls into the first category.

Barrios is not exempt from the Nietzschean influence. His early fiction,

---

[19] «The *Perdido* as a Type in Some Spanish American Novels», *PMLA,* LXX, No. 1 (March, 1955), 19-36.

especially *Un perdido,* reads like a gloss of Nietzsche's ideas—not without relation to Schopenhauer, of course, as we have seen. Vázquez-Bigi, in his psychiatrically-oriented article «El tipo sicológico en Eduardo Barrios y correspondencias en las letras europeas», which owes much to the «types» of the German psychiatrist, Ernst Kretschmer, acknowledges Barrios' debt to Nietzsche, «uno de los autores predilectos de Barrios, cuya obra contiene muchas alusiones o referencias directas a la dualidad en su propia siquis o "naturaleza"».[20] Though Vázquez-Bigi bases his case on the ideas of Kretschmer, it is not without reference to Nietzsche's *Doppelgänger* conceit which is at the root of Barrios' characterisation: «I know both sides, for I am both sides... This double series of experiences, this means of access to two worlds that seem so far asunder, finds an exact reflection in my own nature—I have an *alter ego:* I have a "second sight", as well as a first. Perhaps I even have a third sight.»[21] Through the contrasting characters of Blanco («My humanity is a constant self-mastery». *Ecce Homo,* 8, 830) and Luis («But I need solitude... The whole of my *Zarathustra* is a dithyramb of solitude». *Ecce Homo,* 8, 830), Barrios echoes the words of Nietzsche. This desire for solitude and escape from other men is at the root of Luis' attitude. When he discovers that his father is equally timid, he locks himself in his room: «Diríase que necesitaba defender su soledad contra un peligro que le persiguiera» (I, 283), reflecting the words of Nietzsche from *The Wanderer and his Shadow:* «The solitary man speaks: in compensation for much disgust, discouragement, boredom, which stems from an isolated life without friends, books, obligations and passions, we enjoy those brief moments of profound communion with ourselves and Nature.»[22] As Vázquez-Bigi has shrewdly pointed out, one doubts if Luis has the spiritual qualities necessary to experience the kind of cosmic mysticism of which Nietzsche speaks. In fact, this profound communion of the protagonist is rather a reflection of the genius of the author than an authentic personal experience:

> Y entonces, como el ojo de Dios en las viejas estampas del teólogo, asoma por un desgarro de la bruma la roja pupila del sol: tiende unos instantes su mirada, abanico de flechas encendidas, sobre la solemnidad de la alta mar, y desaparece de nuevo.
> En Luis ha ido perdiéndose la personalidad. La dominación que ejercen los tornátiles aspectos le ha ido diluyendo el alma en el ambiente. Ya no es él, es una nota tremolante de la inmensidad encantada. (I, 297)

When Barrios does develop his characterisation in the later novels (Morales in *Tamarugal* and Valverde in *Gran señor y rajadiablos*), it seems

---

[20] *Revista Iberoamericana,* XXIV, No. 48 (julio-diciembre, 1959), 277.
[21] *Ecce Homo,* from *The Philosophy of Nietzsche* (New York: The Modern Library, 1937), pp. 817 and 821 (trans. Clifton P. Fadiman).
[22] Translated from *Sämtliche Werke* [*Complete Works*] of Nietzsche (München: Hanser, 1960), I, No. 200, p. 956.

to be specifically in the light of, and based on, Nietzsche's theories of the will to power and the superman.[23] Even in his autobiographical essay, «También algo de mí», he specifically acknowledges his debt to Zarathustra whose inspiration supports him in his struggle for life: «¿Cómo llegaré a la montaña?, se interroga Zarathustra. Sube y no mires atrás» (I, 29).

Nietzsche, in *Thus Spoke Zarathustra* (Second Part) in the section «On Self-overcoming», comes to the conclusion that all human behaviour can be reduced to a single idea, viz. the will to power: «Only where there is life is there also will: not will to life but—thus I teach you—will to power.»[24] The whole process of will to power, however, is inextricably bound up with the idea of «self-overcoming» or sublimation. Overcoming is part of man's desire—to help him to escape from his present state of weakness. It is man's nature to want a more powerful state of being—hence the obvious analogy between the Barrios *débil/perdido* types and Nietzsche's herd/slave types. If Nietzsche's superman wants to perfect himself, to re-create himself, to become active rather than passive, to become a creator rather than a creature, it is no wonder that types like Gálvez's Carlos Riga and Barrios' Luis Bernales do not fit the master mould. For Riga «la verdadera y única gloria consistía en penetrar en el corazón de los hombres, conmover, hacer llorar, hacer reír, servir de asunto a los que se amaban para inspirarles nuevos motivos de amor. Ser leído y comprendido por almas sensibles que daban, al autor del libro que las conmovía, un lugarcito en su corazón» (p. 51)—hardly the stuff of the Nietzschean superman. Riga's soul-brother Luis is similarly lacking in ambition—hence his inability to understand Nietzsche's philosophy of the superman (I, 388), a type with whom he cannot identify. Luis, unable to cope with life's problems, can never reach the high state of the *Ubermensch* who has overcome himself—a passionate man in control of his passions, the creator who uses

[23] These are but two of the ideas of Nietzsche that, out of context, would be attractive to the Nazis. His sister twisted many of his notes and presented them to Hitler who published, for propaganda purposes, anthologies which were really a perversion of his thought. Walter Kaufmann, in his article on Nietzsche in *Encyclopaedia Britannica* (1965), suggests that several key images of Nietzsche have been distorted, e.g. (i) the *hammer* image does not mean adopting a sledgehammer technique but posing questions with a hammer to hear as a reply the hollow sound; (ii) the *master* morality/*slave* morality. The assumption was that he was for the «master» morality. KAUFMANN states in the chapter «The Improvers of Mankind» in *Twilight of the Idols,* that Nietzsche showed that this was not the case; (iii) «immoralist» does not mean that he favoured lack of discipline. His immoralism was in the main rather an impassioned non-conformism. He chose the word because morality generally designated a social code that equated being moral with conformity. My great debt to Kaufmann here and elsewhere is acknowledged.

It was Barrios' fate to be associated with Nietzsche as well as another misunderstood thinker, Freud, whose equally simplified and distorted views have also been generally accepted at a superficial level. Thus, it is not surprising that Barrios' novels have not always been fully appreciated by the public and the critics.

[24] *The Portable Nietzsche,* trans., ed., intro., by Walter Kaufmann (New York: Viking Press, 1966), p. 227.

his powers creatively. Luis, who does not have the propensity to the master morality, is constantly by-passed and outwitted by those—Anselmo («un fuerte, un triunfador instintivo» I, 441), Rojitas («uno de esos hombres alegres y satisfechos de la suerte» I, 473)—who seek the higher state. Those who achieve sublimation will find the glory of success: «Success in individual cases is constantly encountered in the most widely different places and cultures: here we really do find a higher type, which is, in relation to mankind as a whole, a kind of overman» (*The Anti-Christ*, Section 4, p. 571). Luis cannot belong to this group since he does not aspire to great actions. In Anselmo, his brother and foil, who finds success in both his military and romantic life, is the seed of Barrios' more balanced character Valverde, who, thirty years later, is a deliberately drawn counterbalance, excelling in passions and enjoying the Dionysian pleasures of great actions in the fields of agriculture, justice and the military life.[25] Valverde, however, in his pursuit of Positivist tenets,[26] does not abandon the consolation of religion, especially in its satisfaction of emotional needs.

Blanco, on the other hand, in *Un perdido*, reflects more directly and closely the Nietzschean strain of Barrios' philosophy, with his views on God and the eternal recurrence. Zarathustra's advice to the potential superman: «Remain faithful to the earth, and do not believe those who speak to you of otherworldly hopes! » is an indictment of the God-oriented universe. The superman ought to be much more concerned with the problems of this life. Man should spend his time trying to perfect himself rather than worshipping «perfection», in the name of God. As Blanco constantly pointed out to Luis, the world is not governed by any purpose: «Nos mueven efectos determinados, por causas entretejidas desde el principio de los siglos, sin

---

[25] This Dionysian idea and its converse the Apollonian are the key concepts of Nietzsche's *The Birth of Tragedy*. WALTER KAUFMANN, in his *Nietzsche: Philosopher, Psychologist, Antichrist* (New Jersey: Princeton University Press, 1968), p. 128, differentiates them thus: «Apollo represents the aspect of the classical Greek genius extolled by Winckelmann and Goethe: the power to create harmonious and measured beauty; the strength to shape one's character no less than works of art; the principle of individuation; the form-giving force, which reached its consummation in Greek sculpture. Dionysius, in Nietzsche's first book, is the symbol of that drunken frenzy which threatened to destroy all forms and codes; the ceaseless striving which apparently defies all limitations; the ultimate abandonment we sometimes sense in music. In *The Birth of Tragedy* the Apollonian power to give form is further associated with the creation of illusions, while the Dionysian frenzy carries with it a suggestion of blind will: in other words, both are coloured by Schopenhauer's destruction of the world as will and representation.»

However, as Kaufmann has also pointed out (*Encyclopaedia Britannica* article), in Nietzsche's later works the early Dionysian (flood of passion) / Apollonian (serenity) contrast is modified to the extent that the Dionysian represents passion controlled and creatively employed (as opposed to negation of the passions, of the body and of this world), which in Barrios' fiction is best represented by the balanced figure of José Pedro Valverde in *Gran señor y rajadiablos*.

[26] The idea of the superman does not necessarily entail faith in «Progress» which Nietzsche calls «merely a modern idea, that is a false idea» (*Anti-Christ*, Section 4, p. 571, *Portable Nietzsche*).

que nuestra voluntad entonces para nada interviniese» (I, 506). It is merely a senseless drama, eternally repeated at great intervals, in which we all have the same roles to play. Luis had already partly come to this conclusion by his intuition: «Ya entonces entrevió Luis que la vida involucra una ley inflexible, indiferente y dura. Estas penetraciones sutiles de sus catorce años, sentimentales o intuitivas, en ningún modo ideológicas, dejábanle suspenso y asustado» (I, 268). Rooted in the earth, then, the idea of the superman is a negation of God,[27] just as the idea of a pointless, absurd existence and the eternal recurrence of the same events denies the Christian view of time and history: «la vida volvió a parecerle un camino absurdo que recorría una caravana de seres vendados, arreada por una ley dura e imperturbable, que tenía previstos aún los latigazos de castigo a nuestras rebeldías» (I, 429). This attack on Christianity is reinforced by Nietzsche's view of what he calls «otherworldliness» as an escape for the weak who, not being able to fulfil themselves in this world, need the crutch of «another life». Luis' burden is doubly hard to bear since he does not even have the compensatory religious prop to give him some means of support. As Morales, the Positivist spokesman for reason and science, implied in *Tamarugal* in the important philosophical discussion with the seminarian Javier, the voice of religious faith and emotion, Christianity is born of weakness and is made up of those failures (slaves) who would militate against the successful (masters). Religion is the haven of the mediocre, the unambitious, and of the fettered mind which «has waged deadly war against this higher type of man...; Christianity has sided with all that is weak and base, with all failures...; it has corrupted the reason even of those strongest in spirit by teaching men to consider the supreme values of the spirit as something sinful, as something that leads into error—as temptations. The most pitiful example: the corruption of Pascal, who believed in the corruption of his reason through original sin when it had in fact been corrupted only by his Christianity» (*The Anti-Christ,* Section 5, pp. 571-72).[28]

In his critique of Christianity as a religion of vengefulness, judgment

---

[27] Cf. the atheism of Schopenhauer. «Schopenhauer reinterpreted Christianity in a pessimistic sense, and then assimilated it to the religions of the East, in order to draw it into the orbit of his own philosophy: but this philosophy itself was atheist. The 'will' is not God: there is no God in Schopenhauer's world of will and idea» (HOLLINGDALE, pp. 34-35).

[28] What Gonzalo Sobejano has to say about the influence of Nietzsche in Catholic Spain summarises well the points of contact not only with Latin America in general but with Barrios in particular: «En la controversia con el cristianismo, en el replanteamiento de los valores morales y vitales, en la comprensión de los motivos fundamentales del obrar, en la aversión hacia la democracia y el socialismo, en el anhelo de una sobrehumanidad futura, en el culto a la voluntad de poderío, en la visión del tiempo y de la eternidad, desapego al romanticismo, condenación de la decadencia, sin lograr rebasarla, interpretación de las artes y en otros variados aspectos secundarios, la huella de Nietzsche se trasluce...» (*Nietzsche en España* [Madrid: Ed. Gredos, 1967], p. 10).

and negation, anti-rational and anti-scientific, and embracing a faith that involves self-deception, Nietzsche is attacking in particular the religion of Blaise Pascal.[29]

BARRIOS AND PASCAL: THE HEART OF THE MATTER

To Eduardo Barrios many spiritual fathers have been attributed, especially in the French literature of the nineteenth and early twentieth centuries. His debt to Flaubert has been perceived and treated by some critics,[30] while others see in him the influence of Hugo, Zola, Balzac, Daudet, and the French Decadents, especially in the early works like *Del natural*.[31] Barrios himself is of no help, and merely denies his literary ancestry: « ¡Oh los padres espirituales de un escritor! Los míos son muchos, son demasiados; tantos, que ni los distingo. Leo a todos, siguiendo la norma de Balzac, para no parecerme a nadie» (*También* I, 30-31). He maintained this attitude, even when faced with accusations of plagiarism, as in the case of his *El hermano asno*.[32]

Few critics go beyond the nineteenth century in French letters to find the sources of literary formation that produced works like *Un perdido*, *El hermano asno*, and *Gran señor y rajadiablos*. One can, however, go back three hundred years, and draw some of the parallels that exist between Barrios and the French religious thinker, Blaise Pascal (1623-1662), picking out the analogies in their work and thought, and showing the similarities in their view of the world and religion. Nowhere does Barrios admit the influence of Pascal, but it seems highly improbable that he, who quotes Fénélon, Balzac, Hugo, and knew thinkers like Kant, Schopenhauer and Nietzsche, should not have read Pascal. In any case, Barrios' concept of the world is Pascalian in tone, and I should like to suggest that Barrios had assimilated, consciously or unconsciously, Pascalian ideas from direct or indirect sources.

[29] In spite of this strong criticism, it is rather interesting that Nietzsche should have cited Pascal as one of the French writers (along with Montaigne and Stendhal) that he held in high esteem. This ambivalence is further strengthened by his confession that «he finds Socrates, Plato and Pascal to be great men, but so highly ambiguous that they must be evaluated in opposite ways, depending on the circumstances in which they appear». He goes on: «When I speak of Plato, Pascal, Spinoza and Goethe, I know that their blood flows in my veins» (Quoted in *Nietzsche* by Karl Jaspers [Tucson: University of Arizona Press, 1965], pp. 34-35).

[30] CARLOS LOZANO, «Paralelismos entre Flaubert y Eduardo Barrios», *Revista Iberoamericana*, XXIV, No. 47 (enero-junio, 1959), 105-16.

[31] NED J. DAVISON, «The Significance of *Del natural* in the Fiction of Eduardo Barrios», *Hispania*, XLIV, No. 1 (March, 1961), 27-33.

[32] Barrios was accused of plagiarising from two French novels: *Le Visage émerveillé* by the Comtesse Matthieu de Noailles, and *La Rose de Grenade* by Jean Rameau, both with a convent setting. Apart from the atmosphere of the former, and the repetition of the name Lazare in the latter, the similarities are superficial.

At first glance they appear unlikely kindred spirits. Pascal, especially after his conversion in 1646, devoted his life to religion, the expression of which we find especially in his *Pensées*. Barrios, on the other hand, could hardly be termed a religious man, in the accepted sense of conventional religion. Religion plays no great part in the autobiographical details that we have of his life («También algo de mí»), nor in the biographies,[33] though religion figures prominently in the main works. Apart from being a divorcee, Barrios was, according to his friend, Fernando Santiván, a mason, with a concept of God as a great architect or geometer: «Me parece que fue masón, y como tal se explicó el mundo, su origen y su fin, bajo la moción de un Gran Arquitecto.»[34] It is a significant fact that papá Juan is described at the outset as «un masón de corazón cristiano y cerebro determinista» (UP I, 224). These allusions to masonry are found elsewhere in his novels.[35] Pascal, too, was a deviant from orthodox Catholicism, being an associate of the Jansenists of Port Royal.[36] His father, who was a renowned mathematician, had nurtured in the young Pascal his vocation as a geometer. Having received also a good solid religious education, he was able to maintain apart the domains of faith and reason: «Cet esprit si grand, si vaste et si rempli de curiosités, qui cherchait avec tant de soin la raison et la cause de tout, était en même temps soumis à toutes les choses de la religion comme un enfant.»[37] This was the agonising problem that Barrios' intellectual, self-analytical Fray Lázaro, in *El hermano asno,* was tormented with, and the solution of which he admired in the implicit faith of his simple fellow-monks: «En religión, mientras menos se piensa más se sabe» (HA II, 557). This ability to maintain science/knowledge apart from religion, which divided the seventeenth century, Barrios reaffirms in *Tamarugal:* «La religión marcha... ajena a la ciencia, independiente de ella, por otra ruta» (II, 689), states Barrios' spokesman, Javier, the young seminarian. Pascal, more akin to Javier, did not have to endure the problems of Fray Lázaro. After his first conversion (i. e. intellectual) in 1646, the young Pascal led a life of contradiction, with the scientist still living alongside the religious convert. Over-zealous in his first years, he became involved in an ecclesiastical court case, *l'affaire Saint-Ange,* in which an old Capuchin, who professed an alliance of faith and reason, stated that dogma could be

[33] JULIO ORLANDI y ALEJANDRO RAMÍREZ, *Eduardo Barrios* (Santiago, 1960), NED J. DAVISON, *Eduardo Barrios* (New York: Twayne, 1970), BENJAMÍN MARTÍNEZ LÓPEZ, *Eduardo Barrios: vida y obra* (Río Piedras, Puerto Rico, 1977).

[34] «Eduardo Barrios y su tiempo», *Atenea*, CLIV, No. 404 (1964), 96.

[35] TAM II, 679; PF I, 53.

[36] Followers of Jannsen, bishop of Ypres, who produced in 1640 his *Augustinus,* to intervene in the grace-free will controversy, affirming that grace is all-powerful, and is reserved for those who are predestined to receive it.

[37] Mme. PÉRIER (Pascal's sister), «Vie de Pascal» in the *Pensées,* Brunschvicg edition (Paris: Garnier, 1958), p. 7. All other references to the *Pensées* are from this edition and are indicated in the text.

4

understood by reason. Pascal, stating that faith surpasses reason, won his case. In his new religious pride, however, he had forgotten the virtue of charity. Barrios was to re-introduce the Capuchin in *El hermano asno* as a vision to tempt Fray Rufino, accusing him of saintly pride.

After his second conversion (i. e. mystical) in 1654, Pascal settled at Port Royal, and continued his studies, producing for the children there an elementary manual, *Premiers Eléments de géométrie,* and a short treatise, *De l'Esprit géométrique,* in which he situates geometry in his new Christian conception of the world. This geometric spirit pervades all the work of Barrios. In «También algo de mí», discussing differences of opinion with regard to art, he prefers to use geometric terminology: «Parece que todos estuviéramos situados en sucesivos puntos de una elipse», with some critics on «... un arco de la elipse...», and others on «... el arco opuesto» (I, 29-30). In *Un perdido,* Blanco's whole conception of the world is rendered in mathematical, geometrical terms: «Veo el humo de mi cigarrillo. Forma como una vía láctea. De ello se desprenden espirales, elipses, círculos; cada cual, un universo de chispas... Y como las leyes físicas rigen igualmente los cuerpos microscópicos y las grandes esferas, allí se moverá todo del mismo modo que en los sistemas planetarios» (I, 366).

It is in this treatise *De l'Esprit géométrique* that we find Pascal's celebrated passage on *les deux infinis.* All his study in the monastic atmosphere of Port Royal, scientific, geometrical, philosophical, is subordinated to a superior order, i. e. the glory of God. In this passage on the two infinites, «l'une de grandeur, l'autre de petitesse»,[38] Pascal seeks to convert the atheist, and to convince man of his nothingness in comparison with the greatness of God. To do so he employs geometrical proofs and terminology: «Quelque mouvement, quelque nombre, quelque space, quelque temps que ce soit, il y en a toujours un plus grand et un moindre: de sorte qu'ils se soutiennent tous entre le néant et l'infini, étant toujours infiniment éloignés de ces extrêmes...» (Michaud, p. 22). Barrios makes constant use of this idea of the two infinities to prove that there is something beyond reason, and quite specifically, in *Tamarugal,* to prove the existence of God. The seminarian, Javier, trying to convince the atheist, ironically named Jesús Morales, quotes Kant to support the Pascalian theory of *les deux infinis:* «Y Kant declaraba que... cuando contemplaba el firmamento infinito y volvíase a continuación a considerar el fondo vivo de su conciencia, todo el pensamiento se le empequeñecía» (TAM II, 680). Luis, in *Un perdido,* was very aware of his «pequeñez en medio de la grandeza del espacio. Sentíase primero insignificante, como un insecto» (I, 255). Blanco, with his physical view of the world, states que «la tierra es apenas una bolita de barro lanzada en el espacio infinito» (I, 312). As Pascal had put his mathematics and his geometry at the service of God, so too does the

---

[38] Guy Michaud, *L'Oeuvre de Pascal* (Paris: Hachette, 1950), p. 21.

young seminarian seek to convince the unbeliever in *Tamarugal* with mathematical proofs to show that something exists beyond scientific reason, and that there are things that our finite minds cannot grasp: «Pero cuando le hicieron dividir diez entre tres, se encontró con tres, tres, tres... hasta lo infinito. Supo entonces que había números racionales y números irracionales. Claro, matemático, ¿verdad? Luego, hay algo que está más allá de la razón. —Un número infinito...» (II, 681). Thus, Barrios is reiterating the standpoint that Pascal had taken up in the Saint-Ange affair, i. e. dogma cannot be understood by reason. We, with our puny, finite minds, cannot rationalise ideas that are beyond our scope—in the infinite. We have, therefore, to accept them by faith, as faith surpasses reason.

As Barrios had used variations on the two infinities theme, he also made use of the famous *pari* (bet, wager) of Pascal, which was a kind of corollary of *les deux infinis*. In an attempt to convince the sceptics, Pascal suggests that, since man, without God, is miserable, man should take a chance on the existence of God. Man stakes his human life, which is finite, i. e. nothing. What can he win? Eternal happiness, which is infinite, i. e. all. There is nothing to lose. If God exists, he has gained everything. «Si vous gagnez, vous gagnez tout; si vous perdez, vous ne perdez rien» (Brunschvicg, p. 136). Thus, one must bet. In *Tamarugal*, the young seminarian, trying to convince the atheist of the existence of God, asks him: «¿Cree usted en la suerte? ... ya cree usted en algo que escapa a la razón. ¿Y se explica usted la suerte? ... —Imposible. Pues mire usted, algunos a la voluntad de la suerte la llamamos voluntad de Dios también» (II, 690). If the atheist believes in luck, which cannot be explained by reason, why not just take a chance (bet) and call the will of luck the will of God. There is nothing to lose, since neither can be explained by reason. Like the infinite numbers, they are «más allá de la razón».

This struggle between reason and authority, between science and religion, between knowledge and faith, which was a burning problem for the Baroque (cf. Sor Juana), we find in Barrios as in Pascal. In his *Traité du vide,* Pascal distinguishes expressly between authority and reason: «Il n'en est pas de même de sujets qui tombent sous le sens ou sous le raisonnement: l'autorité y est inutile: la raison seule a lieu d'en connaître. Elles ont leurs droits séparés...» (Michaud, p. 11). Fray Lázaro, the introspective Franciscan of *El hermano asno,* sees, like Sor Juana, that knowledge is a barrier to salvation, and prays for innocence and ignorance: «Líbrame, Señor, del análisis: él mata la instintividad de las acciones. Hazme claro y simplifícame» (II, 549). To try to rationalise things that cannot be known is the mistake that the theologians make (like Frère Saint-Ange). This is the sin of pride, since it is impossible to reason the ways of God, as Fray Lázaro sees: «Analizando, Señor, los moralistas, doctos en orgullo, pretenden interpretarte, sin ver que fragmentan tu Total Designio...» (II, 549).

Fray Lázaro's constant plea was to be freed from his intellectualising. Before his crisis, Fray Rufino had seen clearly that the less one thinks on religious matters, the more one knows. This is merely stated another way by José Pedro Valverde, the hero of *Gran señor y rajadiablos,* when he says that «sólo hay una manera de tener fe: creyendo sin discurrir» (II, 969). As his priest-uncle had said earlier, «Sin fe, no se cree... no hay más verdad que la fe» (II, 795). In later discussion with the sceptical journalists, Valverde feels, like Fray Lázaro, that «las iglesias han cometido el error de racionalizar sus religiones» (II, 934-35). It is significant that Pascal, in his famous prayer, the *Mémorial,* prayed to «Dieu d'Abraham, Dieu d'Isaac, Dieu de Jacob, *non des philosophes et des savants*».[39]

Religion, then, for Pascal and Barrios is not something that can be rationalised. It is outside the field of reason, and does not stem from the brain. It is of the heart, as opposed to the head, something that is felt. As Pascal says, «C'est le coeur qui sent Dieu, et non la raison. Voilà ce que c'est que la foi: Dieu sensible au coeur, non à la raison» (Brunschvicg, p. 147). It is in this philosophy of the heart as the centre and source of religion—the predominance of emotions, sentiment and instinct—that Barrios and Pascal go hand in hand. Every major novel of Eduardo Barrios reiterates this theme, and acts as a kind of commentary on the fundamental *Pensées* concerning the submission of reason. By the nature of Pascal's life, the role of the heart as a guide, as being superior to reason, will be confined to the religious sphere. In the works of Barrios, however, this heart-centred idea is carried into all spheres of life, as we shall see, especially in Chapter 3. A key part of the work of Barrios on this theme is the discussion of Valverde with the free-thinking journalists in *Gran señor y rajadiablos.* He starts off with the basic assumption that «Vivimos de nuestras emociones» (II, 933). He accepts the label of «un sentimental», if being sentimental means being convinced that ideas do not spring out of the brain like mushrooms, but are conceived in our emotions: [40] «La emoción es el principio. Y la idea, sólo sirviendo a la emoción, su madre, hace doctrina, vive» (II, 933). He staggers his listeners by asking the unusual, but telling, question: «¿Se le ocurrió a nadie nunca pintar el Cerebro de Jesús? No, por cierto. ¡El Corazón de Jesús!» (II, 933). The brain has a part to play, of course, but, as Schopenhauer also saw, the great thoughts have already been pre-felt. The brain only organises them. This concretising function of the brain is an important one, as Pascal too saw, but it is secondary.

Valverde's statement (II, 933) is almost a gloss of Pascal's *pensée* on

---

[39] MICHAUD, p. 18, my italics. This was a prayer that was found on Pascal's person after his death. It was the result of a mystical experience that he had undergone on 23 November 1654.

[40] Cf. BARRIOS in *También* I, 27: «yo soy un sentimental...».

the same subject: «Nous connaissons la vérité, non seulement par la raison, mais encore par le coeur... Et c'est sur ces connaissances du coeur et de l'instinct qu'il faut que la raison s'appuie, et qu'elle y fonde tout son discours» (Brunschvicg, p. 147). When Valverde goes on to state that «hay una zona sensible pero no razonable» (II, 934), he is echoing Pascal, who says that «Le coeur a ses raisons, que la raison ne connaît point...» (Brunschvicg, p. 146). The sum of Valverde's argument is that «En el campo religioso, el sentimiento es la base y el impulso. La idea, sólo un medio expresivo. Los racionalistas discuten y pulverizan las ideas religiosas; mas nada pueden contra el sentimiento religioso» (II, 934). This rationalisation of religion was the great error committed by the church, says Valverde. As Pascal knows, «Si on soumet tout à la raison, notre religion n'aura rien de mystérieux et de surnaturel» (Brunschvicg, p. 146). This is undesirable, for, as Javier observes in *Tamarugal*, «más allá de la razón hay algo misterioso de mayor alcance» (II, 680).

The heart, then, has its order: «Le coeur a son ordre» (Brunschvicg, p. 148), has its own voices, and «las voces del corazón [son] siempre más poderosas que la del razonamiento» (UP, I, 279), and also has its own truths: «hay verdades del corazón, como las hay del cerebro» (HA II, 579). In the thinking of Pascal and Barrios, therefore, the heart is all-important, even to the extent of dominating the brain. Reason, however, can still have a role to play, as we have noted. «La emoción es la esencia virtual de las cosas» (HA II, 625), but «exclure la raison» would be an excess (Brunschvicg, p. 143). As long as we remember its limitations: («Olvida el cerebro; la sensibilidad, nunca» [HA II, 625]), and bear in mind the words of Fénélon that «nuestra razón no existe sino en nuestras ideas claras» (TAM II, 679-80), reason may have a part to play «como instrumento concretador», as we have observed. Like all apparatus, however, it is sometimes defective, whereas the heart never fails. If we follow our instincts, we cannot err: «Mientras las razonables gobiernan la vida visible y palpable, las indistintas, muy escondidas, nos guían desde el mundo íntimo y suelen llevarnos más lejos» (TAM II, 680). Once we reverse the situation and allow our brain to dominate the heart, and «los principios éticos reemplazan la instintividad de las acciones, no sabemos ya conducirnos, por dócil que nuestro corazón se entregue» (HA II, 575). The constant message is that we must be guided by our heart. If, unfortunately, we should be misled by our heart, we need not fear, for very conveniently, as the gospel tells us, «si nuestro corazón nos condena... Dios es más grande que nuestro corazón» (TAM II, 689). Once again we return to the Pascalian wager—bet everything on the instincts of the heart, for we have nothing to lose. If we go wrong, then God in his magnanimity will forgive us from the depths of His Sacred Heart.[41]

[41] Significantly in *Tamarugal,* the young seminarian has a friend whom Barrios

Our object, therefore, is, guided by our heart, to reach God, but «Nous ne connaissons Dieu que par Jésus-Christ. Sans ce Médiateur, est ôtée toute communication avec Dieu; par Jésus-Christ, nous connaissons Dieu» (Brunschvicg, p. 207). A heart-centred religion means that we can reach God only through his Son, through the Heart of Jesus, as Valverde emphasises. To try to reach God without the help of a mediator is pride. Profiting from his earlier altercation with Frère Saint-Ange, Pascal saw that God can only be proved by experience, and by the experience of charity alone: «Jésus-Christ, Saint Paul ont l'ordre de la charité» (Brunschvicg, p. 148). «En lui et par lui nous connaissons donc Dieu» (Brunschvicg, p. 207). Not only is Christ essential as a mediator, without him life has no meaning: «Non seulement nous ne connaissons Dieu que par Jésus-Christ, mais nous ne nous connaissons nous-mêmes que par Jésus-Christ. Nous ne connaissons la vie, la mort que par Jésus-Christ. Hors de Jésus-Christ, nous ne savons ce que c'est ni que notre vie, ni que notre mort, ni que Dieu, ni que nous-mêmes» (Brunschvicg, p. 208). Jesus Christ is the sole means of salvation, and without him eternal life is unattainable. We must humiliate ourselves and say with Fray Lázaro: «no puedo hacer otra cosa que abrir mi corazón al Corazón de Jesús, y obedecer ciego, con la humildad de Nuestro Seráfico Patriarca» (HA II, 557). If Barrios was a mason (which may imply an anti-clerical spirit, at least), he was, however, like papá Juan, a Christian mason. In spite of Barrios' conception of God as a great Architect, he still had a great love for «Jesús, que era bueno y poeta, más que equitativo juez...» (UP I, 246). One notes that the favourite reading of papá Juan's wife, Luis' grandmother, was «la Imitación de Cristo» of Thomas à Kempis (UP I, 231). In *Gran señor y rajadiablos,* one of the outstanding parts of Valverde's important discussion with the journalists was his striking picture of the Heart of Jesus. He goes on to say: «Nuestro Divino Jesús, con su prédica, su ejemplo, su gran sacrificio, ¿creó y sembró meras ideas acaso? Creó una gran emoción que a modo de llamarada nos ha envuelto, nos ha encendido, nos ha fecundado» (II, 933), and, of course, as Fray Lázaro came to recognise, «la emoción es el alma» (HA II, 625). Both Pascal and Barrios agree, then, on the central position of the Son as an intermediary between man and God. In *Tamarugal,* when Javier talks of «la voluntad de Dios», he is very quick to add «que nos reveló el Cristo» (TAM II, 689).

In Pascal's *Mémorial,* the record of his mystical experience, his first cry was to the God of the Old Testament, and then to the «Dieu de Jésus-Christ... Jésus-Christ... Jésus-Christ... Soumission totale à Jésus-Christ et à mon directeur...» (Michaud, p. 18). His whole prayer, as well as being Christ-oriented, is similar in tone to the tormented *cris de coeur* of Fray

names Pascal (a rather unusual name for a young Chilean). This Pascal, concerned about his friend, Javier, asks, «¿qué pasa en ti? ... En tu corazón?» (II, 697).

Lázaro in *El hermano asno.* Pascal's «Mon Dieu, me quitterez-vous?» (Michaud, p. 18), echoing the words of Christ on the cross, is re-echoed by Fray Lázaro: «Padre, ¿por qué me has abandonado?» (HA II, 620). Fray Lázaro's «pero estoy contigo, Señor, no me abandones» (HA II, 610) is reminiscent of Pascal's plea: «Que je n'en sois jamais séparé» (Michaud, p. 18). From a careful study of *El hermano asno,* especially the suppliant tone of the unhappy friar's pleading to his Maker, one might suggest, with a measure of confidence, Barrios' awareness of the *Pensées* from some source. With the *Mémorial* and another fragment called the *Mystère de Jésus* (Michaud, pp. 113-16), Pascal conveys a religious tone identifiable with that of *El hermano asno.* With an orderly reading of the *Pensées,* one ends with Pascal's affirmation that real conversion can only be accomplished through humility, and that it leads to God, via the Mediator, Christ. «La conversion véritable consiste à s'anéantir devant cet Etre universel...; à reconnaître qu'on ne peut rien sans lui... et que, sans un médiateur, il ne peut y avoir de commerce» (Brunschvicg, p. 194). *El hermano asno* ends with the practical application of this self-annihilation. Fray Lázaro, to protect the good name of the order, and the reputation of the dead «saint», agrees to accept the blame for the sexual crime and depart from the convent. «Humíllese y comprenda» (II, 631), the Provincial counsels Fray Lázaro, who sees that, to be a good Franciscan, he has no other option, as Fray Rufino (ironically enough) had advised, than «cerrar los ojos y servir, servir» (HA II, 557).

Barrios was never accustomed to admit his influences, whether it be Flaubert, Fénélon, Balzac or Hugo. I have tried to show that there are many echoes of Pascal in Barrios' work, especially with regard to religion, his view of man's place in the world, and his relationship with God. Apart from details about names (the Pascal in *Tamarugal*), glosses on individual *pensées,* and spiritual affinities with Saint Paul and Saint Augustine,[42] Barrios manages to convey a geometrical picture of the world (with God as the great Geometer), in keeping with the Pascalian idea. At the same time, however, without contradiction, he portrays, like Pascal, a heart-centred world in which faith, sentiment, emotion and instinct triumph over the brain and reason, in the quest to attain eternal salvation. For both, this salvation can be attained only through Jesus Christ. Herein lie the closest links between Eduardo Barrios and Blaise Pascal.

PHILOSOPHY AND RELIGION

For Barrios to be susceptible to extremes like the atheistic ideas of Schopenhauer/Nietzsche and the religious doctrines of Pascal might sug-

---

[42] Cf. GS II, 797: BRUNSCHVICG, pp. 141, 148, 225.

43

gest at first glance a basic contradiction in his philosophical formation. However, this juxtaposition of philosophy and religion is not as anomalous as it may appear. In fact, Pascal, like Kierkegaard, might be considered a good example of a religious philosopher in the sense that be based his view of life, his philosophical outlook, on religious principles.

Barrios, whose literary and philosophical masters are many, is concerned in his fiction with metaphysical problems, with man's place not so much in society as in the universe. Man, however, though the most interesting thing in the world, cannot be understood on the basis of himself alone. As we confront man's being, we come face to face with his concern for God, or Transcendence, as Jaspers calls it, whose external manifestation is religion. All philosophy is directed towards the same goal—trying to achieve some certainty about Transcendence. Although historically philosophy and religion have been related to each other in terms of opposition or subordination, they need not be mutually exclusive. As Jaspers points out in his essay «On My Philosophy»,[43] if philosophy revolves around Transcendence, it must have some relation with religion—not necessarily total exclusion: «When religion is excluded by philosophy or philosophy by religion; when one side asserts dominance over the other, by claiming to be the sole and most exalted authority, then man loses his openness to Being and his own potentiality in order to obtain a final closing of knowledge, but even this remains closed to him. He becomes, whether he limits himself to religion or to philosophy, dogmatic, fanatical, and finally, with failure, nihilistic. To remain truthful religion needs the conscience of philosophy. To retain a significant content philosophy needs the substance of religion... Philosophy will have to affirm religion at least as the reality to which it, too, owes its existence. If religion were not the life of mankind, there would be no philosophy either.»[44]

Barrios' fiction presents a synthesis of the disparate ideas gathered from thinkers like Schopenhauer/Nietzsche and Pascal who represent the polar opposites of atheistic philosophy and Christ-centred religion. This reconciliation of philosophy and religion in the literary field is merely the manifestation of a compatibility in the metaphysical sphere whose goal was to achieve, no matter the source, an outlook on life that would make the problem of existence at least tolerable—which is all that one can hope for in this world.

Though, like Pascal, not an orthodox Christian, and often anticlerical,

---

[43] Translated and reproduced by WALTER KAUFMANN in his *Existentialism from Dostoevsky to Sartre* (Cleveland: Meridian Books, 1956), p. 152.

[44] Jaspers goes on to reinforce his thesis: «Philosophy from its side cannot wish to fight religion. It must acknowledge it, albeit as its polar opposite, yet related to it through this polarity. Religion must always interest it because philosophy is constantly stirred up, prodded and addressed by it. Philosophy cannot wish to replace religion, compete with it, nor make propaganda on its own behalf against it» (p. 153).

Eduardo Barrios has a deep knowledge of religion, and recognises its value as a formative force and an emotional support. To be capable of writing *El hermano asno* Barrios must have had a profound awareness not only of the Franciscan order but also Christian theology and scripture which is at the basis of the religious conflict of the novel. Barrios has narrated in many places the history of his writing of the novel. Apart from the inspiration of *The Little Flowers of St Francis,* there is a general feeling for the doctrinal fathers of the church, St Thomas Aquinas and St Augustine, as well as the mystical writings of St John of the Cross and St Teresa of Avila. Vázquez-Bigi detects also «una activa vena protestante» in the novel, e. g. allusions to predestination and criticism of confessional forgiveness.[45] This he probably inherited from his maternal grandfather Hudtwalcker who was a Protestant and who, as we have seen, had a great influence on Barrios' formation. Especially in *El hermano asno,* which has the religious setting of the monastery, Barrios demonstrates his knowledge of, and the value of, religion as a force, especially for tragedy. In his later view of life in the second trilogy, Barrios, in his mellowing years, utilises religion much more often to portray the balance long sought after. In *Tamarugal,* for example, the young seminarian Javier demonstrates the need for religion in life, and quotes Kant, Fénélon and St John of the Cross to prove his point (II, 679-80). Barrios, contrasting Morales, the atheist, with his two sentimentalists, Jenny and Javier, implies the desirability, even the necessity, of religion in life, as indicated in the discussion on Pascal. In *Gran señor y rajadiablos,* even Valverde, the hell-raiser, the self-proclaimed dispenser of justice, and disciple of Positivism, values his Catholic education. In an outburst of emotion he affirms the indispensable worth of religion, centred on the Pascalian heart (II, 932-35, 940), which in no way detracts from his anti-clericalism and Positivist tendencies.

Thus, religion has a role to play, and is an integral part of life and Barrios' view of it—and in no way clashes with his philosophical education. However, as Barrios sees it, it is only one force of many and should be maintained in its proper perspective, i. e. as a balancing force: «Todas las religiones son buenas. La religión cristiana es la que me gusta más; es muy buena para ayudar la personalidad... Creo que lo estrechan mucho los católicos y lo llenan mucho de demasiadas fórmulas.»[46]

Though not a religious fanatic, then, Eduardo Barrios sees the value of religion in life. It is significant that Barrios' attitude to religion matured as he grew older and developed a more balanced view of the world. The religious arguments of the enthusiastic young seminarian *(Tamarugal)* and

---

[45] See VÁZQUEZ-BIGI's «Los conflictos psíquicos y religiosos en *El hermano asno*» (II), *Cuadernos Hispanoamericanos,* No. 220 (abril, 1968), 120-45, and, in particular, 129-31.

[46] See Note 35, p. 131 of VÁZQUEZ-BIGI, «Los conflictos psíquicos...», for which see note 45, above.

the emotionally charged apologia of Valverde (*Gran señor y rajadiablos*) are a long way from the anti-religious—even anti-morality—tract of the *Del natural* prologue. One notes that his early heroes (*el niño,* Luis, Adolfo) derive no consolation from religion. Even Lázaro, though living the religious life of a monk, derives no spiritual comfort from his surroundings because of lack of charity and excess of spiritual pride. Only when emotion/faith replaces analysis/reason does he manage to get to the threshold of even being able to tolerate life.

One feature of religion, which Barrios treats especially in the first trilogy, is the role of emotion in religion—which spills over into his metaphysics. In *Un perdido,* for example, Luis, whose adolescence and adulthood show little preoccupation with religion, derives much sensual pleasure from its trappings—the music, the flowers, the candles, the stained-glass windows—but the overall impression is one of sadness and anguish: «Más que de rezo, eran aquéllos para él momentos de percibir sensaciones nuevas... pero la impresión total resultaba más bien triste, de una angustia suave y enfermiza» (I, 253). This superficial pleasure, having no strong basis, soon disappears, and the vague sadness gives way at the end of the novel to a sceptical pessimism, nurtured by his reading of the Book of Ecclesiastes, which confirms his view of life (I, 523, 529).

The other aspect of religion which appeals to Barrios the artist is the inherent poetry, the aesthetic implications of the beauty of religion. Papá Juan, stressing the importance of emotion as a guide («el corazón, como una linterna ciega, nos guía en la obscuridad», I, 246) links religion with art in the analogy of «la bondad y la poesía que son hijas de la inocencia, [que] ahondan más que la justicia» (I, 246). Goodness and poetry are born when reason falls down. Certain things have to be felt, not analysed. This is Jesus' particular role, as opposed to God the Father, because with His Heart He is the poet *par excellence:* «Jesús, que era bueno y poeta, más que equitativo juez, acertó siempre» (I, 246). Even Luis, who gained only the most shallow emotional respite in religion,[47] recognised something of the beauty of church ceremony, if nothing else. For papá Juan it was something even more lofty: «Don Juan acudía también por recibir la poesía de la liturgia y de las almas cándidas. Era sensible a la grata emoción que causa el sentir a una muchedumbre de almas obscuras, gruesas y torpes, afinarse, aun cuando ella sea temporal y artificiosamente en un concierto apacible de gesto, visión, perfume, color y sonido» (I, 256). In this sensual atmosphere which prefigures the ambience of *El hermano asno,* a sense of elevation invades and saturates everything: «¿Divinidad? ¿Poesía? ... ¡Lo mismo! Para Don Juan las dos palabras tenían igual significado» (I, 256). Apart from the spiritual role to be played by emotion in

---

[47] «Con los perfumes del incienso, de la cera y de las flores, tranquilizábanse sus nervios, armonizando en el fluido ambiente, lánguido, sedante» (UP I, 255-56).

the field of religion, once again the metaphysical is linked to the aesthetic when he stresses the communicative role of emotion: «La Verdad sería siempre inaccesible; la emoción de ella, no. Y ésta era la Poesía» (I, 256). To solve the mystery of life was impossible, and to know absolute truth was beyond man's ken. The next best thing is to work out a way of life that makes existence bearable. By means of the heart, the basis of religion and the repository of sentiment and tenderness, one can strive to communicate, through feelings, the emotional rendering of truth.

Barrios, if not always won over by human examples of the Christian religion, appreciated the poetry, the mystery and the symbolism of the Catholic church. *El hermano asno* is a long hymn to the beauty of the external manifestations of the religious life and the monastic setting. From the quietist prologue of Amado Nervo, which sets the mood, Barrios presents, almost in Modernist terms (in reverse), an exposé of religion as art, as I shall demonstrate further in Chapters 3 and 4.

Though his view of life is basically Romantic, therefore often vaguely critical of the divine pattern, and his feelings are often violently anticlerical (UP I, 259-60), Barrios sees the function and the value of religion, as he evolves his metaphysical vision. Though religion figures in the early novels, the protagonists receive little spiritual consolation from it in their travails. In the second trilogy the more mature Barrios introduces the corrective, formative qualities of religion. Valverde, for example, in *Gran señor y rajadiablos,* despite his barbaric outbursts and moral defects, seeks and finds consolation in his religion: «Entonces, tras de renegar contra "la canalla actual", se tranquilizaba sólo con inmersiones en su sentimiento pío: tal como el cura durante sus días postreros diérase a la contemplación mística y a los contactos con Dios, él buscaba paz en su yo religioso, en aquella zona o tonalidad donde la secreta raíz de su ser conseguía entonar dentro del gran arcano» (II, 978). Throughout his life, Barrios was keenly aware of the aesthetic qualities of religion which, being emotion-based, must have some good qualities (given the general role of the heart in Barrios' philosophy), especially communicative, if only in the field of art. Since aesthetics is always at the service of metaphysics in Barrios and constitutes the peak of religious worship and liturgy (Christ as poet), one can draw the obvious conclusion that religion, like art, offers a way of escape from the tragedies of the world. Barrios' novels are a reminder that religion, in both its spiritual and aesthetic manifestations, need not clash with philosophy, whose underlying commentary indicates the metaphysical concern of Barrios' fiction.

BARRIOS AND THE GENERATION OF '98

If Barrios seems to have affinities with the Generation of '98 it is not coincidental. His use of terminology to define and contrast traits of character is reminiscent of the '98 writers who were in vogue in Latin America at this period. The Romantic discovery, which was at the root of the pessimism of the nineteenth century, was underlined by the national crisis that befell Spain with the loss of the vestiges of her great empire in 1898—Puerto Rico, Philippines and Cuba. This disaster provoked a soul-searching, national and personal, which was the feature of the group of writers, loosely called the Generation of '98,[48] whose common outlook on life was «their collective recognition of the inability of the mind to make sense of human existence» and an «increasingly desperate search for *ideas madres,* for a satisfying pattern of ideas, ideals, and beliefs with which to solve the threefold problem of truth, duty, and finality which they found confronting them».[49]

Having discoursed long and deep on the essence of Spain (cf. Unamuno's *En torno al casticismo*) and analysed its character and its failings (cf. Ganivet's *Idearium español*), notably abulia, one is not surprised that they turn to the Germans to define the pessimism of their character. Antonio Azorín, the nihilist *perturbado* hero of *La voluntad,* sees, like his master Yuste, that «comprender es entristecerse; observar es sentirse vivir... Y sentirse vivir es sentir la muerte, es sentir la inexorable marcha de todo nuestro ser y de las cosas que nos rodean hacia el océano misterioso de la Nada...».[50] Azorín extends his view of life to embrace both the metaphysical, analogous to Blanco («no puedo afirmar nada sobre la realidad del universo... La inmanencia o trascendencia de la causa primera, el movimiento, la forma de los seres, el origen de la vida... arcanos impenetrables... eternos» [p. 179]) and the possible aesthetic escape from the anguish («Yo he buscado un consuelo en el arte» [p. 180]) which is treated in tragic fashion in *Un perdido* and is an essential theme of all Barrios' fiction. For Luis «la vida, la verdad no vale la pena de vivirse» (UP I, 485). Later in the same novel Barrios spells out in '98 Generation terms the process of degeneration for Luis: «Bajo la presión de una vida embrutecedora, venía la abulia del que embrutece» (I, 387). The title of Azorín's novel, *La voluntad,* points the way to the other great influence on the generation, Nietzsche,

---

[48] Some writers like Ortega y Gasset and Madariaga accepted Azorín's label, whilst others like Unamuno and Baroja, both Basques, one ought to note, maintained their individuality by refusing to accept it.

[49] DONALD L. SHAW, *A Literary History of Spain: The Nineteenth Century* (London: Benn, 1972), p. 159.

[50] Madrid: Castalia, p. 180.

whose presence in Spain at the turn of the century has been well documented,[51] and whose influence in many spheres was considerable.

Baroja too manifests the Schopenhauerian link with Barrios in his pessimistic outlook and his inability to find a meaningful pattern in life. Vázquez-Bigi in a little footnote, undeveloped, sees Barrios' definitive statement on Schopenhauer/Nietzsche as pure Baroja: «Leyó [Luis] a Nietzsche y lo abandonó sin comprenderlo bien [aquí parece Baroja]» (Thesis, p. 266). Baroja's hero of *La lucha por la vida* suffers, like Luis, an atrophy of the will and fails in his desire to realise himself. All of Barrios' *perdido* types want to succeed but cannot make the decision. At the fancy dress party, dressed as Harlequin, Luis cannot come up with the smart answer that would deflate the boy who was teasing him: «El piensa una réplica oportuna, aguda que engríe su amor propio y le reconcilia consigo mismo; sin embargo, otro viene, le espeta nueva broma..., y él aún está perfeccionando, puliendo *in mente* la réplica anterior ya perdida» (I, 243). This lack of spontaneity, of naturalness, which goes hand in hand with excessive rationalisation, is also at the root of the character of Baroja's hero of *El mundo es ansí* whose own lack of security and confidence he defines thus: «Cualquier cosa que otro resuelve instintivamente, yo tengo que resolver por razonamientos. Desde ponerme los pantalones hasta salir a la calle, he de ir calculando todos los días si sería mejor hacer o no hacer.»[52] Vázquez-Bigi has pointed out an interesting parallel between the masquerade episode of *Un perdido* and a similar incident in Baroja's novel where Arcelu confesses to an incident strangely close to Luis' experience: «De pequeño, una cosa que me preocupaba era el Carnaval; creía que bastaba ponerse la careta para que uno se sintiera vivo, ingenioso, lleno de gracia. Un domingo de Carnaval, en el Puerto de Santa María, me vestí de máscara y salí a la calle. Vi pasar a un amigo y me acerqué a él dispuesto a embromarle. ¡Adiós! ¡Adiós! le dije, y no pude salir de ahí. Avergonzado, fui al paseo de la Victoria, me quité la careta, me senté en un banco y casi estuve a punto de romper a llorar» (*El mundo*, p. 158).[53] In the same tradition as Arcelu, Luis is the abulic hero *par excellence*, one of those tortured souls who, through his bad experiences and intercourse with other countercharacters (Blanco, Anselmo, Rojitas), suffers a development of consciousness that leads to a new insight which is almost always negative: «Esta vida no vale la pena tomarla por lo serio» (I, 505). Sacha, Baroja's heroine, like her male counterparts, Arcelu and Luis, comes to the same conclusion: « ¡El mundo es ansí! Es decir, todo es crueldad, barbarie, ingratitud... el mundo todo es brutalidad, dolor,

---

[51] PAUL ILIE, «Nietzsche in Spain 1890-1910», *PMLA*, LXXIX, No. 1 (March, 1964), 80-96; and GONZALO SOBEJANO, *Nietzsche en España,* already quoted in note 28, above.

[52] *El mundo es ansí,* ed. D. L. Shaw (Oxford: Pergamon, 1970), p. 158.

[53] VÁZQUEZ-BIGI, «*El tipo sicológico...*», p. 269.

pena... Todo es dureza, todo crueldad, todo egoísmo... El mundo es ansí» (pp. 133-34).

Barrios' German background gave him a special feeling for the German philosophers who were instrumental in provoking, if not shaping, the minds of the '98 Generation. As Schopenhauer had flirted with and praised the ideas of Buddhism, reflected in Barrios (UP I, 391-92), so too did the vague notions of Krausism, brought to Spain from Heidelberg by Sanz del Río, which pronounced the theory of *panenteísmo* or the doctrine of «todo en Dios, según el cual el mundo se concebía como conjunto de las manifestaciones de la esencia divina en el tiempo y en el espacio. La Naturaleza y el Espíritu se unían en la Humanidad y la vida humana es una ascensión hacia la armonía que Dios representa, cuya meta se alcanza a través de la Humanidad racional y del espíritu científico».[54] This partly rational philosophy, with mystical or pseudo-mystical implications, took root in Spain and has its counterpart in Latin America. Barrios, in the last part of *Un perdido* when Luis is on the downgrade, devotes several pages to a similar kind of alternative to established religion, led by a *sevillano* named «El Teósofo», founder of a «Liga de Bondad» whose metaphysical system «abarcaba desde una cosmogonía vasta, compleja e inductivamente lógica, hasta una evolución de la materia conocida muy conforme a la ciencia experimental; y de aquí, sutilizando y sutilizando, conducía la evolución al espíritu por escalonados y a la vez compenetrados planos de incorporeidad que ascendían hasta lo absoluto en el más pleno vértigo de poesía» (I, 529). Luis, like the *perturbado* heroes of the '98 Generation, Antonio Azorín, Andrés Hurtado *(El árbol de la ciencia),* and Alberto Díaz de Guzmán (Ayala), «... veía en el fondo de aquello una vana inquietud por saber, sólo un ahínco ingenioso por estirar la curva que parte del impenetrable pasado y a la tiniebla del más allá torna» (I, 529). Luis, much more convinced by the basic unhappiness of life and the scepticism of the Book of Ecclesiastes, for him «un hallazgo monumental», sees little hope for man in the false promises of pseudo-mystical ideas, and is more in sympathy with Azorín's *enfermo.* For him *la angustia metafísica* is the only reality: «Una gran tristeza, una angustiadora y rebelde tristeza que se resolvía en el más negro de los tedios, he aquí lo que producía el espectáculo de la humanidad» (I, 533); and death the «meta ineludible y única» (I, 531). The verses of Lautaro García sum it all up: «Por todos los caminos llegamos a la muerte / Este camino mío también me ha de llevar» (I, 531).

In his manifestation of the tragic sentiment of life, Barrios is, of course, close in spirit to Unamuno, who, according to Borges, is the only Spaniard who feels and senses metaphysics («único sentidor»), especially as it is rooted in the formative years of childhood—cf. *el niño,* Luis, Adolfo,

---

[54] ANGEL DEL RÍO, *Historia de la literatura española,* tomo II (New York: Holt, Rinehart and Winston, 1963), p. 224.

young Valverde, Charlie. Unamuno's affinity with Pascal[55] places him, by extension, on the same metaphysical level as Barrios. It has also been suggested that Barrios may have been influenced by Unamuno's *Tres novelas ejemplares y un prólogo* in *Los hombres del hombre,* in Unamuno's choice of the seven *yos* who live inside every being: «Y es que todo hombre humano lleva dentro de sí las siete virtudes y sus siete opuestos vicios capitales: es orgulloso y humilde, glotón y sobrio, rijoso y casto, envidioso y caritativo, avaro y liberal, perezoso y diligente, iracundo y sufrido. Y saca de sí mismo lo mismo al tirano, que al esclavo, al criminal que al santo, a Caín que a Abel.»[56] Barrios, of course, follows this technique, giving his inner man the seven names with which *el hombre* was baptised.

It is clear, then, that there was a literary connection between Barrios and the Generation of '98. Although the crisis of the generation was initially a national crisis, there is at least some feeling that the influence is even a little more widespread, perhaps even a «larger cultural sympathy based partly on heritage and partly on the realisation that the grave spiritual crisis of Spain in the 1890s and 1900s was largely paralleled in Spanish America. The social criticism in the *perdido* is often what meets the eye first, as materialism is described again and again, while the authors either say or imply that what the country needs is a return to simplicity, sincerity, telluric strength and so on. At all times the impression is given that these are times for decision; and thus an atmosphere is built up like that which Ganivet describes, or Pérez de Ayala.»[57]

Pérez de Ayala, like Baroja and others, long under the influence of Schopenhauer, portrays this loss of faith and vital confidence in his early novels like *Tinieblas en las cumbres* (1907), so instrumental in the literary and philosophical formation of the younger Barrios. Guzmán, who has much of Gastón Labarca of the *Del natural* period (anti-clerical, artistic, weak) and Luis Bernales («insignificante», «confuso»), seeks to escape his anguish, in *perdido* fashion, through sex with prostitutes (Rosina becomes a mother-figure like la Meche for Luis), and alcohol, before accepting Travesado's (cf. Blanco's) view of the world that «Todo es ciego, vertiginoso y fatal», which is confirmed, as in the case of Luis, by his own reading of the Book of Ecclesiastes. In his last years, like Barrios, Ayala struggled back to get some balance in his life: «En la primera mitad de la vida, el hombre se revela ansioso contra los valores establecidos por autoridad... Esta experiencia analítica le sirve... para que al llegar a la altiplanicie de la edad madura reconozca... los valores eternos...» (*Principios*

[55] See F. R. MARTÍN, «Pascal and Miguel de Unamuno», *Modern Language Review,* XXXIX, No. 2 (April, 1944), 138-45 and JUAN LÓPEZ-MORILLAS, «Unamuno and Pascal: Notes on the Concept of Agony», *PMLA, LXV,* No. 6 (December, 1950), 998-1010.

[56] *Tres novelas ejemplares...* (Madrid: Austral, 1958), p. 21.

[57] ARNOLD CHAPMAN, «The *Perdido* as a Type...», p. 33.

y finales de la novela [1958]).[58] Apart from the '98 terminology which is obvious,[59] it has already been suggested that Barrios was influenced even by the language of his Spanish counterparts, not just in his concern for purity and correctness but also in his use of Peninsular modes of speech —*leísmos,* and other Peninsular pecularities of language, including the dative *laísmo.*[60]

The linguistic analogy is superficial and, like the terminological, weighs little in comparison with the principal affinity of which it is a manifestation, i.e. the philosophical. Though Barrios' work lacks the concern with a national crisis which was the catalyst for the Generation of '98, his view of life, rooted in the same spiritual seed, Romantic pessimism, and nurtured by the same philosophical masters, Schopenhauer and Nietzsche, was akin to that of Azorín, Ganivet, Baroja, Unamuno and Pérez de Ayala, and reflects the same metaphysical concerns. That Barrios was able to reconcile philosophy and religion, to absorb all of these disparate influences (Pascal, Schopenhauer, Nietzsche, Generation of '98) in a synthesis of ideas that best fitted his own metaphysics, is a tribute not only to the man and the writer but also to the philosopher.

---

[58] Madrid: Taurus, pp. 131-32.

[59] Apart from the many examples already quoted, one can cite at random: «teníanle cohibida, laxa la voluntad» (I, 410), «el sentir muy laxa ya la voluntad» (I, 452), «mi voluntad era ya una cosa fofa» (I, 522).

[60] It is rather interesting that in both Chilean editions (*Obras completas,* 1962 and the Zig-Zag edition of *Un perdido,* 1965), the dative *la* of the 2 vol. Madrid edition, Espasa-Calpe, 1926, has been changed to *le*: «un día la hermana la dijo» (II, 182) and «Lucho sólo veíala el brillo de los ojos» (II, 190). Cf. OC UP I, 467 and 471-72 for corresponding American versions.

CHAPTER 3

THE METAPHYSICAL EVOLUTION

The Metaphysical Novel

Manuel Gálvez perhaps expressed it best when he affirmed that the essential quality of a novelist is «su visión de la vida».[1] Barrios has not been reticent about this aspect of the writer's vocation: «No escribamos sino cuando realmente tengamos algo que decir.»[2] Barrios, as we have seen, has generally gained renown in literary circles for his contribution to what has been loosely called the «psychological» novel. The characters who stick in the reader's mind are generally the «abnormal», the weak, the abulic heroes of *El niño que enloqueció de amor, Un perdido* and *El hermano asno,* psychologically misfits and mentally out of step with their peers—types that one would now label as emotionally disturbed. Barrios' value as a psychologist has been well demonstrated.

I should like to stress, however, that rather than revealing a morbid preoccupation with rare types, Barrios' novels are about life in general and reflect his attitude to it.[3] In his novels he has used many settings—the city,

[1] Prologue to *Un perdido* (Madrid: Espasa-Calpe, 1926), pp. 9-13, and reproduced in Zig-Zag edition, Santiago, 1965, pp. 7-9. Cf. the statement of SIMONE DE BEAUVOIR, «Littérature et métaphysique», *Les Temps Modernes,* Vol. 1, No. 7 (1946), pp. 1153-63; «tout romancier a sa vision du monde» (p. 1161).
It is significant that two of the novelists with whom I draw parallels in this study, Baroja and Mallea, should have suitable aphorisms for this point of view: «Yo creo que para ser escritor basta con tener algo que decir» (BAROJA, *La noche del Buen Retiro,* Chapter 23, *Obras completas,* Madrid, 1946, VI, p. 633); «La piedra de toque de un gran novelista consiste en las dimensiones de su *Weltanschauung*» (MALLEA, *Poderío de la novela,* Buenos Aires, Aguilar, 1965, p. 177). DONALD SHAW, who quotes both in his article «Baroja y Mallea: algunos puntos de contacto», *Actas del Tercer Congreso Internacional de Hispanistas,* México, 1970, goes on to point out: «Los dos autores, pues, subrayan sobre todo la importancia del contenido de sus novelas y como base del contenido (siendo los dos esencialmente novelistas de ideas) la ideología del escritor» (p. 949). Barrios, however, goes far beyond Baroja y even Mallea (who is no primitive despite his alleged opting for *hondura* before *belleza*), in his search for a suitable aesthetic form to render the important content, as we shall see in Chapter 4.
[2] «La saturación literaria», first published in the initial number of *Atenea* (abril de 1924), 48-52 and reproduced in CLIV, No. 404 (abril-junio, 1964), 73.
[3] His admiration for Hernández Catá, with whose point of view he felt so much

53

the nitrate regions, the rural area, the monastery, etc.—but all merely as a backdrop for his comments on life. As Edwin Muir has correctly observed, setting is no more than a background for the human drama, whose protagonists colour the scene, against which and closed in by which, one always sees them.[4] That is precisely what Barrios' novels are about—the struggle for life, and man's (including Barrios') search for a meaningful existence. The essential business of fiction is not really to provide us with a picture of man in society, of masses, of man in his public pursuits or in his relations with other social classes. It can be a part but is not the essence of fiction. The description of the setting can be of value to the reader in what it helps to reveal and what it helps to present of the story, thus achieving a better understanding of the characters involved and their life. Thus, the setting has only secondary significance as the scenario for the drama of human life. Percy Lubbock, in his pioneer work of criticism, *The Craft of Fiction,* describes it thus: «A novel is a picture of life, and life is well known to us; let us first of all "realize" it, and then, using our taste, let us judge whether it is true, vivid, convincing—like life itself.»[5] Several critics have tried to isolate the background of Barrios' novels and lend them a quality which has little meaning—hence the emphasis on Barrios' *Gran señor y rajadiablos* as a novel of the land, and on the American qualities of his fiction in general by critics like Torres-Ríoseco. Even Gálvez, who underlines the importance of the metaphysical in the novel, cannot resist the temptation to highlight the social value of *Un perdido:* «en él está casi todo lo esencial de nuestras sociedades americanas» (p. 9).

Barrios has written about many topics in his novels—a child going mad with love, a weak, sentimental boy who grows up to be an alcoholic lost soul, sexual temptations in a monastery, a youth working in an undertaker's office, life of young people in the northern mining regions, an historical novel of nineteenth-century Chile, a father-mother-son jealousy triangle. These are the superficial themes of Barrios' main novels, but they tell us little about the real theme of Barrios' fiction. The true meaning of Barrios' novel lies below the surface of the narrative and is to be found in the philosophical commentary. Although Barrios has tended to play down his own standing as a thinker, we have seen his awareness of philosophical currents and their influence in his fiction. Unamuno, for example, considered true philosophy (that is, of flesh and blood) closer to poetry than scientific thought, and to be found in great novels and epic poems. When Borges

sympathy, prompted him to write the aforementioned prologue for the latter's *Sus mejores cuentos* (1936). It is significant that what impressed him about Hernández Catá was his capacity to link life and literature: «Conozco pocos escritores cuya obra se halle tan estrechamente ligada a ellos en cuanto hombres» (p. 8).

[4] *The Structure of the Novel* (London: Hogarth Press, 1928), pp. 64-67.
[5] London: J. Cape, 1921 (1954 ed.), p. 9.

paid Unamuno the compliment of being the only Spanish writer who was genuinely metaphysical, he was quick to add: «and is therefore—and because of other sensibilities—a great writer.» [6] Barrios' philosophical findings, combined with the experiences of his own life, which provided much of the basic material for his novels,[7] has produced what I should like to call the metaphysical novel, i.e. a fictional work of art rooted in the problems of life, with philosophical commentary. In a word, literature is about life, and reading or writing a work of fiction should be connected somehow with the business of living. As Guillermo de Torre puts it: «la novela —como cualquier otra expresión literaria, por supuesto—debe responder tanto a una necesidad literaria como a una exigencia frente al mundo».[8]

Simone de Beauvoir, in an article significantly entitled «Littérature et métaphysique», has so clearly seen the connection between literature and philosophy as exemplified in the works of Eduardo Barrios: «Si certains écrivains ont choisi de retenir exclusivement un de ces deux aspects de notre condition, élevant ainsi des barrières entre la littérature et la philosophie, d'autres, au contraire, depuis bien longtemps ont cherché à l'exprimer dans sa totalité» (p. 1153). Barrios clearly belongs to the latter group, and writes, no matter the setting, what Simone de Beauvoir calls *le roman métaphysique.*

Good fiction, therefore, has a role to play in the business of living and deserves our respect. It is not discontinuous with reality and is not, as might appear, a kind of retreat from the harsh world of existence. In the same way that tragedy in the theatre purges us of our fears and emotions in cathartic fashion, the narrative art has its role to play too: «While fiction alters the facts of experience, a fundamental purpose of those alterations, as the first and greatest esthetician, Aristotle, realized, is the achievement of an imaginary world more lifelike than life itself, more directly and honestly concerned with essential problems, more supple in its expression of every aspect of man's nature, less burdened by distracting

---

[6] Quoted by ANTHONY KERRIGAN in «Borges/Unamuno», in *Prose for Borges* (Evanston: Northwestern University Press, 1972), p. 239. In his *Diario íntimo* (1895-1902), Unamuno asks the question as to what philosophy is anyway. He answers himself: «Metaphysics, perhaps.» KERRIGAN adds: «A class of fiction, perhaps» (p. 240).

[7] Though one should beware of too much preoccupation with autobiographical matters in the creation of fiction, it is not possible, as Sartre would like to see, to have the artist refine himself out of existence. What Leon Edel has said about Joyce applies equally to Sartre, Barrios or any novelist: «The disassociation is not complete. He [the artist] remains after all within, behind, above or beyond the work—and not too far beyond. He is like those dreams we have in which we are both the actor and the audience: in which we act and also stand by watching ourselves in action. So a work of fiction, if not autobiography of the artist, is still a particular synthesis created by him and by no one else» (*The Psychological Novel:* 1900-1950 [New York: Lippincott, 1955], p. 179).

[8] *Doctrina y estética literaria,* «Los géneros literarios» (Madrid: Ed. Guadarrama, 1970), p. 548.

irrelevancies.»[9] Or as Unamuno put it: a novel will provide a truer description than any chapter of philosophy of how a person himself dies, dies «for himself» (Kerrigan, p. 244). Rather than an escape, then, the world of fiction provides us with a means of dealing with metaphysical problems, including those that we might not face in real life. The outstanding quality of great fiction is to present these problems in their most essential terms, without the distractions and irrelevancies that come between us and our problems in everyday life and so prevent us from seeing clearly. In the world of fiction we have concretised and formalised in articulate fashion our most fleeting impulses with their consequences and implications. In the imaginative sphere of fiction we are better able to deal with our problems by approaching them in different ways, changing circumstances to find out what the different results might be—a luxury seldom afforded us in everyday life. Through the material of fiction, which objectifies and externalises our problems, posing them in concrete terms and in an orderly fashion, we are provided, usually in terms of individualised human beings, with images of our own emotional problems. Viewed from a distance, these personal problems are more easily solved: «Il [le bon roman] permet d'éffectuer des expériences imaginaires aussi complètes, aussi inquiétantes que les expériences vécues. Le lecteur s'interroge, il doute, il prend parti et cette élaboration hésitante de sa pensée lui est un enrichissement qu'aucun enseignement doctrinal ne pourrait remplacer» (Simone de Beauvoir, p. 1155).

The novel, then, does not merely entertain, though to give pleasure has certainly always been one of its aims, as of all literature, from time immemorial; nor is it merely therapeutic, though it does mitigate anxiety. In the shared experience of reader-novel-author, the work of art touches on life. One should add that the metaphysical development takes place in both the author and the reader. The writing of the novel for Barrios, for example, is his way of hammering out a meaningful approach to life in the sense that every novel he writes is a manifestation of his evolving attitude to the rigours and mysteries of existence. The reader, too, by means of the novel and the fictitious material presented therein, learns to confront life with a greater degree of clarity, and thereby heightens his perception. Through this freshly gained knowledge he has new outlooks which better enable him to live his own life in the light of the literary experience shared: «on espère... dépasser sur le plan imaginaire les limites toujours trop étroites de l'expérience réellement vécue. Or ceci exige que le romancier participe lui-même à cette recherche à laquelle il convie son lecteur...; le roman ne revêt sa valeur et sa dignité qu'il constitue pour l'auteur comme pour le lecteur une découverte vivante» (Simone de Beauvoir, p. 1156).

[9] SIMON O. LESSER, *Fiction and the Unconscious* (New York: Vintage Books, 1957), p. 54.

Writing is, as Henry Miller cogently expressed it, a voyage of discovery like life itself, whose adventure is of a metaphysical kind. It is an indirect way of approximating to life, of acquiring a total vision of the universe. It is in this sense that Barrios' works are metaphysical novels which transcend the regional level, from the geographical point of view, and the costumbrist level from the generic point of view. The author has to believe in his novel, he has to see the truths emerge, as the novel advances, the questions posed, to which the answers will be ultimately revealed. Only then will the true metaphysical novel appear «comme une authentique aventure spirituelle» (to restate Henry Miller). It is this authenticity which distinguishes the truly great novel from the mere clever story and characterises the great work of art. Louise Rosenblatt, in her book *Literature As Exploration,* the title of which extends the Miller-de Beauvoir image, describes it thus: «A great work of art may provide us the opportunity to feel more profoundly and more generously, to perceive more fully the implications of experience than the hurried and fragmentary conditions of life permit.»[10]

Thus, in Barrios, as in any great writer, literature and philosophy are not incompatible. In fact, they are indistinguishable since it is the philosophical commentary that gives Barrios' novels their universal value. It is by living the adventure of existence that one builds up a philosophy of life. In the case of Barrios, it was an evolving philosophy based on his reading (of philosophers, amongst others), on experience and observation, rather than a formulated structure grafted on to the literary form. Without the aesthetic literary vehicle, the philosophical novel remains but a collection of rigid theories without free development. This is what distinguishes a Barrios from a Freud.[11] Even when the philosophic debt is proved, as in the case of Barrios and Schopenhauer/Nietzsche, the distinguishing feature is aesthetics.

A similar analogy can be made between the novel and metaphysics: «La métaphysique n'est pas d'abord un système... En réalité, "faire" de la métaphysique c'est "être" métaphysique, c'est réaliser en soi l'attitude métaphysique qui consiste à se poser dans sa totalité en face de la totalité du monde. Tout événement humain possède par delà ses contours psychologiques et sociaux une signification métaphysique puisque, à travers chacun d'eux, l'homme est toujours engagé tout entier, dans le monde tout entier...» (Simone de Beauvoir, pp. 1158-59). Every Barrios novel is about life and portrays a metaphysical situation. It is significant that in almost every novel, Barrios underlines the role of children (*el niño*, Luis, Adolfo, José in «Pobre feo», young Valverde, Charlie) who experience these metaphysical

[10] New York: Appleton, 1948, p. 45.
[11] SIMONE DE BEAUVOIR draws a similar parallel between Proust and Ribot (p. 1158)

happenings and discover their place in the world. In fact, in his neglected little theatrical piece «Papá y mamá» the children actually play out the roles of the parents. In true Wordsworthian fashion («The Child is father of the Man»), Barrios goes on to demonstrate that these metaphysical situations define their characters more than their psychological aptitudes: «l'enfant découvre concrètement sa présence au monde...; à travers ses joies, ses peines, ses résignations, ses révoltes, ses peurs, ses espoirs, chaque homme réalise une certaine situation métaphysique qui le définit beaucoup plus essentiellement qu'aucune de ses aptitudes psychologiques» (Simone de Beauvoir, p. 1159).

Although Barrios has merited the «psychological» label, one ought to take care not to underline the psychological traits to the exclusion of his philosophical and metaphysical concern. The two terms are not mutually exclusive. In fact, it is often within the metaphysical point of view that the psychological and the social, which fail so often to come together and which, taken by themselves, are incomplete, can best be reconciled. In the case of Barrios one can go one step further by suggesting that the psychological and the social, which have often been the most highlighted aspects of his fiction, are subordinate to the metaphysical, which best demonstrates Barrios' preoccupation with the human condition and man's state in the world, not just in Chile or Latin America.

If Barrios' novels reflect his metaphysical view, one should expect to see a certain growth or evolution in his vital outlook, reflecting his changing sensibility. Having observed his literary and philosophical development, one should be able to detect Barrios' changing view of the world from his novels which span, as we have seen, almost half a century.

THE EARLY PERIOD

«Del natural»: A Promising Beginning

Barrios began his literary career with the publication of *Del natural* (1907), a collection of three short stories and a short novel, all in the Naturalist/Decadent mould, as we have seen. Although the work is of limited artistic value, as Barrios himself confessed later, it is important as a point of departure for a study of Barrios' fiction because it presents for the first time in embryonic form the characters, themes and techniques later to be developed in his main novels.

The three short stories which open the collection are of little value, being merely Naturalistic exercises in the portrayal of stereotyped characters, modelled on French Decadents, in luxurious settings peopled by sensuous women. The mysterious, Byronic, satanic types of the short stories give way to better characterisation in «Tirana ley», a more successful short novel, which tells the story of Gastón Labarca, a young painter who finds love and inspiration in a beautiful young widow, «la angelical Luz Avilés», who finds in Gastón and his work «la síntesis de [su] ideal: el artista unido al hombre fuerte» (I, 89). After a temporary setback, when Gastón places art before his love for Luz and goes off to Paris, they are reconciled and reunited, after the birth of their baby, and all live happily ever after. Apart from the hackneyed theme, there is a great deal of self-conscious over-writing with Modernist influences: «The descriptive passages suggest a pastiche of the poorer *Rubenianos* who imitated *Azul...*»[12] However, and herein lies the merit, this Modernist influence will be developed and refined in the beautiful prose of later works, especially *El hermano asno*. One notes here his use of religious imagery and terminology to describe the physical beauty of Luz («hierática», «sublime»), mixed with Modernist concern for exotic, elegant sensuality, as in the picture of the couple in their love nest «iluminado por una luz beatífica y tranquila, luz de santuario que, partiendo de una lamparilla de aceite y azulándose a su paso por una pantalla chinesca de cristal pintado en forma de biombo...» (I, 121). Apart from the theme of art and the role of the artist (which I shall develop in Chapter 4), the basic themes that Barrios treats are the role of sex (from the Modernist point of view), the theme of jealousy, particularly with regard to paternity (to be developed later in *Gran señor y rajadiablos* [cf. Marisabel, Antucho] and especially in *Los hombres del hombre*), and, most important of all, the role of the heart and emotion vis-à-vis reason which they displace—a key concept in Barrios' philosophy of life: «Cada día me convenzo más de que el mejor guía para el hombre es el corazón. Si siguiéramos siempre sus impulsos en vez de obedecer al cálculo, siempre convencional..., seríamos menos desgraciados» (I, 123-24). The most potent manifestation of this trait is to be found in the character of Labarca, who, apart from being the protagonist of the novel, is the prototype of the future Barrios heroes—with variations, of course. In his *falta de firmeza* and his *debilidad de carácter,* he is a precursor of Luis Bernales of *Un perdido,* but with the saving grace of an artistic temperament and training. There is much too of him in the sensibility and indecisiveness of *el niño,* Adolfo, Javier, and *el hombre*/Charlie. As we shall see, *Tamarugal* and *Gran señor y rajadiablos* are conscious efforts to redress the balance by depicting more stable characterisation. However, Barrios, if he does not condone, at least sympathises with this weakness of Gastón as being a source of artistic sensitivity. Gastón, who appears a *desequilibrado* to his friends, considers himself «un ser más natural, más franco que ellos, quizás un poco débil, pero por lo mismo más humano. Si no tuviésemos debilidades, los artistas ¿tendríamos ilusiones, dolores, goces, fuente de inspira-

---

12 NED J. DAVISON, «The Significance of *Del natural* in the Fiction of Eduardo Barrios», *Hispania*, XLIV, No. 1 (1961), 28.

ción, en fin?» (I, 139). This Romantic notion is repeated in Barrios' last novel, *Los hombres del hombre,* and indeed is implicit throughout his work.

This weakness of character is underlined not only by the mood of the novel but also by the atmosphere created by the Schopenhauerian references and also by the implications of the nineteenth-century philosophical currents discussed in Chapter 2: «La expectativa de hallarme solo un rato, entregándome libremente a saborear mi dolor, me sedujo más que la de respirar a plenos pulmones el aire perfumado del campo» (I, 129). Though the novel concludes with a comparatively happy ending—the return of the young couple to Paris where he is to pursue his studies—Schopenhauer has the last word, the advice to be followed: «Es muy cuerdo gozar lo más posible del presente, el solo momento de que se tiene seguridad, puesto que la vida no es más que un gran pedazo de presente y lo mismo que él, pasajera» (I, 142). One remembers that for Schopenhauer the only possible escape, albeit a temporary one, from a meaningless existence, is the world of art. This coupled with Gastón's final attack on conventional morality and a hypocritical society, is a fair summary of the young Barrios' feelings at this time: «Yo sé cuanto más vale una unión como la nuestra, hecha por un amor sublime y a toda prueba, que uno de esos contratos sociales que vulgarmente se llaman matrimonios honrosos» (I, 141).[13] With his accustomed technique of confronting his weak protagonist with a counterlocutory foil (cf. Luis/Blanco), Barrios makes use of Gastón's friend, Jorge, as the voice of energy: «Todo depende de que tengas voluntad. Ya hallaremos el modo... Es preciso ser enérgico alguna vez en la vida» (I, 114). In response to the exhortations of the Nietzschean mouthpiece, Gastón, face to face with his own weakness («Mi sensibilidad ha quedado tan quebrantada, tan falta de energía», I, 135) sees that decisions have to be made: «Veo que un esfuerzo, un llamado a la energía... me ha bastado para obtener el dominio de mi voluntad» (I, 137).

Del natural is not a masterpiece, but it is an important first statement, in spite of Barrios' self-denigration,[14] of his then view of the world—not from the social, ethical, moral point of view, which is the concern of his prologue, but of key concepts that are the seeds of his future novels. Apart from the interesting form—largely a first person narrative, the use of the diary technique—and the initial use of the themes of sex and jealousy, the book has value for its Romantic concern with emotion, and the heart/brain

---

[13] Cf. also this attack: «Dolor de tener un hijo sin padre reconocido: vergüenza por la sociedad, por aquella legión de cristianos incomprensibles que nos acompañan mientras somos felices y nos escupen cuando caemos en desgracia» (I, 122).

[14] «Me parece que sobre *Del natural* sería suficiente decir que fue mi primer libro... que, como tal, resulta la obra del escritor joven, la que se celebra *como una bella promesa*» (in a letter to Davison, quoted in Note 5, p. 32 of the *Hispania* article referred to above in Note 12).

contrast;[15] the Modernist preoccupation with art and the role of art in life; the characterisation of the protagonist Gastón Labarca and his '98 Generation affinities with the *abúlico/fuerte* contrast rooted in Schopenhauer and Nietzsche; all of which are the stuff of the future major novels and which provide a key to Barrios' metaphysical vision of the world.

«El niño que enloqueció de amor»: A Little Poetic Tragedy

«El niño que enloqueció de amor», as the title suggests, is a tragedy. Published in 1915, this beautifully-written short novel takes up not only the mood and atmosphere of «Tirana ley» but also the Romantic theme of love, the tyrannical law of the title, which it develops to its extreme, culminating in the ultimate madness of the protagonist. Rooted in the seeds of «Tirana ley», «El niño que enloqueció de amor» is the study of a sensitive, emotionally repressed personality, whose weakness and sentimentality are not alleviated by any meaningful counterbalance, like Gastón Labarca's art. This is not possible, or hardly likely, in the case of the nine-year-old boy whose tragedy sets the tone of Barrios' later work.

The basic theme of the short novel, and the key to all of Barrios' work, is the importance of emotion, especially emotion as a force for evil which in this case and in others (Luis, Olga, José) leads to tragedy. As we have seen, this view of emotion as a vital value is basically a Romantic notion. The treatment of Romantic love in «Tirana ley» demonstrates its existentialist importance. As the Romantics, and later the Modernists, were to show, when human love dies there is nothing left. For Barrios emotion is the key to life: «La emoción es la esencia virtual de las cosas. La emoción es el alma» (HA II, 625) and elsewhere: «La emoción es el principio» (GS II, 933)—in his last novels as in his first. When this emotion is directed into wrong channels, as in «El niño que enloqueció de amor», tragedy takes place. What makes this tragedy doubly bitter is that it is an ironic tragedy. For an adult to lose his sanity over love is tragedy enough; for it to happen to a child is an affront to existence. The anti-religious, anti-clerical, anti-morality outbursts of «Tirana ley» take on a deeper dimension in «El niño que enloqueció de amor», becoming almost the Romantic cry to the heavens, the raised fist challenging God with a criticism not only of life itself but of the providential pattern. That Barrios was not just describing the emotional life of an abnormal, psychologically disturbed child is patent in the many instances of identification with the

---

[15] Luz, the idealised heroine, has, like Emma Bovary, a Romantic view of life, formed by the reading of romanesque novels (I, 93).

[16] In the many interviews granted to scholars (Dulsey, Decker, Fogelquist), Barrios relates several incidents in which strangers have approached him claiming to be «el niño que enloqueció de amor».

metaphysical experience narrated.[16] Though based on an incident in his own life, in true Romantic fashion he was not only fulfilling the emotional needs of his readers but also identifying with them and helping them to cope with their emotional problems. That it was indeed a Romantic tragedy is borne out by the «Elogios sentimentales que los poetas escribieron al niño que enloqueció de amor». Daniel de la Vega, Gabriela Mistral, Claudio de Alas, Carlos Préndez Saldías, Roberto Meza Fuentes and Angel Cruchaga Santa María all paid homage to the subject, «aquel pájaro que cantó en la noche y no tuvo mañana» (I, 245).

Like his predecessor Gastón Labarca, el niño suffers «una desesperación grande», undergoes the physical effects of his angustia, and in true Schopenhauerian fashion, like his successor Luis Bernales, wants to suffer more: «Tengo mucha pena y quisiera tener más» (I, 147). With the acute psychological analysis one expects from Barrios, the child's relationship with his Romantic ideal, suitably named Angélica,[17] is traced through the first person narrative—Barrios uses the diary technique again—the jealousy, the misery, the daydreams, the hopes, the happiness, the shattering disillusionment and the recognition of the worthlessness of the girl, which underscores the irony of the tragedy. The probing of his implied illegitimacy and its effect on his condition, the hints at the causes and results of possible masturbation, and such like psychological elements in the novel, pale before the metaphysical reality of a child who seeks pain and solitude from an emotional situation he cannot control. The precocity of the child, who sees through the equivocation of the adult double-talk, heightens the tragedy: «Los grandes dicen que todo lo hacen por el bien de uno, y mientras tanto no saben sino quitarle a uno los gustos que tiene. Dice mi mamá que lo hacen para que uno sea feliz cuando grande; pero otras veces dice que los grandes nunca pueden ser felices, que la felicidad no dura sino mientras uno es chico» (I, 157). El niño learns early what Luis is to find in adolescence—that life is tragic and that there is no escape. This awareness of death as an escape from the tragic sentiment of life shocks us: «¡Ay, qué bueno sería que me muriese y le dijeran y que me había muerto por ella!» (I, 164). Barrios' technique of using the diary form to portray the oncoming madness provides an insight into the childish mentality which underlines the tragedy for us the readers, and by extension the participants, since the novel is a picture of life. With the growing death wish («ganas de morir»), the approaching fever, and the classic symptoms of hearing bells, madness comes on with a rush. Whilst the narrator/Barrios/reader preserve the memory of this affront to existence «como una llaga en carne viva, siempre irritada y sangrienta» (I, 167), the tragedy unfolds.

---

[17] Many of Barrios' women characters are symbolically named thus: Luz («Tirana ley), Blanca (Un perdido), Gracia (El hermano asno).

«El niño que enloqueció de amor» is a fascinating novel from the psychological point of view. Barrios' analysis of the causes and effects of the madness of a sensitive child, deprived of parental guidance, has been lauded and well documented by other critics. The linguistic skill with which Barrios portrays the boy's awareness of his own tragedy is beautifully done by use of diminutives and simple style. His use of the diary as a therapeutic medium, as well as heightening the intensity of the tragedy, prefigures his later novels. These, of course, are only techniques, and as Sartre so aptly observed, a fictional technique always relates back to the novelist's metaphysics. It is the critic's task to define the latter before evaluating the former. In «El niño que enloqueció de amor» Barrios is beginning to formulate a tragic view of life that will reach its peak in the next novel, *Un perdido*.

«Un perdido»: A Naturalistic Tragedy

If «El niño que enloqueció de amor» concretises the nineteenth-century vision of the world that was implicit in «Tirana ley» and from which Gastón Labarca escaped through love and art, *Un perdido* strengthens Barrios' pessimistic view. The protagonist, Luis Bernales, represents a more detailed portrayal of the type of child embodied in *el niño*—a timid, sentimental boy leading a sheltered life with his mother and grandparents in Quillota, with the inevitable consequences: «De ese modo formóse imaginativo, debilitáronse sus fuerzas de acción. Habituándose a soñarlo todo y a quedar satisfecho de lo ilusorio, se hacía tímido. No alentaba nunca deseos de realizar algo; suponerlo érale suficiente. Hay un instinto que enseña a los tímidos que sólo en sueños es todo perfecto, sin dolores ni fracasos» (I, 229). With the death of both grandparents and the mother in succession, he is obliged to live in the garrison town of Iquique with his equally timid father, from whose forced severity he flees to the arms of prostitutes like la Meche. Here too he meets Blanco whose ironic and deterministic philosophy of life fits Luis' preconceived notions of life as he found it. With the death of his father, he is obliged to live with his paternal grandparents in Santiago, where he attends military college against his will (and temperament). After an unsuccessful love affair with the symbolically named Blanca who marries his well-adjusted brother Anselmo instead, he finds employment at the library, meets another stray like himself, Teresa, who also rejects him, this time for his friend Rojitas. Drinking excessively, Luis searches for her unsuccessfully, never recovers his poise and ends a confirmed dipsomaniac on the way to a tragic death.

This mere outline gives little idea of the drama of human tragedy of Luis Bernales or of the artistic value of the novel. As Wellek and Warren so rightly state: «There are few works of art which are not ridiculous or meaningless in synopsis.»[18] As we shall see in Chapter 4, content should not be equated with a synopsis of it. The artistic effect of a novel does not reside in what is generally called its content. It is the synthesis of content and form, the aesthetic rendering of metaphysical problems that distinguishes Barrios from other Latin American writers of his generation. As Gálvez stated in his prologue to *Un perdido,* Spanish America (at that time) had few novelists. What are generally called novels are mostly novelesque poems, since Spanish American novelists tended to compose beautiful phrases rather than reproduce life.

Un perdido is unique, being significantly better than other novels of the same period and being based on philosophical insight, following the European tradition.[19] Rather than painting a series of tableaux of Chilean society, *Un perdido* has merit in that it expresses Barrios' view of life as hinted at in «Tirana ley», and developed in «El niño que enloqueció de amor», especially in the characterisation of the protagonist. If the literary orientation is French, then undoubtedly much of the philosophical mood springs from the pessimistic determinism of the German thinkers, Schopenhauer and Nietzsche. The subtle blend of literary and philosophical influences produces not only Barrios' first major work of fiction but also the most finely drawn of his *perdido* types, already suggested by minor characters like Ernesto («Los celos bienhechores»), Gastón Labarca, Ramiro («Canción» and *Vivir*), José («Pobre feo»), and Carlos *(Lo que niega la vida)*.[20] Luis is the peak of these post-Romantic heroes who suffer on account of their excessive sensitivity and lack of will power, as opposed to the positive, struggle-for-life hero in the Hernani/Rastignac mould. As the century progresses the process of the intellectualisation of Romanticism grows with the doctrines of thinkers like Schopenhauer and Nietzsche whose pessimism struck a responsive chord in those who felt perhaps everything was not for the best in this world, as the eighteenth-century optimists had induced people to think. Barrios' stature as a novelist stems not just from the semi-autobiographical narrative nor from the psychological details but from the metaphysical view of the world which he reveals by means of the narrative, psychological analysis, and characterisation. His view of the universe Barrios achieves generally by the fusion of the narrative and

---

[18] RENÉ WELLEK and AUSTIN WARREN, *Theory of Literature* (New York: Harcourt, Brace, 1949), p. 140.

[19] Much has been written about the influences on this novel. Cf. NED J. DAVISON, *Eduardo Barrios* (New York: Twayne, 1970), p. 46: «There is little question that his main inspiration was derived from France. In the work he combines the Realist traditions of the French and Spanish novels with an easily discernible portion of Naturalistic determinism.»

[20] Though Barrios' drama and short stories are inferior to his fiction, they are of value in that they give Barrios an opportunity to develop his characterisation. As literature, his theatrical works are most concerned with social problems, whilst the short stories have no real merit beyond the portrayal of the psychological.

philosophical commentary. The story of Luis' life, the constant failure, tragedy and disillusionment cannot but hammer home the message that there is an evil force in the world. This is reiterated with even more consistency than in «El niño que enloqueció de amor» where the protagonist, mercifully, suffers only a comparatively short time.

Un perdido takes us further along the path of life which is strewn with even more pain than in the case of *el niño*. Though *el niño* was aware of the presence of evil and suffering, Barrios channels the tragedy into one major episode—his abortive love affair. When that fails, his life (and, by definition, his tragedy) ends. Luis, as the synopsis indicates, emerged from the same kind of sentimental background, but had to travel farther along the path of life, to experience quantitatively more individual setbacks, though his consciousness of the absurdity of the world and his own helpless position in it was just as acute. In this sense, *Un perdido* is a more intense novel and more pessimistic since, being longer, it offers Barrios more opportunities to present his point of view. It has even been suggested that the novel is too long and might well have been shortened by half, since the character of Luis, developed so well in the first part, changes little in the second.[21] Given his emotional make-up and Barrios' view of life, Luis' fate is well mapped out in advance. Also, given Barrios' nineteenth-century attitude, *Un perdido*, rooted in the sentimentality of the Romantic novel, with its converse Realism, is excessively pessimistic. Luis, his literary creation, seeks answers to his metaphysical problems in emotion.

Like other great philosophical novelists, Baroja and Mallea, Barrios expresses his insight by means of a spokesman, in this case the figure of the lieutenant Blanco, who comments on life, fate and destiny, and whose conclusions are all part of the great Romantic discovery that life is basically tragic and governed by deterministic laws (I, 365-66). Since every human action is preordained and there is no such thing as chance, then man is powerless. Man has two choices of belief: either there is no Divine Providence or, if there is, it is hostile and evil. Though a highly exaggerated view of life, it is an important one, since Barrios often uses mouthpieces like Blanco (cf. the freethinkers in *El hermano asno* and *Gran señor y rajadiablos*) to articulate essential philosophical arguments like this one, which is a key to Barrios' view of life *at this time*. As the novel progresses, Luis comes to the awareness that the words of Blanco, the truth of which he had glimpsed, were being realised. Life itself, its experiences and its tragedies were underlining the basic pessimism of Blanco. Through his own insight Luis comes to the conclusion: « ¡Qué absurda, qué absurda la vida! » (I, 347). Linked with his awareness of the blind cruelty and absurdity of life is the equal awareness of his own character and the collapse thereof: «Soy un tipo sin voluntad. Pero ¿cómo me contengo?»

---

[21] DAVISON, *Eduardo Barrios*, p. 60.

(I, 354). The others too see him thus, rudderless in the ocean of life, bearing the cross of his loneliness, faced with a cruel destiny in a hostile world: «Porque es un "solo". Eso, un "solo". Y no le comprenden» (I, 449). Luis is a product of his age and his environment. To try to understand the problems of life and his own failings and to find solutions thereto, he has recourse to Nietzsche whose views on the will to power he does not understand, and promptly turns to Schopenhauer from whose melancholy and pessimism he derives some comfort (I, 388).[22]

In the post-Romantic malaise, like other anti-heroes, he finds no comfort in religion, therefore derives no inner strength from spiritual convictions. Unlike Gastón, he finds no fulfilment in the path of art. One recalls that papá Juan had early, and constantly, exhorted him to cultivate an art: «Cuando seas ya hombre, trata de cultivar un arte. La poesía, la música, la pintura... ese arte será nuestro más fiel compañero» (I, 224). Nor does he find consolation in the ultimate Romantic escape—love. Despite his emotional needs and his intense hunger for affection, rooted in his childhood fondness for kissing and fondling in the sheltered haven of the sentimental home of his grandparents, his emotional life is a catastrophic disaster. As his emotional needs grow into adolescence and end constantly in disillusion, his intellectual perception and insight into the world grow along with them, and are heightened to the point where he accepts Blanco's view of the world, which seems the one that best fits his pattern of life. This is reinforced when the providers of that tenderness, papá Juan, his grandmother, and his mother, are all quickly and dramatically removed from him, thus strengthening his despairing picture of the world and the belief in his own inadequacies. With nothing more than the advice of papá Juan—to let his heart be the guide (I, 246) and to allow emotion to prevail over the voice of reason—Luis' relations not only with his father but with the women in his life are total failures.[23] The death of his father and the disappearance of the prostitute la Meche destroy any possible chance of rehabilitation, of finding any means of support. This novel too, like «El niño que enloqueció de amor», is an ironic tragedy in the sense that the only meaningful, consolatory relationship that he strikes up as an outlet for his emotional needs should be with a prostitute. Even this hope, however, disappears with the flight of la Meche who, having contracted syphilis, prefers to abandon him rather than subject him to the dangers of the dreaded disease.[24]

[22] Cf. Gastón in «Tirana ley»: «entregándome libremente a saborear mi dolor» (I, 129).

[23] The father/son relationship is a favourite theme of Barrios. See, for example, Valverde/Antucho (Gran señor y rajadiablos) and el hombre/Charlie (Los hombres del hombre).

[24] Like Luz in Tirana ley, la Meche is a mother-figure for Luis who lost his own mother at an early age. This parent/child relationship, prefiguring the links with

Barrios skilfully weaves together the two threads of the narrative and the psychological development so that, as the events happen, not only does Luis suffer but the suffering produces insight. Each emotional setback adds to and clarifies his metaphysical view of the absurd, inimical world, and brings him nearer to complete consciousness not only of the hostility of life but also of his own weakness. This awareness of his own position helps him to gravitate to his own kind, like the *fracasado* Pepe Robles in the library: «Principalmente, habíale unido con Lucho la circunstancia de ser ambos pesimistas y de considerarse ambos perseguidos por implacable mala suerte» (I, 454).[25] Blanco's philosophy is increasingly imprinted on his mind and provides, in its deterministic theories, the convenient escape that Luis' lack of will power seeks (I, 429). Rejecting personal blame for his actions, Luis shifts the burden of responsibility on to destiny or fate: «Yo nací sentimental, infelizmente sentimental, demasiado sentimental para correr la suerte que corrí después» (I, 522). As Ned Davison succinctly expresses it: «At this moment the possibility of his personal regeneration ceases» (*Eduardo Barrios*, p. 56). As if to underline the Romantic basis of the novel, Barrios sets Luis up twice more to hammer home, in contrasting fashion, the message that need not have been spelled out. The final degradation could have been left unsaid, but Barrios, in his youthful pessimism, seems resolved to take Luis (and the reader) along the path of total awareness of life's hostility and his own weakness. The beautiful Blanca, his «ideal de belleza» (I, 431) and the Romantic ideal woman, is presented not only as another example of Luis' unattainable emotional satisfaction but also as an example of strength of character as a prerequisite for emotional stability. It is significant that Barrios allows her to be won over by Luis' brother, Anselmo, the *fuerte,* as opposed to Luis, the *débil.* His last effort to establish some kind of emotional relationship indicates the depth to which he has fallen. He picks up Teresa, a *mujer burlada,*[26] who satisfies a sensual need and diverts him temporarily from the other manifestation of his degradation, alcohol. With the foreseeable infidelity and desertion of this shallow girl,[27] his downward movement is almost complete—not without the rounding out of his illuminating self-awareness and his metaphysical vision of the world. He has finally come to accept totally Blanco's view of life: «Y tengo el corazón llagado, muy lleno de pus. Necesito reposo,

---

Freud's theories, is an important aspect of the psychological values of Barrios' novels.

[25] This is a good example of the *pobre feo* theme, exemplified in the story of the same name.

[26] Another favourite type of Barrios. Cf. María Rosa, *la mujer burlada* of his play «Lo que niega la vida».

[27] BARRIOS' description of the failure of the last prop, love, is suitably Romantic: «Apagado por la angustia, como desde el fondo de un abismo, salió de Lucho un sonido horrible» (I, 496).

olvido. Necesitaría... el no ser... La vida es mala, es madrasta para muchos, y, a la larga, para todos; lo ha sido para mí, lo es para ti...» (I, 537).

The double thread of self-knowledge and metaphysical awareness is complete. Luis' view of the world, based on analysis of his own emotional weaknesses and hard earned by his own experiences, now matches exactly the Naturalistic, deterministic theories of Blanco. Life is tragic, concludes Barrios, especially for weak, timid, sentimental abulics like Luis who follow their instincts in their search for emotional fulfilment. Emotion is an important force in life, but in the hands of lost souls like *el niño* and Luis it can lead to tragedy.

«El hermano asno»: The First Peak

El hermano asno (1922) is generally regarded as Barrios' best single work—almost certainly his best known, at least in his early period,[28] though *Gran señor y rajadiablos* was probably more popular from the «best-seller» point of view. On the artistic plane *El hermano asno* is the peak of his first period, or rather the first trilogy, since *Del natural* is a mere promise of things to come. *El hermano asno* has attained this reputation not only in Barrios' fiction but in Latin American literature in general, not for its apparent worth as a novel about religion, which it hardly is. *El hermano asno* has gained this high prestige because it is the culmination of the aesthetic and the psychological values, rooted in his metaphysical vision, which reinforces with subtle distinctions the mood of the previous novels.

El hermano asno is certainly the most sophisticated and the most complex of Barrios' earlier novels from the psychological point of view, transcending the relatively simple characterisation of *el niño* and Luis by means of a dualism technique not only in the contrast between the two friar protagonists Lázaro and Rufino but in the make-up of Lázaro/Mario himself.[29] The two threads of the novel, which is set in a Franciscan monastery, tell the story of two monks respectively. Fray Lázaro, the intellectual, analytical ex-man of the world (Mario), whose difficult, seven-year-old search for self-fulfilment is hampered by the appearance of María

---

[28] It also gained some notoriety on two accounts: the accusation by church figures that it was anti-religious, a charge that was later withdrawn; and the charge of plagiarism levelled against Barrios. See *Eduardo Barrios: Obras. Estilo. Técnica* by JULIO ORLANDO and ALEJANDRO RAMÍREZ (Santiago de Chile: Editorial del Pacífico, 1960), pp. 51-52, and RAÚL SILVA CASTRO, *Panorama de la novela chilena* (México: Fondo de Cultura Económica, 1955), pp. 128-29.

[29] This multipersonality theme is taken to its extreme conclusion in his last novel, *Los hombres del hombre* (1950).

Mercedes, the young sister of his ex-fiancée, Gracia, is contrasted with the simple Fray Rufino, who represents instinctive, non-rational acceptance of religion, and who has gained a reputation for sanctity and asceticism. Rufino's spiritual struggle, defined in terms of pride by his sinful visions, reaches a shocking climax in his attempted violation of María, the instrument of Fray Lázaro's temptations. Barrios' skilful weaving of the two strands of spiritual and psychological development is brought to an equally skilful climax in which the good name of the «saint», the order and the church is protected, whilst Fray Lázaro accepts blame for the crime and leaves for another monastery.

Though far superior to *Un perdido* from the point of view of construction, technique and style, there is little doubt that from the philosophical point of view this novel is related to the previous ones in its attempt to define Barrios' attitude to life. Emotion, the key to Barrios' fiction, is at the root of the problems that plague both Rufino and Lázaro. Rufino, following in the tradition of papá Juan's homily to Luis, represents «the intuitive religious spirit, the sentimental, non-rational, instinctive devotion to the ideals and commandments of the Franciscan Order» (Davison, *Eduardo Barrios*, p. 62). Lázaro, on the other hand, is characterised by his excessively analytical approach, not only to religion, but life in general. However, he too has his emotional struggles, not only in his affair with the young girl María, but also in his dealings with the other monks whom he considers less intellectual, therefore less spiritual. Lázaro's tragedy is that, despite his conscious desire to abandon the vanities of the outside world, and despite his awareness of the need for simplicity in order to be a good Franciscan, he cannot step down from his intellectual pedestal to join his fellow-brothers in the ways of St. Francis. In *El hermano asno*, which in a sense is as much an odyssey of a sick soul as *Un perdido*, Fray Lázaro cannot find peace and serenity either. His is the tragedy of insight struggling against emotion. Although he begs to be liberated from the demon of analysis, he clings to his intellectualism as a counter-balance to the feeble-minded simplicity of Rufino and the shallow faith of Fray Elías, in both of whom he questions the manifestation of the Divine Will, and so adds the sin of spiritual pride to intellectual conceit.

The real pathos of the novel, as Donald Shaw has so accurately perceived, lies in the struggle between emotion and emotion, in the inability of Lázaro to cast off human emotions on entering the monastery. The appearance of the temptress resurrects the Mario he thought dead, and adds to his spiritual struggle an emotional struggle. In Barrios' depiction of Lázaro's growing emotional involvement with the girl, his self-deceit, the depression, the rising hopes, etc.—what Sor Juana calls *los efectos irra-cionales del Amor*—he approaches the great psychological novelist, Stendhal, whose theories of crystallisation are concretised in this novel by Barrios' acute analysis not only of Lázaro but by his subtle hints as to the possible fate of Rufino.[30] As Fray Rufino appears to be on the downgrade, Fray Lázaro begins to see some light in the tunnel. From now on his evolution seems to take an upward trend. He accepts the situation, offering his feelings for the girl (and hers for him) as a sacrifice to God. For the first time in his religious career he experiences a genuine Christian feeling of unselfishness, offering his suffering to God and praying that she be exempt from pain and grief. It may be an ironic comment on Barrios' part that Lázaro achieves religious and spiritual fulfilment by means of an emotional involvement. Through a liaison of concupiscence which is refined, through possible love, to friendship, and to genuine Christian feeling, Mario is finally buried and the new man born. This spiritual conversion is reinforced by the second climax, when Fray Rufino cracks under the weight of the pride/lust cross and sexually attacks María—the ultimate self-debasement which should lead to absolute humility and the final destruction of the legend of sanctity. The double irony is that the church authorities suppress the truth for the sake of the «saint» and the church, whilst Fray Lázaro assumes responsibility for the attempted rape—a more credible solution given Mario's sensuous background—and offers his sacrifice as a penance. This second offering, also rooted in the stirrings of the flesh, guides Lázaro further along the path of salvation. By a skilful development of character Barrios has neatly reversed the roles—the saintly ascete succumbing to the temptations of the flesh, whilst the proud intellectual, bowing to the dictates of the heart, yields to two acts of selfless love that reveal his humanity, his heroism and, dare one say it, his possible saintliness. At least, by taking the advice of Fray Rufino to humiliate himself, he is well on the way to becoming a good Franciscan. Only at the end does the symbolism of Fray Lázaro's name gain full significance, when he rises from the death of physical lust and intellectual pride to a new life of simplicity, tenderness and love.[31]

One, however, should not ignore the fact that El hermano asno is a tragedy, in the sense that at least three lives are indelibly marked by the events described, one of which ends with the death of Fray Rufino: «Ha sido absurdo. Ha sido trágico. Ha sido absurdo, trágico y grotesco» (II, 628). Barrios has a penchant for grotesque death scenes especially in the religious

---

[30] The psychological master touches of Barrios have been well treated by NED DAVISON in his article «Conflict and Identity in El hermano asno», Hispania, XLII (December, 1959), 498-501.

[31] The name symbolism in the novel, which is quite significant, has been touched on though not fully developed by JOHN R. KELLY in a short article entitled «Name Symbolism in Barrios' El hermano asno», Romance Notes, XIII, No. 1 (1971-72), 48-53.

This is also an example of Luther's doctrine (whose influence has already been noted in Chapter 2, especially Note 45): pecca fortiter—sin strongly, and in the end you'll be a saint!

setting.[32] This comment on the clerical life and organised religion can be extended even to include oblique criticism of the Divine pattern, the immutability of one's fate, as in Blanco's view of the world in *Un perdido*. Lázaro/Mario, as well as being a sensualist in his Modernist delight in the senses (colour, sound, music, fragrance, etc.), is a self-confessed Romantic, who underlines his relationship with the previous heroes by giving a copy of *El niño que enloqueció de amor* (II, 566) with the inscription that comes back to haunt him: to the *colegiala* «que ojalá no sea tan romántica como su hermana» (II, 585), and which serves as a catalyst for his own emotional crisis. The whole novel is the story of his attempt to win over his *alter ego* and become a good Franciscan, with the metamorphosis implied not only in his character but in his attitude to life and humanity.

The theme of emotion which is a vital factor in *El niño que enloqueció de amor* and *Un perdido* is continued in *El hermano asno* not only in the evolution of the characters of the two protagonists but in a way that has become a favourite technique in Barrios' novels, underlining its link with the European tradition (cf. Baroja and Mallea), i.e. the philosophical discussion. Like the Valverde/journalists and Morales/Javier confrontations of his later novels, this discussion between the rationalist engineer and the monks hinges on the antithesis of heart/brain, faith/reason, instinct/analysis, and the Pascalian belief, reiterated by Barrios' characters from papá Juan to Valverde, that there are truths of the heart as well as of the brain, an argument that the mathematical scientists can neither refute nor accept.

Closely related to the vital issue of emotion is the theme of the child,[33] since to become pure of heart one has to become like little children, «mansos, humildes, simples» (II, 579), without whose innocence one cannot attain any kind of salvation. This view of the child as the fount of innocence and truth is another key issue in Barrios' novels, almost all of which are devoted to child psychology and the role of the child face to face with the world. Although *El hermano asno* is not a narrative of a sentimental, sensitive youth, Barrios devotes long pages in discussion to this very theme. Fray Bernardo is Barrios' spokesman in *El hermano asno* for his theories on heart-inspired love, a love that emanates from the belief that one can love all men if one sees them as children (II, 548-49). This idea is strengthened by the description of Fray Bernardo as «un corazón que comprende, lo cual es más que un cerebro que comprende» (II, 548).

Emotion, then, is the keynote. Used in prudent fashion, channelled into worthy causes, it can be a source of love, happiness and success. In Barrios' novels of the early period, stemming from his pessimistic view of the world,

[32] Cf. the grotesque death of Luis' grandmother in *Un perdido*, when she falls from the altar in the church. See also JERRY BENBOW, «Grotesque Elements in Eduardo Barrios», *Hispania*, LI, No. 1 (March, 1968), 68-91.

[33] See NED DAVISON's article «El niño», in *Sobre Eduardo Barrios y otros* (Albuquerque: Foreign Books, 1966), pp. 62-72.

it is generally a force of evil that leads to tragedy. *El hermano asno* is a tragedy too in the sense that injustice seems to prevail, the innocent suffer, whilst an unconcerned God watches indifferently. Rufino dies tragically, absurdly, grotesquely while Fray Lázaro, unfairly, one feels, has to accept the blame. Why does he have to accept the blame?, Barrios seems to ask. The answer is *el mundo es así (ansí?)*—there is an evil force in life that causes pain and suffering. In this light *El hermano asno* is an extension of the metaphysical picture painted in *El niño que enloqueció de amor* and *Un perdido,* in its portrayal of the tragic aspect of life. However, compared to *El niño que enloqueció de amor* and *Un perdido* (which is the peak of his pessimistic-deterministic period), there is a slight but perceptible change in his vital outlook in *El hermano asno.* Though tragic, for the reasons stated, Barrios appears to give a ray of hope in the open ending, with Fray Lázaro partially redeemed through love and charity after his emotional crisis which he survives. The novel ends with Mario now dead and Fray Lázaro donning Rufino's ascetic mantle of the true Franciscan, to some extent liberated from the torment of rational analysis and intellectualisation, and reconciled to humility. There is a certain irony in Barrios' reversal of the roles of Rufino and Lázaro, but he is consistent in his view that undisciplined emotion usually leads to tragedy. The climax also confirms Barrios' oft-expressed opinion that religion can be a valuable formative force.

«Páginas de un pobre diablo»: The Light in the Darkness

Páginas de un pobre diablo (1923), which marks the end of Barrios' first productive phase, is made up of two short novels, the title piece and «Canción», plus the short stories «La antipatía» and «Como hermanas», which is a version of «Amistad de solteras» already published in *Del natural* (1907). Although not published till 1923, «Canción», written around 1912, reflects Barrios' literary and philosophical concerns of that period—not to mention his standard and technique of writing. Both from the point of view of chronology and development it fits somewhere between *Del natural* [34] and *El niño que enloqueció de amor,* though it is also closely linked to Barrios' drama and its concern with the position of women in society. In fact, *Vivir* (1916) is a continuation of «Canción», the story of Olga, the innocent young girl who falls in love with Ramiro, the man of the world (imperfect anagram of Mario?), who leaves her. The play-sequel brings out the nervous, desperate character of the emotionally immature girl, fraught with anxiety and sexual frustration which precipitates the crisis and her eventual breakdown. The preoccupation with sex and exces-

---

[34] Gastón Labarca, the protagonist of «Tirana ley», is one of the characters of this short novel.

sive sentimentality looks back to *Del natural,* and «Tirana ley» in particular, whilst the neurotic character of Olga is clearly in the line of *el niño* and Luis whom she prefigures. Though the novelette adds little to our appreciation of Barrios or to his view of the world, it is interesting as a statement of themes already presented and as a foretaste of his mature novels. Apart from recalling the anticlericalism and antimorality of *Del natural* («... sus abuelos, viejos católicos de moral rancia, rígida e infanzona, quisieron hacerle sacerdote; pero a él molestárale tanto la gramática latina como la teología...» [I, 195]), it looks forward to the religious views of *Un perdido* and the anti-rationalism and excessive analysis of *El hermano asno;* and the heart-centred instinctiveness as a guide to life («Pero... hay algo en los corazones de los demás que una lo siente, algo que da pruebas, aunque no se oye traducido en palabras ni se palpa convertido en hechos...» [I, 199]) which is at the root of Barrios' fiction and his attitude to life and love: «Hay quien asegura que sólo amamos una vez, la primera, y que luego experimentamos únicamente reacciones de aquel amor que para siempre quedó latente, allá, en el fondo de nuestro corazón. Para mí, el amor es más bien algo inherente a nosotros, un sentimiento inseparable, esencia y razón de la vida...» (I, 207). This analysis of the ways of love, reminiscent of Stendhal's *De l'Amour,* sets the mood for the much more analytical treatment of the theme in *El hermano asno,* the psychological peak of the first period: «Para amar, no precisa ser amado. El amor no es siempre aroma de dos almas que comulgan en lo humano para elevarse a lo sublime. Cuando mucho, esto, que es la "obra maestra", podría ser el ideal de los enamorados. El amor para nadie tiene realidad fuera de su yo propio. Es una batalla en la que sólo combaten los heridos. Deseamos conquistar cuando hemos sido conquistados; anhelamos hacer nuestro un corazón porque él nos ha hecho de antemano víctimas de un vértigo, de una gran sed de ternura.»[35] Defective as a work of art, «Canción» is an interesting contribution to the metaphysical evolution of Barrios' novels, though it in no way reflects the true state of Barrios' growing philosophical maturity in 1923 when the revised form was published.

The previously unpublished short story, «La antipatía», is perhaps more typical of what many critics have come to expect of Eduardo Barrios. It is a psychological study of human emotions—or rather one emotion, antipathy or repugnance, a theme that greatly interested Barrios.[36] The story of the medical student who, motivated by his dislike of a family, hastens the death of a patient, is, for many, vintage Barrios. Despite its technical excellence, convincing setting and acute psychological penetration, «La an-

[35] I, 208. Cf. also: «Creemos en la virtualidad sentimental del amor, sabemos gozar y sufrir; tenemos una filosofía estética, amable, llena de gracia y de bondad» (I, 215).

[36] Cf. the short piece «Pobre feo», and the treatment of Chela Garín in *Los hombres del hombre.*

tipatía» adds little to Barrios' view of life, being rather a psychological *tour de force,* perfectly capable of standing alone and being judged separately from Barrios' other fiction. The Poesque mood, the gothic atmosphere and the grotesque elements of this successful short story are closely linked with the main piece of the collection, «Páginas de un pobre diablo».

On the whole, *Páginas de un pobre diablo* has been neglected by the critics, even by those who have written extensively on Barrios, like Torres-Ríoseco, Fernando Santiván, Jefferson Rea Spell and Carlos Hamilton.[37] Raúl Silva Castro and Milton Rossel give it the briefest mention, whilst Vázquez-Bigi, concentrating as he does on the psychiatric aspects of Barrios' work, ignores it in his emphasis on *el niño* and Luis Bernales. Only Ned Davison has given more than superficial treatment to this work—but generally in a way that highlights the aforementioned psychological value (*Eduardo Barrios,* pp. 83-89).

The *pobre diablo* of the novel is Adolfo, an orphan who takes a job in a funeral parlour owned by Milton López. The novel is the story of Adolfo's reactions not only to the behaviour of the undertaker and his wife but to the macabre atmosphere of corpses and coffins, and to the theme of death itself. Rooted in the Realistic tradition of the nineteenth century with strong Dickensian overtones, the novel owes much to the influence of the Russian writers of the turn of the century, especially Gorky, as Davison and other critics have pointed out.[38] The psychological analysis of the tormented mind of the youth from his insomnia, to hallucination, to potential insanity, if he were to stay in this gruesome setting, matches the best of Barrios' better-known psychological works. This portrayal of the «abnormal» aspects of the human mind is in keeping with the general atmosphere of the first trilogy, and ties up with the weakness and madness of *el niño,* Luis, Olga, and Fray Rufino.

As the title and the opening lines indicate, this is a novel about a *perdido* type: « ¡En fin! Hay que ser hombre y dominar el miedo... ¿acaso un muchacho infeliz y solo como yo... tiene derecho a mimar un corazón asustadizo de mujercita? ... Sé fuerte, sé hombre, vamos, ¡todo un hombre! » (I, 169). I use the term reservedly, however, since I intend to show that Adolfo, although the novel is in the tradition of the previous trilogy, and although he follows in the footsteps of his predecessors, does not meet the same fate. This subtle shift, which was suggested by the open ending of *El hermano asno,* becomes more evident at the conclusion of «Páginas

---

[37] RICARDO LATCHAM discusses it in a review published in *La Revista Católica,* XLVI (1924), 226-27, only to attack it: «*Páginas de un pobre diablo* es un relato confuso, que se desenvuelve entre cuatro paredes. Se halla escrito con un estilo retorcido y presuntuoso. Hay aciertos y observaciones originales; pero lo daña el alambicado propósito de imitación de los complicados y sutiles novelistas rusos.»

[38] JULIA GARCÍA GAMES, *Como los he visto yo* (Santiago: Nascimento, 1930), p. 121: «Tiene algo de las novelas rusas, el análisis envuelto en piedad de su dolor reconcentrado, feliz en el ahondamiento del abismo humano.»

de un pobre diablo». However, Adolfo, at the outset of the novel, is obviously of the same breed as the previous heroes. Like *el niño* and Luis, he is prematurely thrown into an adult situation which he has to face with his childish sensitivity. In *el niño*'s case it is love. In *Un perdido,* and especially in «Páginas de un pobre diablo», it is death. In contrast with the adult insensitivity we see the perceptiveness of the child which, born of suffering, produces a growing awareness of the world and its values. As an orphan whose parents died in their thirties, Adolfo is more susceptible to the same kinds of emotional problems that beleaguered Luis, *el niño,* Olga, all of whose lack of normal parental care, Barrios suggests, contributed to their emotional instability and excessive sentimentality. Apart from the diary form, also used in «El niño que enloqueció de amor» and *El hermano asno,* more suited to the inner analysis which is typical of Barrios, «Páginas de un pobre diablo» is a good example of the link between literature and metaphysics, so vital to an understanding of Barrios' fiction. Adolfo's writing is more consciously therapeutic than in other novels. Given the sombre gothic setting of the funeral parlour and the timid temperament of Adolfo, writing is more than a means of whiling away the hours. In his case it is a deliberate attempt to shut out the phantoms and sinister noises of his lugubrious prison. It is the only successful method of warding off fear: «Porque aún dejar de escribir me atemoriza, me entrega al pánico. Para mí, en estas noches, no escribir equivale a quedar más solo» (I, 182). More than a leisure-time activity, more than a method of recording his thoughts, writing for Adolfo is an escape from the grave metaphysical problems that beset him. Writing helps him to cope with the everyday business of living and to mitigate the inherently tragic character of life.

Living in the midst of death and face to face with the suffering that produces it, Adolfo grows and reacts in a way that was foreign to *el niño* and Luis. A certain progression is revealed in his character by his response to the sickness of the child of the servant Celinda, and its treatment by Don Milton and his wife: «Me punzó el alma, la criatura sufriente, tan tiernecita, tan indefensa y tan sufriente» (I, 183). This element of anguished protest which sees in the death of an innocent child an absurdity of nature raises Adolfo to a level never achieved by Luis. His handling of the reality and finality of death, with which he comes to grips by writing about it, indicates a growing philosophical maturity that one never finds in Luis:

> Además, una obstinación capaz de conducir al delirio: pienso a menudo en mi muerte. La muerte. No escapa nadie a ella. Nunca nadie escapará. ¿Es aceptable? ¡Y se vive tranquilo! A mí me soldarán también un día..., una mañana tal vez, una noche, un atardecer..., ¿a qué hora moriré yo? No se me había presentado jamás esta pregunta... Quizás haga un sol sofocante, quizás llueva... A la hora y con el tiempo que sea, a mí me soldarán también dentro de la caja horrible. Después, el nicho, con olor a cal y a ladrillos húmedos, vecino a otros cadáveres, desconocidos y asquerosos; la putrefacción, el frío... ¡Oh! Cuando he ido al cementerio, ese hielo, único, absoluto, de las criptas y los

mausoleos, me ha seguido días y días, impregnado en las carnes, en las venas, en los huesos, en el corazón...

Por último, la muerte... ¿Qué es la muerte? Tiniebla. ¿Y el alma? ¿Qué es el alma? Me la explico yo como la llama del cuerpo. Pero ¿adónde va una llama cuando una lámpara se apaga? A ninguna parte, no *es* más. De manera que mi madre, mi padre, ¿no son ya sino ideas y sentimientos míos? (I, 186)

Whilst Adolfo struggles with the concept of death and the immortality of the soul in a fashion reminiscent of Unamuno, Luis shelters behind the convenient deterministic philosophy of an adverse fate and pre-arranged destiny.

Worn out by nervous tension, insomnia, and repugnance for a job that exploits death with hypocritical euphemisms, Adolfo throws discretion to the wind, and, in an outburst worthy of young Valverde, he resigns his post: «Me tiene ya loco su porquería esta, su funeraria, su asquerosidad. Me largo, señor» (I, 189). When he leaves the funeral home at the end of the novel, Adolfo realises that life is still a struggle and that death is still very much a reality. However, in this his first encounter, he has not gone under nor yielded in a wave of self-pity. Unlike Luis, and more like the young Valverde, he has learnt something from this clash. An innocent youth, faced with the harshness of life, he has emerged from his first traumatic experience with a hope for the future, feeling «el mismo vago temor en las entrañas a la vida nueva, a la lucha renovada» (I, 190). Again it may be said that this novel is open-ended in the sense that we do not know the ultimate fate of Adolfo. However, Barrios points the way with a conclusion that cannot be anything but optimistic. As writing had been therapeutic during Adolfo's confinement in the funeral home (a symbol of the world in general with its sombre, oppressive concern with death), so too does writing suggest a possibility of escape: «Si me dieran algo por estos papeles... Acaso algún escritor...» (I, 190).

As I have reiterated, many critics have not fully appreciated the value of Barrios' fiction, because of their too strong emphasis on the psychological. Even Ned Davison, who is one of the few to see any merit in the novel, in his early work on Barrios attacks «Páginas de un pobre diablo» for its weak ending: «Unfortunately, the abrupt resolution is completely inadequate aesthetically. The reader feels that Barrios became tired of his narration or that he was unable to extricate Adolfo from his conflict and simply gave up. The frivolous ending destroys what might have been a good story» (Thesis, p. 125). Although I agree with Ned Davison that the protagonist Adolfo is the only figure who escapes the «flat» characterisation description (*Eduardo Barrios*, p. 89), I am also of the opinion that the ending is more significant that he would admit.[39] It seems to me that Adolfo's conduct,

---

[39] It is interesting that NED DAVISON in his Twayne *Eduardo Barrios* (published a decade after his thesis findings) modifies his earlier opinion of the ending of

given Barrios' subtle but perceptible shift in sensibility, is in keeping with his evolution—an evolution that reflects Barrios' turning towards a more optimistic view of life. When one comes to look at the second trilogy, this change becomes more clear.

«Páginas de un pobre diablo» is not a great novel, but is important because of its position as Barrios' last philosophical comment of his early literary period. It stands at the crossroads, a kind of link with the past trilogy—the Naturalistic preoccupation with death, the Poesque, gothic traits, and the *perdido*-type protagonist in the *niño*/Luis mould. Adolfo, however, by reason of his conscious effort to do something positive to help himself, looks forward to the strength of character of young Valverde *(Gran señor y rajadiablos)* and the sensitive young Charlie of *Los hombres del hombre,* who finds an escape from the harsh world by means of his intuitive gift of poetry, which gives meaning to life.

The Later Period

«*Tamarugal*»: A Faltering Comeback

After the success of the early trilogy, there is no doubt that *Gran señor y rajadiablos* (1948) was Barrios' next huge success. As *Páginas de un pobre diablo* (1923) tended to be ignored (in comparison with the first trilogy), *Gran señor y rajadiablos* undoubtedly overshadows *Tamarugal,* published four years earlier in 1944, which, though inferior to the others, has a vital role to play in the evolution of Barrios' fiction and in his view of life as reflected in his later novels.

It is not the aim of this section to analyse the causes of the twenty-year-long silence. Although several reasons have already been put forward to explain this so-called quiet period, they are all conjecture. I would caution prudence, therefore, to those critics who read Barrios' novels as autobiographical works and who are forever searching for clues to link the biographical data on the novelist with his fictional creations. One of the weaknesses of the criticism of Latin American literature in general and Barrios' works in particular is this reluctance on the part of many critics to permit the artistic entity a life of its own. Too close an identification between novel and biography can have a vitiating effect.[40] However, the

«Páginas de un pobre diablo» by omitting his criticism of the unsatisfactory resolution of the story.

[40] ANDERSON IMBERT provides the antidote to this attitude, more specifically with regard to Literature/Biography in his *La crítica literaria contemporánea* (Buenos Aires, 1957), pp. 77-78: «No hay duda que la biografía es muy útil... por cuanto nos da noticias relativas a la vida privada y pública de un autor. Pero una cosa es la biografía como género literario o como contribución a la historia y otra el método psicológico» (p. 77).

facts about Barrios' own life during these twenty years are well known and can be sketched briefly. In 1925 he was a member of the literary group *Los Diez,* and became the first editor of *Atenea.* He served the dictator Ibáñez in various posts—Director General de Bibliotecas y de la Biblioteca Nacional, Ministro de Higiene, and Ministro de Instrucción. With the fall of Ibáñez in 1931, Barrios resigned his government posts, and till 1943 was engaged in the cattle business as a ranch owner and an administrator, experiences that provided him with material for *Gran señor y raja-diablos.* Apart from regular contributions to the Santiago newspapers *El Mercurio* and *Las Ultimas Noticias* (editorials, reviews on themes as varied as politics, literature, language, cinema, opera, sports, etc.), he was deeply involved in other cultural work and organisations—reason enough, some would think, for not publishing any new fiction during these years.

When he did finally publish *Tamarugal* in 1944, it was not related to his recent experiences, but was based on his adventures as an administrator in the Oficina Salitrera Tarapacá, in the north of Chile in 1904. The action takes place in the office of the British-owned nitrate company, la Tamarugal, near the town of Huara, in the province of Tarapacá. The administrator of the Tamarugal office, the materialistic Jesús Morales, nicknamed *el Hombre* (a disciple of the Positivist school), decides that he should marry Juanita Arlegui (who prefers to be called Jenny),[41] the daughter of one of the employees, a sentimental girl of eighteen. Whilst preparing for the wedding, Jenny feels attracted to the equally sentimental young seminarian, Javier del Campo, who visits the mine with his priest-uncle. In spite of their feelings for each other, both decide tearfully to pursue their chosen vocations. An epilogue, some forty years later, sees Jenny, a rich old widow, living in Santiago, with the comfort of her three professionally successful sons, and the consolation of her friend and confessor, monsignor Javier del Campo.

Tamarugal is not a great novel. In fact, it can hardly even be called a good novel. Some of the major critics give it scant or no mention (Zum Felde, Anderson Imbert, Fernando Alegría, Luis Alberto Sánchez). Chilean scholars like Carlos Hamilton and Fernando Santiván give it the briefest attention. There is no major article devoted to the novel, and those critics who do treat it are divided in their views. For Orlandi and Ramírez «*Tamarugal* es una obra de la edad madura escrita con la agilidad de la juventud»,[42] whereas for Jaime Peralta «es una novela no conseguida... Es una obra débil, muy poco convincente».[43] For Salvador Dinamarca, «*Tamarugal* es una novela de valor permanente... Barrios no ha perdido nada de su

---

[41] BARRIOS has a liking for English names, e.g. Charlie in *Los hombres del hombre.*

[42] *Eduardo Barrios* (Santiago, 1960), p. 63.

[43] «La novelística de Eduardo Barrios», *Cuadernos Hispanoamericanos,* No. 173 (1964), 365.

genio creador, ni de la maestría de su estilo»,[44] yet according to Raúl Silva Castro «hay cierta regresión de las aptitudes creadoras».[45] In the opinion of Jefferson Rea Spell «la última escena es magistral, en su brevedad»,[46] yet according to Dinamarca «hasta la última escena... la novela está muy bien... El fin tan brusco de *Tamarugal* es lo que la mata como gran novela» (pp. 175-76).

This difference of opinion amongst the critics would have pleased Barrios. One remembers his observation in «También algo de mí»: «Y si los críticos no están de acuerdo sobre mi obra, me siento más dueño de mí; porque recuerdo a Wilde: "Cuando los críticos difieren, el artista está conforme consigo mismo"» (I, 29). In spite of these conveniently facile remarks, Barrios was too much of an artist to insist that *Tamarugal* was a great novel, stylistically or structurally. There are far too many flaws, defects and weaknesses in the construction of the novel for it to be placed alongside *Un perdido, El hermano asno,* or even *Gran señor y rajadiablos,* a later work.[47] In spite of its few merits, then, *Tamarugal* is a weak novel. However, this does not detract from its important role in the changing view of life as evolved by Barrios, from the early trilogy culminating in *Gran señor y rajadiablos* and *Los hombres del hombre.* Herein lies the significance of *Tamarugal,* as yet another step in Barrios' realisation of the importance of emotion in life (for good and evil), and yet one more step in his changing vision of the world.

The most evident function of the novel is to portray something of the nitrate regions of the north of Chile. In a letter to Jefferson Rea Spell, Barrios says «es una parte que faltaba en el panorama chileno de *Un perdido*» (Spell, p. 143). Barrios genuinely felt that this region had been neglected.[48] In an interview with Donald Fogelquist he confesses: «yo tenía que escribir esa novela».[49] Since no one knew that era and the life there, he felt compelled to write about it so that it would not be lost from memory. His experiences there gave him first-hand information, and one suspects that, if not *Tamarugal,* at least parts of it and the stories that were published with it («Santo Remedio» and «Camanchaca») were actually written at this

[44] Reseña de *Tamarugal, Revista Iberoamericana,* X, No. 19 (noviembre, 1945), 176.
[45] *Panorama de la novela chilena* (México, 1955), p. 127.
[46] Reseña de *Tamarugal, Revista Iberoamericana,* XIV, No. 27 (junio, 1948), 142.
[47] e.g. NED DAVISON in his *Eduardo Barrios* (New York, 1970), feels that: «... the overall focus of the novel is uncertain. It lacks a density of interrelationships. The link between the principal figures and their environment is inadequately realised. And the characters seem curiously one-dimensional» (p. 102).
[48] This feeling is shared by other Chilean writers. Writing in *La Nación,* 28 November 1935, JOAQUÍN EDWARDS BELLO states: «Falta en nuestra naciente literatura la emoción profunda del salitre... Creo que la novela no es un oficio, ni una ciencia, sino la confesión patética de cosas vistas y soñadas en la forma exaltada por la invención.»
[49] «Una visita con Eduardo Barrios», *Cuadernos Americanos,* CXVI, No. 3 (1961), 238.

time and revised later for publication—in spite of the fact that Barrios claims not to have brought to life any of his earlier efforts which were very bad.[50]

On the most obvious plane, then, as we have seen, *Tamarugal* looks like a *novela minera* in the tradition of Zola, and also a novel of northern pampa *costumbrismo*. Superficially in the same vein as Baldomero Lillo's *Sub-terra* (1904),[51] the poems «La huelga» and «De vuelta de la pampa» of Carlos Pezoa Véliz (1905), and the Naturalistic stories of Víctor Domingo Silva's *La pampa trágica* (1921), Barrios treats the same incidents—the terrible fires, the industrial accidents (cf. «Santo remedio»), the suicides, etc. Here Barrios «rises» to the heights of the Naturalists with his description of the mangled remains of bodies caught in machinery. Equally painful are the suicides—the mechanic who places his head under the hydraulic hammer; the workman who puts the stick of dynamite in his mouth, lights it like a cigarette, and blows off his head (II, 676). These were normal events which had to be portrayed, and were not depicted for propaganda purposes. As far as the social questions of the workers are concerned, Barrios states that «allá el obrero no estaba maleado por el odio de clases todavía» (II, 706). This judgment would not have been shared by his more militant contemporaries, and is obviously the opinion of the conservative Barrios of the 1940s, looking back on the events of some forty years before. This is a good example of the eclectic nature of the novel—the contemporary commentary intercalated with events of a previous era (and parts of it probably written then too and revised). One is impressed too by his brief but telling descriptions of the natural conditions of the pampa: «un páramo afiebrado de torridez y esfuerzo, áspero y cruel» (II, 681). Barrios, a self-confessed sentimentalist, obviously felt, like Jenny, the solitude, the beauty and the anguish of that remote, arid region, and one cannot refute his keen desire to express it artistically. As a work of pampa *costumbrismo* it has some

---

[50] «... todavía me acuerdo de unas libretas de hule negro que me servían en la soledad de la pampa para escribir unos cuentos muy malos y muy largos que felizmente tuve el buen criterio de no mostrar a nadie», *Boletín del Instituto de Literatura Chilena*, Vol. II, No. 3 (1962), 23.

As NED DAVISON points out also (*Eduardo Barrios*, p. 103), «Santo remedio» was probably part of the original version of the novel *Tamarugal*.

[51] Lillo was never able to fulfil his ambition to write a novel about the exploitation of the nitrate workers. Although he visited the north, did his research, and set out to write *La huelga*, it remained an unrealised dream, even an obsession, for the rest of his life. He confessed to Barrios: «No sé bastante de ese ambiente... No lo he asimilado como el de las minas de carbón.» See «Baldomero Lillo», *Revista Chilena*, XX (1923), 416.

Orlandi and Ramírez have an interesting theory that Barrios delayed the publication of *Tamarugal* in the hope that his friend would finish *La huelga*. If this is the case, it would confirm my suspicion that much of the novel pre-dates by a long stretch 1944. In fact, these two Chilean critics state that «... razones estilísticas la ubicarían entre *Del natural* [1907] y *El niño que enloqueció de amor* [1915]» (p. 63).

merit in its treatment of a neglected area and a forgotten epoch. In spite of the realistic background and the social themes, however, the value of the novel lies elsewhere.

Making use of old material and experiences of his past life, Barrios, in a sense, has indulged in a literary exercise, flexing his artistic muscles, in an attempt to come out of his long retirement. As a work of art, *Tamarugal* was no great success. Stylistically, structurally and aesthetically, it falls below the level of the earlier trilogy.[52] However, there is some value in the fact that it was written and gave Barrios an opportunity to renew his labours. What is most important about the novel, and herein lies its main merit, is that it is a groping attempt by Barrios to take up again his commentary on life and to formulate his changing view of the world. In this sense the novel serves as a link between the novels of the first period and the new metaphysical outlook manifested by Barrios in *Gran señor y rajadiablos*. In other words, it is a bridge novel between the ideas of the younger Barrios and the new philosophy of life which emerges in *Gran señor y rajadiablos*. Thus it becomes clear that the background is less important, the social questions less relevant. What really matters is the life of the three main figures, their feelings, their emotions—and, of course, Barrios' analysis of their characters. Basically, then, it is yet another Barrios novel on the role of emotion in human life—but with a difference.

In this truncated novel, Barrios appears to be trying to formulate his new philosophy of life, more balanced, and less black than in his previous novels. Twenty years of literary inactivity had obviously provided him with the experience and maturity that cause this change in sensibility. If the theme of the first trilogy is that emotion is a vital force in man's nature (for good and for evil), twenty years later Barrios is looking for a way to express his new view of life, less black, less negative, less likely to lead to tragedy. He is searching for a compromise without abandoning his belief in the importance of emotion as a vital force. Two decades of idleness have left their mark on the artist, but have matured the philosopher. Four years later, with *Gran señor y rajadiablos,* having had his practice and training on *Tamarugal*, the writer was to emerge again, improved, and with a clearer metaphysical perspective.

The struggle in *Tamarugal,* as always in Barrios' novels, is between emotion and strength. As Luis in *Un perdido* was contrasted with the

---

[52] When the Chilean critic Alone pointed out the defects of the novel, Barrios, in an interview with JORGE ONFRAY, «Perfil de Eduardo Barrios», in *Revista Zig-Zag* (30 de mayo, 1946), took the opportunity to attack Alone for what he considered his lack of objectivity: «Antes de publicar este libro, él y yo habíamos tenido un disgusto personal.» Alone counter-attacked with «Una aclaración», *Revista Zig-Zag* (6 de junio, 1946), pointing out that Silva Castro and De Luigi had treated it much more harshly.

strong types like his brother Anselmo, so too do we have the same comparisons in *Tamarugal*—but with subtle differences. Jesús Morales, the
administrator, represents strength, energy, will power, all the good qualities
that were lacking in the previous Barrios heroes like *el niño* and Luis.
However, Morales too is incomplete, since he lacks the complementary
qualities that would have balanced his strength, i.e. emotion, tenderness.
In other words, the very qualities that lead to tragedy in the abulic heroes
of the early novels are those that are lacking in Morales, *el Hombre,* who
appears to be almost a robot, completely devoid of feeling.[53] To balance
this, Barrios counteracts with the female protagonist, Jenny Arlegui,[54] young,
romantic, sentimental, more in the tradition of Barrios' early characters:
«Entonces caía sobre Jenny la tristeza. Solía ponerse angustiosamente triste.
Era, en el fondo y por encima de todo, una sentimental» (II, 662). Lonely
and sad, she sees in this strong man of high social standing in the com-
munity an opportunity to escape the boredom of pampa life. *El Hombre*
lacks temperament but at least he is intelligent and sincere. Not until the
portrayal of José Pedro Valverde in *Gran señor y rajadiablos* was Barrios
able to synthesise the two contrasting qualities of strength and tenderness.
Another defect in *el Hombre*'s character is his lack of religion. His frank
boast of atheism goes hand in hand with his lack of tenderness, since the
theme of Barrios' other novels is that emotion is the basis of religion.
To underline this lack of sentiment, and to emphasise the importance of
religion, Barrios introduces his third main character, the seminarian Javier
del Campo. Through Javier and his affair of the heart with Jenny, Barrios
draws the contrast with Morales: «un fuerte, para el mundo. Vencedor
de todos los trances, inteligente de las cosas y de los hombres, del dine-
ro y de la técnica» (II, 699), i.e. the man of reason. Barrios also utilises
Javier as the spokesman for heart-centred religion in the long debate with
Morales, who represents science, reason, atheism (in the very important
chapter XVI).

Jenny, in love with Javier, and affected by the accidents of the pampa
life, is touched by the emotion which is at the root of the Christian life:
«Habíala emocionado la doctrina cristiana...» (II, 692). Now both she
and Javier, united in love, emotion and religion, are set in contrast with
the materially successful Morales. However, and here we see one important

---

[53] I cannot agree with MARIANO MORÍNIGO, *Eduardo Barrios, novelista* (Tucumán:
Universidad Nacional de Tucumán, 1971), who finds *el Hombre* «uno de los esbozos
más interesantes creados por Barrios» (p. 36).

[54] Without stretching the imagination too much, Arlegui is obviously a form of
Arlequín, the masquerade role that Luis liked to play in *Un perdido* (I, 240).
Barrios' symbolic names are always worthy of attention. Apart from the irony of the
atheistic materialist's name, Jesús Morales, and the role of Pascal (in Chapter 2),
the young seminarian's too has symbolic overtones. Javier del Campo's role as a
rural redeemer becomes more explicit with the appearance of Barrios' novel of the
land, *Gran señor y rajadiablos,* a comment on life set in the country.

aspect of the change in Barrios' new attitude to life, in this particular case emotion does not lead to evil or tragedy. In spite of their awareness of their feelings for each other, the young lovers subordinate their feelings to the voice of reason, both choosing dutifully to adhere to their selected vocations—respectable, bourgeois marriage for Jenny, and the priesthood for Javier.

Thus we see that at this stage Barrios was not yet able to blend the desirable human qualities in one character. The emotion, religious feeling, and counterbalancing strength and energy had to be portrayed by means of three characters. Not till his balanced portrayal of Valverde in *Gran señor y rajadiablos* will Barrios be able to bring all of these attributes together in one fictional creation.

Tamarugal is not a good novel, as some critics have realised. However, it is an important work not merely for its contribution to the *novela minera* and northern pampa *costumbrismo*, but more especially for its place in Barrios' fiction. It serves as a link between the earlier novels and his more mature *Gran señor y rajadiablos*, in which he finally formulated his new philosophy of life. Although not a work on which Barrios' artistic reputation will be founded, *Tamarugal* is an essential preparation for the balanced characterisation of José Pedro Valverde, and the metaphysical evolution of Eduardo Barrios.

«*Gran señor y rajadiablos*»: *Redressing the Balance*

Gran señor y rajadiablos (1948), though recognised by Raúl Silva Castro and Fernando Santiván as a best-seller, and lauded by Milton Rossel (OC I, 24) and Carlos Préndez Saldías as «la mejor novela de América»,[55] or at least «la más completa y perfecta novela campestre que se ha escrito en Chile» (Silva Castro),[56] as a work of art its qualities are more doubtful. Donald Fogelquist sees no conflict in his seemingly contradictory remarks that «la maestría artística está en el estilo mismo» despite the fact that there is «alguna tendencia hacia la prolijidad».[57] For Anderson Imbert, «aunque bien escrita, la novela está mal compuesta».[58] Although Silva Castro praises the novel, he also feels that «carece de intriga, trama o conflicto propiamente novelesco» (*Panorama*, p. 123), whereas Carlos Hamilton affirms that «la técnica y el estilo de Barrios lo sitúan, con Güiraldes, a la cabeza de los novelistas de América» (p. 289).

[55] Quoted by CARLOS D. HAMILTON, «La novelística de Eduardo Barrios», *Cuadernos Americanos*, LXXXV, No. 1 (1956), 287.
[56] «Eduardo Barrios (1884-1963)», *Revista Iberoamericana*, XXX, No. 58 (1964), 244.
[57] «Eduardo Barrios, en su etapa actual», *Revista Iberoamericana*, XVIII, No. 35 (1952), 20-21.
[58] *Historia de la literatura hispanoamericana*, vol. 2 (México: Fondo de Cultura Económica, 1966), p. 117.

Thus the two most salient features that emerge from the criticism of the novel are its *americanismo* or *criollismo* and the division as to its artistic merits. American it certainly was, and perhaps the most consciously American novel he wrote, and thus related to the regional novels of the 1920s, though superior to them, according to Orlandi and Ramírez.[59] Angel Manuel Vázquez-Bigi goes even further: «Si Barrios hubiera invertido el orden de su creación, si *Gran señor y rajadiablos* hubiera aparecido en 1915, 1917 o 1922, ... tendríamos hoy más estudios sobre Barrios que sobre ningún otro escritor americano» (Thesis, p. 9). Being a rural novel, it is atypical of Barrios, since his other main works might be more easily classified as urban novels. Though his most popular novel (perhaps because of the nostalgic, escapist elements), the general consensus of criticism would certainly not rate it as his best achievement artistically. Where the critics have agreed, however (with the exception of Anderson Imbert),[60] is in their estimation of the finely-drawn character of the protagonist, José Pedro Valverde—«uno de los varones mejor logrados...» (Silva Castro, RI, p. 253), «una figura perdurable» (Jaime Peralta),[61] and certainly the most finely drawn of the many human beings who people the novel (Orlandi and Ramírez, p. 71). Arturo Torres-Ríoseco touches on the real crux of the matter, without developing the point: «Lo que sí logra el novelista es cierto equilibrio en la existencia sentimental del héroe, que mantiene dos actitudes opuestas sin contradecir su autenticidad sicológica.»[62]

Herein lies the key to the novel, and it is mainly through the character of Valverde that I shall try to demonstrate the significance of *Gran señor y rajadiablos*. More than a novel of the American soil, or a stylistic work of art, *Gran señor y rajadiablos* has lasting value as a philosophical document, as a comment on life by Barrios. In this sense, then, *Gran señor y rajadiablos* is more related to the first trilogy than one would imagine at first glance. If these earlier novels are novels of the city, then *Gran señor y rajadiablos* is apparently a novel of the land, in the accepted sense of this overworked term, but with a difference. If *Don Segundo Sombra*, *La vorágine* and *Doña Bárbara* are the three great regionalist novels of the 1920s, then *Gran señor y rajadiablos*, written in 1948, must be an anachronism. Barrios, however, was too much of an artist not to recognise that the novel was written out of its time. I should like to suggest that this key novel was a deliberate attempt by Barrios, using a past genre, to make a comment on life; and

---

[59] *Eduardo Barrios* (Santiago: Pacífico, 1960), p. 68.

[60] «El carácter del protagonista se ve menos que el panorama social e histórico del campo chileno...; como la creación de un personaje va junta con la creación de una trama, los defectos compositivos malogran la personalidad del héroe» (p. 117).

[61] «La novelística de Eduardo Barrios», *Cuadernos Hispanoamericanos*, No. 173 (1964), 366.

[62] *Ensayos sobre literatura latinoamericana*, segunda serie (Berkeley: University of California Press, 1958), p. 192.

that it was to serve as a counterbalance to the mood and tone of the earlier tragic novels and the view of life expressed therein.

On a very superficial level Barrios almost gives the impression in *Gran señor y rajadiablos* of being weary of the tragic fate of his earlier protagonists, and having a great desire to write at least one novel about «normal», well-balanced characters. Having achieved artistic renown with *El hermano asno,* in *Gran señor y rajadiablos* Barrios might even appear to be writing his swan-song, an attempt to terminate his literary career with a popular best-seller. However, something more profound is involved —a shift in sensibility. In his youth Barrios, brought up in the Naturalistic school, expressed only the black, negative side of existence. Perhaps, as in the case of Sábato and Pérez de Ayala, it was this very quality that gave his earlier works their extreme force. However, one can fittingly apply to Barrios Sábato's affirmation about his own *Sobre héroes y tumbas* as compared to the earlier *El túnel:* «Pero me parece que el hombre, al final, se inclina más por la esperanza que por la desesperanza.»[63] Man, as he ages, mellows, and views life differently. Moreover, *Gran señor y rajadiablos* is an attempt by an old man to write a novel whose hero is an incarnation of the author *par compensation* in the Stendhalian tradition. As the great French psychological novelist endowed his heroes, Fabrice, Julien Sorel and Lucien Leuwen, with the energy and other qualities that he obviously lacked, so too does Barrios re-live in Valverde the life that he would like to have led. Timid, sentimental, conservative, even reactionary, Barrios, whose own marriage was a disastrous failure, whose political life was identified with the régime of the dictator Ibáñez whom he served and admired, lived out his *rajadiablos* elements in his literary creation, Valverde. As in all men who have the propensity to good and evil, the barbaric lay just beneath the civilised surface.[64] In a psychologically sound fashion, Barrios was able to channel his suppressed violence into the fictitious figure of Valverde, and thus purge himself of his own latent violent excesses.

Although too much has been said about the autobiographical elements in Barrios' novels, it is obvious that there is much of Barrios' life in all his works: «Mis libros, todos, tienen historia, aun *El hermano asno,* que ha recibido las emociones de mi amor, del definitivo, de este que hoy me da una felicidad que me asusta, que me causa el espanto de la eternidad *El niño que enloqueció de amor* recogió un episodio de mi vida cuando apenas contaba yo nueve años. Y así, *Vivir, Lo que niega la vida* respondió a una siembra que la vida realizó en mí» (*También* I, 27). According to Manuel Vázquez-Bigi, to create a literary character like Luis, one

---

[63] *El escritor y sus fantasmas* (Buenos Aires: Aguilar, 1967), p. 22.
[64] «Poseía el don del superior. ¡Ay! ..., para el bien como para el mal» (GS II, 710). For further discussion see my article «The Theme of *civilización y barbarie* in *Gran señor y rajadiablos*», *Hispanófila*, No. 42 (1971), 57-68.

7

would have to have something in common with him—at least a certain amount of *refracción sicológica* (Thesis, p. 68). Just as the basis of «El niño que enloqueció de amor» was rooted in his own life, and Gastón Labarca in «Tirana ley» represents the sentimental reality of the author, by his own admission and by the biographical data, *Gran señor y rajadiablos* obviously contains much of Barrios' life and his way of thinking. Torres-Ríoseco, paradoxically, having praised the balanced character of Valverde, considers the novel inferior to «El niño que enloqueció de amor» and *Un perdido* for its excessive *costumbrismo* and its distortion of history. More grave, however, is his claim that «el defecto más grave del libro es... la actitud subjetiva de Barrios que le identifica con su héroe...» (p. 194). Torres-Ríoseco would appear to want the best of both worlds, applying the self-confessed sentimentalism of Barrios to his weak characters, but refusing him the right to arrogate to himself (if only by desire) similar, plus complementary, qualities in Valverde. We know that Barrios' experiences as the manager of a *finca* in the central valley of Chile (1937-43) undoubtedly provided him with much material for his rustic novel, which also proves to be a document of historical and social importance. Like his literary predecessors, for example Stendhal in *La Chartreuse de Parme,* he was skilful enough to set the scene in a past era, perhaps to avoid too obvious personal identification and political involvement, and at the same time make his hero more convincing and artistically authentic. Appropriately he chose the nineteenth century, the age of the *caudillos* whose strength was the admirable quality in the Latin American male. If Barrios had written another novel of the city in the vein of *Un perdido,* with a twentieth-century setting, this time portraying the antithesis of the Luis type, i.e. with counter-balancing strength, energy, and the capacity to withstand the rigours of life, the volte-face would have been too pronounced and could have strained the readers' credulity. In fact, one of the criticisms of *Un perdido* was that the Naturalistic elements were exaggerated. *Gran señor y rajadiablos,* therefore, is an attempt to strike the balance, as we see from the first pages of the prologue with its antithetical portrait of Valverde. To choose the nineteenth century, and so make it an anachronism, allows Barrios to paint his characters a little larger than life, and still maintain their credibility. This, after all, was the era of characters like Rosas, Facundo, Urquiza, and even Sarmiento, a self-confessed civilised gaucho himself. This was, in a sense, a heroic past with larger-than-life heroes whose prestige rested on their virility and the *rajadiablos* elements that Barrios portrays in Valverde.[65]

---

[65] One remembers the attitude of the governor who, though admiring the civilising work of Valverde the engineer and *gran señor,* seems much more impressed with his *rajadiablos* qualities: «Pues me parece un rajadiablos estupendo este mocito Valverde... Son éstos los tipos que nos hacen falta, los que nos dejaron felizmente, sembrados por aquí y por allá, los conquistadores, y que luchan a vencer o morir, incansables, a veces crueles, pero crueles consigo mismo también, y van creando,

This is a genuine nostalgia for bygone days and past values, in the same way that *Don Segundo Sombra* (1926), also an anachronism, written long after the gaucho ceased to exist as a force, is an artistic attempt to recreate a heroic past.

Like *Don Segundo Sombra*, *Gran señor y rajadiablos* is not merely an American novel of the land, nor is it just an aesthetic recreation of a heroic past and its admirable values. It is not merely the costumbrist elements of the rodeos, the cock-fights, the country dances and the folklore, nor the poetic prose that makes both novels works of art. Güiraldes also has some observations to make on life, on man's attitude to nature, destiny and death. What Fabio learns as a *gauchito* equips him for the business of living. So too will the tough apprenticeship of young Valverde prepare him for the hard life ahead.

The full philosophical significance of *Gran señor y rajadiablos* becomes apparent only when related to the novels that precede it. Thus it acquires great importance as a last-ditch effort by Barrios to give some order to his view of the universe, and to salvage some meaning from life. In *Gran señor y rajadiablos,* with the experience of age and life, Barrios does not abandon his faith in emotion and the heart, but tries to graft something on to it, to complement the instinct and the tenderness that will enable his characters to respond meaningfully to life. Valverde is still ruled by his heart, but has the disciplinary counterbalance of action, energy and will power that Barrios underlines with the consistency of a '98 Generation writer.[66] Barrios gives to his new well-balanced hero, Valverde, the qualities lacking in *el niño,* Luis and the other timid souls, i.e. the gifts of strength, energy and the capacity to act—all the while counterbalanced by the all-important emotion.

The balance is suggested in the title of the novel, and becomes more explicit in the prologue, where we meet Valverde: «Duro y tierno, serio y tarambana, demócrata y feudal, rajadiablos... pero gran señor» (II, 710). The whole novel is an attempt to produce a well-balanced character, with a propensity for good and evil, with vices and virtues, with strengths and weaknesses: «Sus temeridades aventureras como sus miedos católicos, sus ternuras humildes como sus cóleras lívidas, sus delicadezas paternales como el diabolismo de su vino, su distinción en sociedad como sus desentonos de huaso bizarro, todo lo suyo se acomodaba en conjunto de *valores complementarios*» (II, 710; my italics). If Luis and company end tragically because

de espaldas a la política, entre delirios, barrabasadas y porfías, un futuro fuerte y rico para Chile» (II, 856).

[66] In a seldom-quoted article «La saturación literaria», published in the first number of *Atenea* (1924), of which Barrios was the original editor, he underlines the theme of the early novels and points the way to the corrective of *Gran señor y rajadiablos:* «El corazón sin disciplina nos pierde, se destroza con sus propias fuerzas.»

of their lack of strength, then Morales, the atheist of *Tamarugal,* is deficient too, since strength without the compensatory force of tenderness is useless. Valverde, in spite of his violent outbursts, his barbaric behaviour, and his sexual promiscuity, is repeatedly rescued by the saving grace of emotion.[67]

Barrios draws the parallels between Valverde and the previous heroes right from the earliest years. Products of their different backgrounds, they emerge as different types. Even as a child, Valverde, reared by men and without the comfort of the feminine petting and fondling to which *el niño* and Luis were subjected, grows up hard, courageous and ready to face the world. The traumatic experiences of youth have the opposite effect on the two types. Hardened by the drowning of his little friend and the murder of his father, young Valverde meets violence with violence. Luis, in the face of the death of his parents and grandparents, refuses to face up to life. In Valverde's case, suffering matures, as in *Martín Fierro,* whereas in the case of Luis it precipitates the flight to alcohol, sex, and the illusory world of dreams. In spite of the apparent advantages of a military college education (to instil backbone), Luis emerges as *un tipo sin voluntad,* whilst Valverde, paradoxically, the product of a seminary, emerges strong and fearless, under the home influence of his militant priest-uncle. In their attitudes to women the contrasts are further drawn. Luis, product of a feminine ambience, has no success with women. Valverde, deprived of maternal love and subject to male influences, runs roughshod over his women and is a veritable *potrito de campo* (II, 747). José Pedro Valverde is a sexual desperado who uses women merely for his own gratification, whereas Luis, «cuyas necesidades eran más sentimentales que de sexualidad» (I, 388), desperately in need of emotional support,[68] is referred to as Luchita by his prostitute friends. Even Luis' having to resort to prostitutes highlights the contrast between the two types. Luis' sexual adventures are unsatisfactory, paid for, and consummated in the city. Valverde's are free, satisfying and enjoyed in the wholesome air of the country. In this key novel Barrios seems to reiterate the Horatian idea of the advantages of country life over city life developed by Güiraldes, especially in *Raucho.* It is significant that *Gran señor y rajadiablos* is the only rural novel that Barrios wrote—as if to hammer home his comment on life, and to underline

---

[67] There are many examples of this contrasting behaviour in the novel. In one incident, resorting to violence to chastise a servant, Valverde catches sight of his wife, whereupon the violence melts away (II, 960). Also, after the symbolic shattering of the alcohol still, typifying his struggle with the law, the violence again yields to tenderness at the sight of his wife: «Una ternura, en ola de paz que cubre y aquieta las emociones violentas, le invade entonces el pecho, le sube a la garganta y le pone a riesgo de sollozar» (II, 966). See also II, 790-91.

[68] Luis has neither the sexual ardour nor the stamina of Valverde, nor does he seek the same kind of satisfaction in the sex act: «No constituía para él una dicha. Era demasiado fugaz y no persistía mucho su deseo. Más que la sensación misma, él amaba la conciencia durante la sensación» (I, 329).

the contrast between this novel and the previous novels of the city, and also the normality of Valverde as opposed to Luis and his kin.

Having endowed Valverde with the emotional stability and the sexual satisfaction that is denied to his abulics, Barrios emphasises the point and tries to restore the balance by further philosophical comment, and portrayal of Valverde as the full, mature character. Although Jesús Morales is not lacking in strength, energy or will power, he is still not the complete man, since he lacks, conversely, the complementary quality that would have rounded off his character—emotion, tenderness. Being an atheist («carezco de sentimiento religioso») (II, 683), Morales does not have the vital force of emotion, the basis of all religion, as we have seen. Valverde, whilst recognising the value of the brain, sees the heart as a superior guide. Educated in the seminary, he is always a staunch Christian, in spite of his sexual excesses, his barbarous practices and his cacique mentality. Though apparently anti-catholic, Barrios sees the value of religion, especially Catholicism, as a balancing force in life, as a means of helping character formation.[69] Before Valverde Barrios' heroes show scant regard for religion, being often overtly anti-religious. Barrios' own attitude, especially in *Un perdido*, appears to be at least anti-clerical. The grotesque manner of the death of Luis' grandmother (I, 258) is an ironic comment on the fate of those who devote their lives to religion. Luis' reaction to the pious clichés of the priest after her death (I, 259), his sardonic comments on the decision of Pepe's sister to be a nun (I, 480), all denote his cynical judgment of God's representatives on earth, if not a direct comment on the divine pattern itself.

By 1948, however, Barrios has formulated a philosophy of life that embraces the necessity of religion, rooted in emotion and heart-centred, as before—not the religion of the philosophers, like Fray Lázaro who prayed to be released from the torments of intellectualisation, but a religion that can be felt. José Pedro Valverde symbolises this new type. Although equipped with the essential complementary quality of strength, he is no paragon, however, and does not wear his religion easily, handling his rosary like reins—which Barrios does not find absurd or contradictory. Even the representative of religion in *Gran señor y rajadiablos* is different. José Pedro's priest-uncle, who is atypical, is drawn as a corrective to the whited sepulchres of *Un perdido*. He is the priest of action, like the fighting clerics of the Middle Ages, proud of his conquistador heritage, derived from Pizarro, as opposed to the analytical, anguished Fray Lázaro of *El hermano asno*. Clearly, since Fray Lázaro represents Barrios' point of view at that time, Valverde, the hopeful product of his maturity, reflects the new Barrios as he would like to be—anxious to see things less black and to

---

[69] «Los conflictos psíquicos y religiosos de *El hermano asno*» (II), VÁZQUEZ-BIGI, *Cuadernos Hispanoamericanos*, No. 220 (1968), 131, note 35.

moderate the pessimistic tone of the earlier trilogy. Seeing the difference between right and wrong, the priest Valverde intervenes in the temporal field and survives, while more timid souls like his brother (José Pedro's father) and his symbolically named servant, Pacífico, are destroyed by the assassins who scourge the Chilean countryside. Heart-rooted, instinctive religion, then, added to the newly-won strength and energy, will be the desirable elements in the make-up of the new character. Armed with this combination, the latest Barrios hero will be able better to face the world.

To Valverde Barrios also gives the ability to escape the harsh world of reality by means of poetry, the path of art denied to Luis. Valverde's years in the seminary inculcate in him a love of the classical poetry of Horace, Virgil, and Ovid, whose winged horse, Pegasus, becomes not only a war-cry (¡Caballo pájaro!) but also a symbol of his desire, and capacity, to escape from barbarism into the civilised world of art and poetry (II, 843). Instinctively he follows the *carpe diem* advice of Horace, «que como él es fuerte y optimista», whilst Virgil acts as a mirror and reminds him of his past loves: *Agnosco veteris vestigia flamae...* (II, 843). A quotation from Ovid—*Video meliora proboque, deteriora sequor*—underlines his ambivalence, highlighting his human weaknesses and strengths as portrayed in the prologue.[70]

It is significant, too, that *Gran señor y rajadiablos* is the only one of Barrios' novels that gives a complete birth-to-death life cycle of the protagonist. *El niño* goes mad at the age of ten, Luis becomes a dipsomaniacal pariah at twenty-six, Adolfo gives up his undertaker's job as a mere youth to wander on, Olga becomes neurotic from sexual frustration, and *El hermano asno* is left open-ended with Lázaro changing convents and accepting blame for a sexual crime he did not commit. Valverde is the only character to be presented to us at all stages of his life. He dies at the ripe age of eighty, showing the two complementary essential qualities of emotion and strength, his deathbed prayers interspersed with outbursts of anger («Yo me muero cuando me da la gana») (II, 982)—a complete, rounded figure, as opposed to the aborted, abnormal lost souls of the earlier works.

Barrios' comment seems to be that emotion, not bad in itself, is insufficient to cope with the pressures of life. Given a free rein, it will, as demonstrated in *El niño que enloqueció de amor* and *Un perdido*, be a destructive force, often leading to tragedy. Other complementary qualities

---

[70] Even without the support of his art or the consolation of religion, Valverde's character was so many-sided that he was capable of turning his energies to other fields. A great admirer of Vicuña McKenna (II, 178) and Sarmiento (II, 196), he devotes his engineering ability and agricultural knowledge to the regeneration of Chile. Various fields that might have constituted for others a single valid response to the post-Romantic malaise were all within his ken—politics (as a member of the congress), social action (a one-man police force), etc.

must be used to offset the excessive tenderness—strength, action, energy and will power. Without discipline, emotion leads to failure and often to tragedy, especially if the character has no other valid support in life. Barrios, more hopeful in old age, as if to compensate for a lifetime of literary *perdidos,* endows his hero Valverde with all the desirable and admirable qualities, and yet at the same time keeps him human by displaying his converse weaknesses. To have done so at the end of his literary life in a best-selling, anachronistic, atypical novel, against the unusual (for him) background of the country, denotes a shift in sensibility on Barrios' part. I am suggesting that this is a conscious attempt by the author to check the Naturalism of his previous novels and the consummate weaknesses of his earlier types, and to give us his more balanced view of life. More than for its creole elements or artistic qualities, the novel has lasting value for its metaphysical view of the world.

«Los hombres del hombre»: A Fitting Finale

Two years later appeared *Los hombres del hombre* (1950), which proved to be Barrios' last novel, and, therefore, constitutes his final comment on life. This novel, which seems more in keeping with the analytical Barrios of *El hermano asno,* had a mixed reception. There had been, until recently, no major article, only a couple of reviews published in 1951.[71] Even the two latest articles, excellent as they are, have concentrated only on a certain aspect of the novel, which I shall treat in Chapter 4.[72] Torres-Ríoseco has nothing to say about the novel, and Silva Castro, in at least four major articles on Barrios, barely mentions it. Vázquez-Bigi in his penetrating studies of Barrios gives it scant attention, preoccupied as he is with the early trilogy, whilst Milton Rossel outlines briefly the psychological elements of the novel.[73] Apart from Hancock and Ned Davison, who can always be relied upon for a solid treatment of Barrios' work,[74] those critics who do touch on the novel—Peralta, Hamilton, Fogelquist—do so to the extent of a mere couple of pages, within the framework of a general article on Barrios. Even amongst them there is no consensus as to the value of the novel. For Jaime Peralta, it adds nothing to the bulk of Barrios'

[71] ENRIQUE RUIZ VERNACCI, «Una gran novela americana: *Los hombres del hombre*», *Repertorio Americano* (San Juan de Costa Rica), XLVII, No. 1126 (15 de mayo, 1951), 81-83; GONZALO DRAGO, «*Los hombres del hombre* de Eduardo Barrios», *Atenea,* C, Nos. 307-08 (enero-febrero, 1951), 196-98.
[72] JOEL C. HANCOCK, «The Purification of Eduardo Barrios' Sensorial Prose», *Hispania,* LVI, No. 1 (March, 1973), 51-59 and «El diario como medio de estructura en *Los hombres del hombre*», *Hispanófila,* No. 49 (September, 1973), 1-9. See also his thesis already mentioned.
[73] In his article «El hombre y su psique en las novelas de Eduardo Barrios», *Atenea,* CXXXIX, No. 389 (1960), 182-207, which constitutes more or less his Introduction to the *Obras completas de Eduardo Barrios,* published in 1962.
[74] In his doctoral thesis and his Twayne *Eduardo Barrios,* both already mentioned.

work, being a mere artificial *tour de force* in the use of language and psychology: «Nada agrega esta obra a lo anteriormente hecho por este autor. Podría no haberla escrito, y el valor literario de Barrios no habría sufrido detrimento por esta carencia.»[75] More recently this criticism has been echoed though tempered by Mariano Morínigo who sees the novel as «una recapitulación de diversos elementos ya ensayados y aplicados en sus novelas anteriores, dentro del patrón psicológico. En rigor, no se agrega nada sustancialmente nuevo, pero no por eso el novelista se repite».[76] Carlos Hamilton, on the other hand, considers it the key to Barrios' whole fiction: «*Los hombres del hombre* es la última novela de Barrios. Lo digo sin conocer los planes de trabajo del joven septuagenario activo y contemplativo. Lo digo porque la novela es final. Es la clave de las otras.»[77] Donald Fogelquist, who interviewed Barrios,[78] leads us to believe that, although he spoke less of this novel than others, Barrios gave him the impression that he considered it «su obra más acabada»: «En *Los hombres del hombre* ha llegado Barrios a su apogeo. Es un libro que perdurará y que con el tiempo irá cobrando relieve.»[79] As always, of course, the truth probably lies somewhere between these extremes. There is no doubt that the novel is a recapitulation of Barrios' views on the psychology of man, in his sophisticated treatment of the Unamunesque conception of the various personalities within the individual being. There is little doubt either that from the point of view of structure, style and language it is not only the peak of the second trilogy but also a fitting conclusion to Barrios' fiction, as I shall demonstrate in Chapter 4.

Although Ned Davison labels it «the most philosophical of Barrios' novels» (*Eduardo Barrios,* p. 114), one cannot but agree with Peralta to some extent that it adds little to his previous work in the sense that it contributes little more to the metaphysical conclusions reached in *Gran señor y rajadiablos.* However, where it does have merit is in its capacity for underlining the philosophical points of view drawn in *Gran señor y rajadiablos,* highlighting the gift for psychological analysis demonstrated in previous novels, and synthesising in an artistic manner the themes and ideas of the earlier fiction. It is in this sense that *Los hombres del hombre* is an appropriate final novel, as well as Barrios' last novel.

At first glance, then, *Los hombres del hombre* appears to have little

[75] «La novelística de Eduardo Barrios», *Cuadernos Hispanoamericanos,* LVIII, No. 173 (mayo, 1964), 367.

[76] *Eduardo Barrios, novelista* (Tucumán: Universidad Nacional de Tucumán, 1971), p. 119.

[77] «La novelística de Eduardo Barrios», *Cuadernos Americanos,* LXXXV, No. 1 (enero-febrero, 1956), 289.

[78] «Una visita a Eduardo Barrios», *Cuadernos Americanos,* CXVI, No. 3 (mayo-junio, 1961), 234-39.

[79] «Eduardo Barrios, en su etapa actual», *Revista Iberoamericana,* XVIII, No. 35 (1952), 25.

in common with *Tamarugal* and *Gran señor y rajadiablos,* with which it is closely associated in time, or with the early trilogy. However, on closer examination, salient features emerge which justify Hamilton's claim to see «una unidad sustancial en toda la obra novelística de Eduardo Barrios» (p. 290)—a theory I have tried to demonstrate throughout this study. No one work of Barrios can be totally appreciated out of context, without relation to his complete philosophical point of view. That is not to say that his individual novels are not self-contained artistic entities. Nevertheless, as a single literary unit, *Los hombres del hombre* is a final, integral part of the philosophic whole—even if it is a device, albeit aesthetic, for underscoring Barrios' view of the world.

The novel presents, again through Barrios' preferred diary form, the anguish of the unnamed narrator, *el hombre,* who after eleven years of marriage, begins to doubt the fidelity of his wife Beatriz and the legitimacy of his son Charlie, named after an English friend of the family who leaves the boy an inheritance. The novel is the exposition of the protagonist's fears and suspicions as he observes both his wife and his son, whilst he and the seven different components of his personality, all named after him, debate with each other. As the narrative develops, the rift between *el hombre* and his wife becomes greater, whilst he and his son draw closer to each other—both relationships heightened by the intrusions of the antipathetic Chela Garín. Torn, anguished by the domestic turmoil and the talk of divorce, he finally finds refuge in his paternity and love for the sensitive, intuitive poet Charlie, who gives meaning to his life. The synopsis, of course, does not do justice to Barrios' skilful use of the multiple personality technique, the subtlety of the psychological self-portrayal of the narrator-protagonist, and the characterisation, especially of the boy Charlie. It is in this description of the character of the boy and his father that the novel points the affinities with Barrios' previous work, and underlines, if not continues, the development of both the fiction and the view of life expressed therein.

The boy Charlie, nicknamed by his father «Cabecita Despeinada», is obviously in the same line as *el niño,* Luis, and Adolfo, and as such deserves study. However, one ought first to examine the role of the father who helps to form his character. *El hombre,* the anonymous protagonist, is an interesting variation on the Barrios hero, and more in the tradition than one would at first suspect. Although, through his obsession with the demon of analysis, he appears more spiritually related to Fray Lázaro, there is much of Barrios' earlier heroes in him. In fact, in this, his last novel, Barrios goes full circle, using themes and notions that appeared first in *Del natural.* The theme of jealousy, related to his suspicions about the paternity of his son, is a restatement of the problem of Gastón Labarca in «Tirana ley». By means of his diary he reconstructs in his mind the incidents of the past, his wife's relationship with the English diplomat, Charles Moore, and her pregnancy. This jealousy, provoked by his self-analysis, makes him question his own virility, which therefore casts doubts not only on his wife's faithfulness but on his son's legitimacy. This theme of jealousy, product of excessive analysis, leads to a kind of derangement. When *el hombre* complains «... analizo... estoy enloqueciendo» (II, 1004); «Estoy loco. También los celos bestiali- zan» (II, 1006), he is expressing with the essence of conciseness the anguish not only of Labarca, *el niño* and Luis, but also the root of Fray Lázaro's problem. Being a first novel, «Tirana ley» (along with the other stories of the collection) was a rather facile presentation of the jealousy-suspicion- paternity theme, which was resolved simply in a welter of Romantic love, with the return of Gastón to Luz. Barrios' treatment in *Los hombres del hombre* is more complex, especially because of the enhanced importance of paternity not just as a theme but as a vital value, rather than a shallow consequence of sensuality.[80] Paternity, or the lack of it, has been implicit in Barrios' novels from the early trilogy after «Tirana ley»—closely allied to the resultant state of legitimacy and illegitimacy and its effect on the children. *El niño,* without legal father, appears to be the adulterine child of Carlos Romero, a situation that provokes the enmity of his grandmother and contributes to his sheltered upbringing, sentimental education, and the tragic circumstances that destroy his sanity. Luis too, reared among women and the sentimental papá Juan, suffers as a result of paternal deprivation. Fray Lázaro, a self-confessed Romantic, in the throes of torment in the monastery, escapes in memory to the dreams of his mother and his special relationship with her—without reference to his father. Adolfo, of course, being an orphan, does not have the consolation of a mother to fill the gap of his deceased father. The neurotic Olga spends her life in the charge of her grandmother for want of parental care. In all of these *perdido* types Barrios seems to be saying that, with the support of a good paternal relationship, their lives might have been at least bearable if not completely happy.

In the second trilogy Barrios takes up the theme again. Jenny, the sentimental heroine of *Tamarugal,* is reared by her uncle but soon suc- cumbs to the marriage proposals of the older, sensible administrator, Jesús Morales, in whom she obviously sees a father-figure. The paternity theme is a key aspect of *Gran señor y rajadiablos* in which the young Valverde, without mother, is reared by his father and his uncle, though it is the tough-minded priest-uncle who firmly guides his steps in the world when his father dies. The father-son motif is strengthened in *Gran señor y raja- diablos* by the older Valverde's decision to adopt his own illegitimate son,

---

[80] Cf. this theme of paternity as a vital force in the aforementioned Naturalistic novel of CAMBACERES, *Sin rumbo;* and, perhaps less obviously, in *La vorágine,* in which the paternity theme is an integral part of the protagonist's «search for values».

Antucho, and thus give him the advantage of a properly-balanced education in the beneficial atmosphere of the home where mother and sisters counterbalance the strong male influence. Thus it is obvious that fatherhood is an important theme in Barrios' novels, as well as an intense preoccupation of his own life. When overcome with the boredom and anguish of existence, he confesses, one hope sprang eternal—to have children: «Mi esperanza se había refugiado en un anhelo único: tener un hijo. Y me casé, ciego, contra toda prudencia... Es preciso haber vivido todo lo que yo viví para comprender ese cansancio tras el cual la posibilidad de un hijo renovador avienta toda cautela... Hice un matrimonio absurdo. Pero tuve el hijo, dos hijos tuve: y por ellos y para ellos viví años y años..., aunque yo sólo sé a qué precio» (*También* I, 27-28). There is much meat here for the literary detective, but undoubtedly Barrios' own experiences helped to shape his views on paternity, as it did in other parts of his fiction.[81]

With this illuminating personal exposé by the novelist, the theme of fatherhood, and fatherhood as a positive value which gives direction to life, emerges clearly. Seeking consolation in his debates with one of his other selves, Fernando the sentimental, one clear-cut fact is revealed: «pues en seguridad o en incertidumbre, padre seré, sin remedio ya, de mi Cabecita Despeinada» (II, 1026). The more he reflects the more he becomes aware of the increasing role his son is playing in his life: «Con qué claridad distingo ahora que la vida de mi criatura estuvo reflejándose dentro de mi corazón, aun cuando yo no lo pesara [sic]» (II, 1029). Face to face with his wife, he finds little sympathy, since he approaches her with an insecurity that produces, as it were, «ciertas perspectivas nocturnas», whilst with his son be feels much more «en pleno día». A subtle and successful move that Barrios makes in his discussion of fatherhood as a meaningful concept in life is his linking of the paternity value with writing as a vital force. His love for his son enables him to escape, in circular fashion, from his anguish by giving him the peace and tranquility to revert to his writing—about love, fatherhood and his son. As we have seen with regard to religion, and shall see in Chapter 4 with regard to emotion, Barrios is able to take a force (in this case, writing) and use it as a vehicle: «Reabro, pues, hoy este cuaderno tan abandonado. Anotaré cuanto he visto vivir a mi chicuelo en el último tiempo» (II, 1030). The diary is a good weathervane as to his emotional stability and happiness. As with *el niño*, Adolfo and Fray Lázaro, the diary is more than just a formal device used by Barrios to better acquaint the reader with the personal feelings that are the essence of the psychological novel. Writing has other functions in Barrios, therapeutic,

---

[81] This procreative urge is not confined to Barrios' male characters. Cf. María, in the play *Vivir*, who used Martín mainly as a device for fulfilling her feminine, biological function, though it provokes social condemnation. One remembers too Unamuno's advice, faced with, to use Barrios' Unamunesque expression, «el espanto ante la eternidad» (*También* I, 28): «Haz chicos.»

cathartic and metaphysical, reflecting the agitated state of the protagonist's mind—even in the non-writing: «Desde luego, en las varias semanas transcurridas a continuación de mi fracaso ante Beatriz, no había yo intentado siquiera poner dos líneas en estas páginas...» (II, 1028).

Apart from the jealousy/paternity theme and the role of art as an escape, there is much of the early sensuality of Labarca in *el hombre*. However, the gap between Barrios' first and last novels is evidenced by his sophisticated treatment of the sensuality described. As Barrios' attitude towards sexuality in 1907 had separated him from the Naturalists, so too does one find a refinement in *Los hombres del hombre* which distinguishes it from the frenetic love-making of Luz and Gastón: «Fue aquella una posesión rápida, brusca, y con ímpetus bestiales a causa de la incomodidad del sofá...» (TL I, 100). By means of *el hombre*'s erotic *yo*, Luis, Barrios is able to portray a sensuality which, if not exactly cerebral, is rendered more potent by the Symbolist power of suggestion and nuance: «Mi erótico... había cogido turno e impulsaba mi sangre con violencia de venas a corazón, de arteria a vasos y por la carne toda. Giró Beatriz así, promesa obscura, insistente, dulce y terrible; mi dolor, mis celos y mi deseo, confundidos en torbellino, alcanzaron intensidad...» (II, 1001). Even when he is explicit in his description, it is done tastefully with a rein on the excesses which produces the end effect of sensuality without naked lust: «Las ropas le ocultaban el rostro, los brazos y las piernas; pero como por intervención de la fatalidad, tenía desnudos el vientre, medio pecho y uno de sus costados pulidos. Esa carne de caliente blancura me hizo temblar» (II, 1001). Thus Barrios, who had learnt much from the Modernists, manages to convey a sensuality that pervades the whole ambience without resorting to pornography, overt sexuality, or over-concentration on the purely physical: «Cosas, colores y atmósfera, todo languidecía enfermizamente voluptuoso allí...; algunos azules de humo; cierta rosa de aurora velada de niebla, y flotando, mezcla de ausencia y presencia, ella con su palidez» (II, 1001). In this bedroom scene the sensual atmosphere has been rarefied without loss of the sense of sexual urgency or the magnetic power of Beatriz's «vórtice carnal, ese algo que gira y envuelve, que no se ve y sin embargo es lo único presente, que los ojos rechazan y los poros reciben con ansia» (II, 1001). With this diaphanous, hazy treatment, none the less powerful, of the sexual urge, Barrios has come a long way from the youthful excesses of «Tirana ley». Creating the nuptial atmosphere of Silva's «Nocturno» in the depiction of «el clima de la intimidad peligrosa» (II, 1001), Barrios shares the Rubenian delight in the senses: «Mis sentidos codiciaban hallazgos en los furtivos contactos. Todo era verla, oírla, palparla con las antenas de la sensibilidad afinada» (II, 1001-02). Though linked to the early novels by the common theme of sensuality, *Los hombres del hombre* transcends them in Barrios' refined handling of what he considers an important factor in life—human sexuality and its fulfilment: «¿Habrá hombre que no haya sufrido ese azote de la sensualidad que sobresalta la carne, da vahido en la cabeza y angustia las vísceras en el silencio de un dormitorio femenino del que la dueña está ausente?» (II, 1002). It is this ability of the older Barrios to rationalise his feelings that produces philosophical discussion on the various kinds of love, culminating in the female response: «"Tuya soy, amor mío, total y para siempre." He ahí entonces la seña del perfecto amor» (II, 1003). Unfortunately for *el hombre,* analysis does not lead to consummation. The interior monologue ends with the anti-climactic, but not surprising, statement, given Barrios' view of life: «Pero anoche nada hubo de tal» (II, 1003).

In the tradition of Barrios' heroes, *el hombre* achieves little success in the field of life, as of sex, because basically, like Luis and company, he is in the *perdido* mould, timid and lacking in decision. This characteristic is underlined by Barrios' technique of contrasting his weak heroes with strong female characters. Although Luz (in «Tirana ley») is described as angelic, she is sexually aggressive and soon adopts a maternal attitude in her relations with Gastón. Luis, of course, in *Un perdido,* is the supreme example of the weak type, cheated and exploited by his female counterparts, whether it be the ideal Blanca or the uncouth Teresa. *El hombre* has no illusions about his strength of character. When his wife commands, he obeys: «Es tan dinámica, y yo estoy tan lacio de voluntad...» (II, 995). Even in the intimacy of the bedroom, with a propitious atmosphere, he fails: «Me invadió la timidez. Esquivé roces y miradas, vacié de significado mis palabras, temblé tanto del hacer como del no hacer» (II, 1002). Also in matters relating to his beloved son's welfare, like his education in the British school, which his wife proposes, he bows to her dominating personality: «No cedí por cierto a causa de argumentos que me convencie-ran... Acepté por..., ya lo dije, por voluntad dulcemente diluida» (II, 1007). Thus, in his sensuality, timidity and abulia there is much of the earlier protagonists in the character of *el hombre:* «Eres un pobre diablo, al fin y al cabo. Miserable y asqueroso, con tu sensual cochino y tu cínico nego-ciante y tus otros granujas emboscados, como tú mismo lo dices» (II, 1080).

As Luis had inherited much of his father's weakness, and Antucho much of Valverde's strength, it is not surprising that Charlie, *el hombre*'s son, reflects the spirit of his father: «Mío, sí, mío, reconozco a este niño. Su delicadeza es mi delicadeza crecida, hecha vena de arte por avance de la generación» (II, 1008). The whole novel is the father's attempt to find a common bond, to seek his identity in his son. Having established a feeling of paternity (legitimate or not), *el hombre* strives to nurture in the child the good qualities that will distinguish him from the herd and help him find fulfilment in life—through the gift of poetry, the ability to look beyond the mundane, and through his perceptiveness in seeing the soul of things.

Recognising his own defects, and their causes, he does not want his son to suffer like him. Although he is opposed to sending his son to the British school, for reasons of jealousy, he sees the value—as well as the faults—of this kind of education as a means of character building and mental formation: «Le convendrá en [sic] cambio para cotejarse. Porque se va formando en soledad y eso no está bien. Sus juegos todos son de infante solitario. Sucede toda su vida en la imaginación. Y si cualquier estímulo de fuera viene a excitarlo, su mente linda con el delirio y hasta con la enfermedad» (II, 1007). Barrios in his final comment seems to be trying to prevent the kind of tragedy that befell el niño and Luis who, as a result of their sheltered upbringing coupled with their extreme sensitivity, found themselves totally incapable of confronting the world, and thus retreated to the false world of dreams and illusions. As in *Gran señor y rajadiablos,* Barrios tries to redress the balance by not having Charlie make the mistakes of his literary predecessors. Young Valverde is the link between el niño/Luis and Charlie, since he represents aggressive strength. Charlie is meant to be a synthesis of the previous heroes. Whilst el niño went mad at an early age, Luis, though he ended a moral and physical wreck, progressed at least into adulthood before succumbing. Adolfo, at the end of «Páginas de un pobre diablo», manages to overcome his timidity and goes off into the world with the hope of achieving independence and a meaningful existence. Young Valverde is Barrios' representation of the strong personality which he accentuated, even exaggerated, to make the contrast with the *perdidos.* Charlie represents a softening of this aggressiveness, an intermediate point between the extreme weakness of el niño and the extreme strength of Valverde. In an altercation with a servant his father sees him thus: «Cabecita la mira, digno y en silencio. No se altera; piensa, nada más. Y tal es su aire, sus ojos establecen tan bien la jerarquía y tan denso trasciende sus pensamientos, que la mujer cierra la boca, se reduce a su plano. El caballerito no ha sido violento, ni áspero siquiera; sólo ha sido superior. Me sorprende su prudente señorío y lo admiro» (II, 1054).[82] Though sensitive and imaginative, he is psychologically stable in the face of life's hardships. However, he can only be so with the help of his father who sees much of himself in his son. *El hombre*'s aim is to prevent his son's sensitivity and imagination from becoming weapons that can harm him, and to channel his gifts towards a happiness and an emotional balance that Luis and el niño never experienced: «Yo también fui chico solitario durante largo período. Me transmutaba en seres de mi fantasía y, ¡oh complicación!, nacieron demasiados yoes en mí. Perturban y desvían desde la infancia estos fantasmas que se nos incorporan» (II, 1007).

---

[82] Cf. a similar situation in *Gran señor y rajadiablos,* and the young Valverde's response to *his* servant: «Tú que abres el hocico y yo que te lo parto a pencazos» (II, 743).

Under the careful observation of his father, and through the medium of the detailed writing of the diary, Charlie emerges as a normal boy with a special gift for appreciating the natural things around him. He differs little from the other Barrios children, and all children, in his preference for illusion, for creations of his own imagination, for fantasy and dream worlds. However, as Ned Davison has rightly pointed out, «tiene... una facultad de autoevaluación que sobrepasa en mucho a las caracterizaciones anteriores» (*Sobre Eduardo Barrios*, p. 70). This faculty of self-evaluation stems from the understanding and the sympathy of his father who, sharing his sensitivity which is at the root of his sensibility, sees much of himself in his son. Whilst the mother recognises only his poetic gifts,[83] *el hombre* recognises both underlying conditions: *fantasía* and *hiperestesia*.[84] Luis failed because, having no artistic temperament, he was unable to follow the path of art which might have provided an escape from his emotional problems. There was hope for Adolfo who not only took decisive action but did so in the direction of a literary career. Although Valverde was strong and experienced some alleviation from the prevailing barbarism through the cultural outlet of his Latin poets, Charlie is undoubtedly the last link in the chain of figures, the poetic peak. Having been endowed with a sensitive, perceptive father that the others lacked, he is permitted to go to the English school which will provide him with the missing qualities needed to equip him for a life that will certainly be harsh and hostile: «Lo forjarán algo más dinámico, enérgico, varoncito de acción. Lo necesita» (II, 1008). With the '98 Generation qualities of energy, action and will power to offset his sensitivity, Charlie has an added quality denied to the rest of ordinary mortals—the gift of poetry which will not only raise him above the herd but will also provide him with an escape tunnel from a cruel world and a hostile environment: «En fin, digamos que ha de subir a la fantasía. La fantasía, Cabecita Despeinada, te abrirá pronto su placer. ¿No te lo abrió ya? Es la puerta para evadirse de la vida. Tú, aunque lo niegues, eres poeta» (II, 1059).

Father and son, then, are kindred spirits. Despite *el hombre*'s tendency to analyse and intellectualise which recalls Fray Lázaro,[85] the lasting message of the novel, as of all Barrios' fiction from «Tirana ley» onwards, is

---

[83] «Es soñador. Beatriz dice que poeta» (II, 999).

[84] This is manifested in his anxiety provoked by his father's suggestion that he speak to his mother about the troublesome Chela: «El miedo a consecuencias con su madre lo enferma. No teme a irritaciones o cargos de Beatriz; le asustan la pena que le ocasionaría y lo difícil que le sería sincerarse. Anda, pues, retorcido entre sus nervios» (II, 1058).

[85] Morínigo subtitles the chapter on *Los hombres del hombre* «más intelectualismo que psicología», seeing *el hombre*'s writing more as an intellectual need: «el escribir no es en el hombre evasión plácida, más o menos reconfortante, sino necesidad intelectiva... No escribir por escribir, por placer... sino por necesidad de minucioso análisis de sus tribulaciones» (p. 124).

the importance of following one's instincts, of listening to one's heart
—despite the tragedies of *el niño*, Luis, Olga, and the like. The point is,
as I have tried to demonstrate throughout, that emotion by itself is not bad.
Without the discipline of other balancing forces, however, it can lead to
tragedy. Barrios' novels are geared to showing the gradual evolution in his
philosophy and his attempt to establish a way of survival without abandoning the virtue of sentiment as a guiding force in life. In other novels emotion
has been shown to be the basis of religion, which provides a positive
element in the formation of character. In *Los hombres del hombre* this
sensitivity and intuitive feeling for beauty, combined with his feeling for
illusion and controlled fantasy, is the basis of Charlie's poetic sensibility.
It is significant that even in his last novel which is, if not the height, at
least the synthesis of his previous novels, Barrios should adhere to the
important role played by emotion, tenderness and instinct.

In his discussion with Mauricio, the mercenary *yo, el hombre*/Barrios
is still preaching the message of papá Juan to Luis: «Sigue al instinto...
No hagas gestos de superioridad. Vale más que nada el instinto. Te parece
rudimentario y obscuro. Pues no; es un vidente, que se nos esconde para
guiar mejor» (II, 992). In a conversation with another side of his *yo*, the
sentimental Fernando, with whom he identifies more than with the practical
Mauricio, he confesses the growing emotion he feels for his son: «También
convengo en tu norma: guiados por la ternura, conducimos a los nuestros
hacia nuestro corazón» (II, 1055). However, given the maturity of Barrios'
later protagonists and the fact that this is the final novel, *el hombre*/Barrios
is quick to add: «Seguiré contigo, pues, previo acuerdo de no incurrir en
el exceso sentimental que obscurece» (II, 1055). In other words, one must
avoid the errors of *el niño* and Luis for whom excessive sentimentality,
without the corresponding discipline, leads to tragedy.[86] This is not to say
that displays of tenderness are forbidden to the later Barrios heroes. Just
as Valverde, the epitome of strength, yields to tenderness at the sight of his
wife, after a particularly grave outburst of violence (II, 966), so too does
el hombre succumb to his emotions at the sight of his son at play, «vibrando

---

[86] Although a self-confessed sentimentalist, as early as 1920 Barrios was attribut-
ing to himself this self-discipline, this will power so necessary to maintain a balance
in the face of life's dangers. This, however, could be more wishful thinking than
reality, in the same way that Valverde of *Gran señor y rajadiablos* represents his
wishes rather than reflects his character: «Siempre hubo en mí una voluntad firme
que me daba combatividad ante los peligros; era una fuerza ciega que me envolvía,
me arrojaba duro de coraje en la brega y me inflamaba súbitamente en medio de
cualquier desaliento. He tenido durante la lucha una extraña y casi inconsciente
tenacidad, acaso la testarudez del bruto, acaso la obsesión irrazonada del iluminado;
en los momentos más difíciles he procedido por raras intuiciones, y a veces como
conducido por alguien que invisible me guiase» (quoted by JULIO CEJADOR Y FRAUCA,
Historia de la lengua y literatura [Madrid: Revista de Archivos, Bibliotecas y Museos,
1920], p. 221).

en igual ternura» (II, 996). The child too, his father's son, faced with the problem of suffering and death (in this case, of animals), responds with a display of emotion which in Barrios is manifested physically: «de todo su cuerpecito la emoción sale, como el vaho de un cofre que arde cerrado» (II, 998). This incident, which reveals his feeling for the suffering of the cow whose calf dies, is a good example of his special awareness of the world around him (II, 998). This rare feeling for life and its mysteries, which the boy enjoys, not only provokes the emotional response of the equally sentimental father but also constitutes the essence of his poetic sensibility. Barrios implies a relationship not only between innocence and poetic intuition, which is the natural gift of the child, but also between sensitivity/sentimentality and the artist, as exemplified in Labarca's case in «Tirana ley». It is not merely Charlie's youth that brings out *el hombre*'s tenderness but his special gifts of metaphor, his dreams, and his obvious awareness of the artistic and emotional identification between father and son: «La emoción me había ensordecido. Mucho lo cogí en brazos. Y sólo sé que ahora, como entonces, mi júbilo, mi ternura, mis lágrimas lo besan» (II, 1039).

Following one's instincts, then, guided by sentiment, one can gain salvation from the potential tragedies of this world. Only through the heart does one gain the saving grace: «Yo me guío por mi ternura... Así guiados, al menos conducimos a los nuestros hacia nuestro corazón» (II, 1047). This role of the heart, as opposed to the brain, is treated finally in *Los hombres del hombre*, with no distinction from its customary role in Barrios' thinking: «Como también que en estos lapsos de tiniebla [el almita] se camina a tientas, la razón ciega y el corazón más despierto que nunca para sentir más. Sabe aun que entonces el corazón se agranda, que llega uno a ser sólo corazón» (II, 1062). By means of the philosophical dialogue technique used in *Un perdido*, *El hermano asno*, *Tamarugal* and *Gran señor y rajadiablos*, Barrios reiterates through Jorge, the humble *yo* (cf. Rufino, Javier) and Mauricio, the analytical *yo* (cf. Lázaro, Morales), the oft-quoted Pascalian proofs for the superiority of the heart over the brain:

> Te falta eso, ver venir las cosas, presintiéndolas en sus horizontes, desde la verdad de su origen, descubriéndoles el paso silencioso en el camino que las aproxima. Puestas bajo la lente, objetivadas, tú las analizas, las describes y crees que las sabes. Mentira, hermano. La verdad de las cosas, en particular cuando pertenecen a la vida sentimental, se manifiesta como en una anunciación, fluye desde cuando ellas nacen y las acompaña iluminándolas no sé qué lirismo en su trayectoria. La sensibilidad capta la onda; la razón, *a posteriori*, a lo sumo comprueba. (II, 1017)

Emotion, therefore, as always, is the keynote. His marriage a mockery, his life a wreck, *el hombre* sees no future with his wife. Deciding to leave, he wonders what he will do with the rest of his life and how he will cope with it: «Vivimos de nuestras emociones: viviré yo de las mejores mías. Y él me las ofrecerá siempre» (II, 1086). The child is the ultimate value, the only source of comfort, the only thing in life that gives meaning to existence. Paternity, though it has never been proved that he is the real father, emerges as a valuable force, confirming the words of one of his *yos:* «No reside la paternidad ni en la criatura ni en su progenitor, sino en el amor que nace, crece y los une» (II, 996). Because of the spiritual affinity and close identification of father and son, life now has a meaning —for both. As the last image of the novel suggests—a neighbouring father and son, both driving their carts (the toy one on the back of the real one) with confidence, independence and dignity—parenthood has a double function. The guiding force of the father on the son is complemented by the existential contribution of the child to the father: «Así vivimos todos. Porque al cabo, las ilusiones de los hombres ¿diferirán para la mirada de los cielos? ... Sí, a mí una sola ilusión puede sostenerme ya: mi Cabecita Despeinada, suave y tibio refugio de mi ternura»[87] (II, 1086). Child, emotion and poetry. The last page of the novel summarises rather well the main concerns of Eduardo Barrios, and points to the main literary and psychological themes of his works, underlining the role they play in his metaphysical evolution.

Los hombres del hombre is the peak of the later trilogy and the last work that Barrios produced. As such it deserves our attention as his final comment on life.[88] Psychologically, it is the most advanced of Barrios' work—through his technique of multiple personality and *yoísmo*. The characters of Charlie and his father, *el hombre,* are amongst his most finely drawn. Aesthetically, as we shall see in Chapter 4, it stands in relation to *Tamarugal* and *Gran señor y rajadiablos* as *El hermano asno* does to *El niño que enloqueció de amor* and *Un perdido*. Since it is a final work it is not surprising that labels like compendium, recapitulation and synthesis suggest themselves as descriptions worthy of *Los hombres del hombre*. Barrios himself commented that he wrote the work with the express intention of capturing «la esencia de toda psicología humana» (Fogelquist, *Visita,* p. 238). Ned Davison praises it for «the brilliance of style and the highly perceptive presentation of human emotion» (*Eduardo Barrios,* p. 122). Although, psychologically and artistically, the novel contains some of Barrios' best writing, the question has to be posed as to what it adds to Barrios' view of the world.

The division amongst the critics has already been noted, but one can add some clarifying remarks as to the role of the novel in Barrios' meta-

---

[87] This mutual influence is suggested in the dedication of the novel where Barrios stresses the *sabiduría/inocencia, sabio/niño* analogy (II, 983).

[88] It is also the peak of a many-sided pyramid: «Artes, ciencias, religiones y filosofías forman una pirámide poliedra» (*También* I, 31).

physical evolution. Although the themes of jealousy, suspicion, paternity and childhood date back to «Tirana ley», Barrios' skilful characterisation in the portrayal of Charlie, in contrast to el niño/Luis, indicates a growth that is manifest in the progressive treatment of el niño, Luis, Olga, Adolfo, and young Valverde. Charlie represents the peak of Barrios' child psychology development in that, although of the same sensitive breed, he is more stable than the early perdidos, and even possesses the poetical intuition lacking in the balanced Valverde. In other words, added to his essential emotion, corrected by the English school-inspired qualities of energy and will power, he is firmly on the path of art denied to Luis, which Barrios offers as an escape from the anguish of life.

One should add, however, that Los hombres del hombre in no way departs from the essentially tragic picture of life that is characteristic of Barrios' other novels. As in Tamarugal and Gran señor y rajadiablos, Barrios is simply pointing out more positive ways of combatting the hostility of the world. The point of the novel is that el hombre, without the support of his love for and of his son, could very well suffer the same fate as the other perdidos. Donald Fogelquist calls him «un hombre decepcionado pero no desesperado» (Visita, p. 238). Charlie, without the qualities of self-evaluation and controlled fantasy, could become another el niño, whom he resembles in sensitivity and fondness for illusion. In Charlie's case, his control over his illusions, nurtured by an equally sensitive father who derives his values from the paternal role and the pure, unselfish love he feels for his son, prevents such a tragedy. Undoubtedly both father and son have the potentiality for tragedy: Fogelquist describes el hombre as «ese padre y marido atormentado, a quien le remuerde una duda, mal fundada e insignificante tal vez, pero capaz, en una persona de su sensibilidad, de cobrar dimensiones de tragedia» (Visita, p. 238). The older Barrios, taking full advantage of his maturity, his knowledge and experience, pours it all into his final literary creation which becomes his final heartfelt plea: «la sabiduría del corazón me guíe y la bondad me vigile» (II, 1059). An unhappy marriage and sexual relationship, combined with a disturbed childhood, which thirty years before would have spawned a Luis, in this last novel is rescued from its tragic conclusion by abiding, mutual, unselfish love.

Los hombres del hombre, therefore, denotes a shift in sensibility that is evident but awkwardly drawn in Tamarugal and later developed in Gran señor y rajadiablos. Los hombres del hombre is an attempt to refine in more typical Barrios fashion, through the psychological novel, an attitude to life that was perhaps hammered out in Gran señor y rajadiablos. Los hombres del hombre is a more finely chiselled, a more exquisite, a more aesthetic comment on life, but none the less authentic despite its diaphanous qualities. Barrios' novels are about life, its hardships, its illusions, its deceptions, its intrinsically tragic qualities, which he recapitulates in summary fashion in *Los hombres del hombre*. They are also his attempts to come to grips with these problems that face man in the world. It is in this sense that aesthetics and metaphysics are inextricably bound up in Eduardo Barrios.[89]

---

[89] Before going on to Barrios' aesthetics, this might be an appropriate moment to recall Jean-Paul Sartre's quotation, justification enough for the order of this study, which stresses the importance of the novelist's metaphysics in relation to his art: «Une technique romanesque renvoie toujours à la métaphysique du romancier. La tâche du critique est de dégager celle-ci avant d'apprécier celle-là» («A propos de *Le Bruit et la fureur:* la temporalité chez Faulkner», *Situations* I, 1947, p. 71, originally written in 1939).

CHAPTER 4

THE AESTHETIC MANIFESTATION

ART AND ARTISTS IN BARRIOS' FICTION

Although *Del natural,* Barrios' first published work, is of inferior quality, it is important, as we have seen, because it contains in embryonic form all the themes and ideas to be developed in the more mature first and second trilogies. Of all the pieces in the first collection the short novel «Tirana ley» is undoubhtedly the most valuable, not just because it is superior to the gothic-type short stories with their *fin de siècle* characters. «Tirana ley» has merit in itself being a precursor of the main novels and an example of Barrios' concern for art and his preoccupation with artists like Gastón Labarca.

In this first collection, whose strident prologue calls attention more to social and ethical abuses, e.g. the position of women in society, attitudes of conventional morality, freedom from censorship, it is significant that Barrios should have chosen as his hero a young artist, Gastón Labarca. The tempestuous, youthful Barrios devotes part of his prologue to an attack on those who would hamper the writer, by means of censorship, in his pursuit of true art, and in his attempts to depict honestly the theme of love, i.e. sexual love, which was of great interest to Barrios at this time. In the novel itself the artist-hero is a painter, which does not surprise us since we know that at one period in his life Barrios wanted to be a painter: «Vagué por el mundo, viajé en pos de mi vocación, buscando los pretextos y los incentivos. Quería pintar, creía que ése era mi destino; y si no llegué a realizarlo fue que nunca hubo la dirección de un maestro ni la cercanía de una escuela de Bellas Artes.»[1] As in the case of the philosophical influences in his life, Barrios absorbed his artistic masters whose traits he synthesised and demonstrated in modest fashion without parading ostentatiously his knowledge: «Hablaban de claroscuros de Rembrandt, de coloridos de Rubens, de elegancias de líneas de Da Vinci, de energía rafaelesca»

---

[1] JORGE ONFRAY BARROS, «Perfil de Eduardo Barrios», *Revista Zig-Zag,* XLII, No. 2149 (30 de mayo, 1946), 25-26.

(TL I, 111).[2] The whole novel is an outline of the struggles of a young painter whose daily effort to make ends meet and win artistic renown as a painter is further complicated by his love affair with the beautiful young widow Luz. In his description of the daily life of the painter Barrios reveals an affinity with, and a sympathy for, the struggling young artists whose routine, poverty, aspirations, failures, successes and discussions he depicts authentically. Amidst the attacks on conventional morality, organised religion, censorship, etc., one finds the Modernist theme of the misunderstood artist, unappreciated by a philistine society. Even Luz, Gastón's muse and model, the source of his inspiration, who had once confessed that Labarca was the synthesis of her ideal («el artista unido al hombre fuerte» I, 89), when she discovers that she is pregnant and apparently abandoned by her lover, reiterates the usual attack on selfish artists: «Los artistas no aman más que a su arte. A él todo lo sacrifican. Si gozan con nosotras es por los ideales que en su imaginación engendra nuestra belleza. Gastón ha concebido conmigo sublimidades de estética que, en su delirio artístico, en sus alucinaciones, me describía entusiasmado... Son éstos, los artistas, los que ensalzan la generosidad de alma. Ellos que son todo egoísmo, que nos engañan y se engañan a sí mismos para acumular observaciones» (I, 122-23). It is not without significance that Barrios, although preoccupied with love and sex in his first novel, should have his hero Gastón, in his struggle between love (for Luz) and art, opt for art and go off to Paris to study—despite his feelings for Luz—but not without agonising and philosophising about his position and his duty as an artist.[3] The youthful Barrios, however, by the fictional machinery of a pregnancy and an inheritance, contrives to bring the two lovers together again. By means of the inheritance, Luz and her baby are able to join Gastón in Paris, thus enabling Barrios to reconcile neatly love and art. The novel closes thus:

[2] Besides detailing Barrios' knowledge of artistic techniques, the following passage is a good example of a favourite Modernist technique, greatly used by Barrios, the *transposition d'art*. In this case he renders in literary form the effect of a painting: «En cuanto al vigor y pureza de las líneas, se mostraba el autor de portentosas facultades. Hábil y originalísimo, rompía las escrupulosas vallas académicas para mantènerse exacto, natural y espontáneo. La corrección y naturalidad del cuerpo de la madre eran verdaderamente mágicas, asombrosas: los pechos, hinchados por el líquido de la vida, aparecían suspendidos por la posición de los brazos, bajo de ellos partía la curva armoniosa y soberbia de su vientre ubérrimo, y seguía, suave, hasta perderse en el agua; en la axila visible en el lienzo, un manchón sepia de vello mojado era una de las filigranas de la obra; y, sobre todo, como última y refinada manifestación del genio del artista, la piel humana, húmeda y engranujada por el frío, estaba tan justamente reproducida, que quien la miraba creía verla despedir un tibio vapor de agua» (I, 91-92).

[3] Barrios, by means of long discussions between Gastón y his friend Jorge, the voice of reason, outlines the problems of the young artist and the importance of money required to achieve one's aims, glory, honour and success (I, 109-13).

La noche había extendido sus alas de misterio sobre los últimos matices del horizonte; entre las plantas, los grillos multiplicaban sus trinos como centenares de cascabeles de plata; y mientras de todas partes parecía salir una bendición para aquellas criaturas obedientes a la ley fundamental de la vida, ellas subían las gradas de la casa, muy juntas, bajo la luna que las adornaba con sus besos blancos. (I, 142-43)

Despite the conventionally romantic ending and the obvious structural and stylistic defects of the novel, «Tirana ley» is important not just because of the basic themes that are to appear developed in later novels. That he should have chosen to devote his first novel to a treatment of the role of the artist in society is an indication of Barrios' concern not only with the day-to-day, material problems of the aspiring painter, but the spiritual problems that face every artist who has to consider where his duty lies, what his priorities and his choices are—in Gastón's case between love and his vocation. Barrios, obviously under the Modernist influence at this period (via the Symbolists and the Parnassians), takes up the theme of art for art's sake in its material and spiritual manifestation. Thus the first steps on the path of art, which is to become a vital theme in Barrios' view of life, are already laid in the first, inferior novel.

Barrios treats again the artistic life in *Un perdido* whose hero Luis Bernales, after a life of emotional disasters, abortive love affairs, and military failure, meets up in the second half of the novel with a group of young artists in the bohemian sector of the city. In this important novel Barrios extends his sway to embrace not only painters like López but also sculptors like Téllez, poets like Braulio, and pseudo-musicians like Don Manuel. The importance of art as a vital force in life, which was implicit in «Tirana ley», becomes explicit in *Un perdido*. Barrios, in his depiction of the final stages of Luis' degradation, places him in the company of artists as if to affirm that if he cannot find salvation in their company then there is no solution to his problems. To this end Barrios describes the hard struggle of the poor painter López who, in spite of his indigent condition, still finds time and means to help the downtrodden Luis. He also, of course, serves as a foil to the abulia of Luis: «López, aquel francote tan rudo y tan generoso, no hablaba sino detonando. Era su modo: violento y preciso, como su carácter. Parecía poner acción, acción rápida, vigorosa y certera, hasta en el lenguaje. Lucho había llegado a quererle; más, a necesitarle» (I, 410). Barrios seems to imply again that the artistic vocation serves to strengthen the character and prepare a man for life. This was also the message of «Tirana ley» where Gastón considers himself superior because of his naturalness, his frankness and his humanity, even if he is a little weak (I, 139). In fact, these very weaknesses are at the root of his artistic temperament. López, however, is not susceptible to these weaknesses, his '98 Generation qualities being exaggerated by Barrios to underline his contrast with Luis.

The real artist has to dedicate himself to art, as Jorge tried to convince Gastón in «Tirana ley» (I, 110), like López whom Lucho cannot understand. When Luis suggests that he take a job rather than starve, López pleads lack of time, being too busy «en asistir a clases, largar[se] al campo a estudiar la luz, hacer [sus] ensayos y embadurnar esas telitas vulgares que todo el mundo hace "para el consumidor"; la vida corre» (I, 413). When Luis questions him as to how he spends his nights, López describes with enthusiasm and sincerity the artist's life, ambitions, dreams and skills:

> Pienso, leo, discuto sobre arte con algún compañero... ¡Ah, las discusiones sirven mucho! Ayudan a esclarecer lo que uno quiere conseguir pintando, que no siempre se sabe bien. Porque pintar como todos..., ¡buena imbecilidad! No. Yo tengo talento. Veo muy bien el paisaje. Voy a ser un original, acuérdate. Por ejemplo, en las tardes, en esos crepúsculos que todo pintamonos ve iguales, yo distingo que hay momentos verdes como vistos a través de una esmeralda muy diáfana, otros como vistos a través de un topacio... En fin, las armonías varían infinitamente. No hay dos minutos idénticos en un atardecer. Estos mil instantes los cogeré yo. Sólo que todavía no puedo. Me falta mucha técnica. Pero nada más que eso. (I, 413)

With more than a superficial knowledge of the artist's vocation, Barrios describes with rare feeling not only the mundane matters of classroom technique and academic learning but also the dreams and desires of the committed artist.

Through his acquaintance with the painter López, Luis moves in a bohemian world, reminiscent of Gálvez's *El mal metafísico*. As Luis' soul-brother Carlos Riga had frequented the literarty coteries of Modernism, so too does Luis come into contact with poets like Braulio, whose dashing military appearance is enhanced by his ever-present sword, which in this case is as mighty as the pen. Luis marvels at the poetic paraphernalia of Braulio's «pieza estrafalaria encumbrada en el confín de caserón tan pintoresco» (I, 416),[4] the centrepiece of which is a bust of José Asunción Silva, presiding over an illustration of «Nocturno» and two lovers projecting «una sola sombra larga». The extravagant picture of the room and the rare dress of the buffoon-poet are counteracted by the sobering presence of Silva, whose suicide was his answer to the overwhelming *angustia* of life. Before leaving

---

[4] This detailed picture of the poet's room indicates the painter's eye and Barrios' keen powers of observation and description: «Los muros, pobremente encalados, cubríanse de retratos: junto a bellezas aristocráticas de altanero y desdeñoso gesto, provocaban las tiznadas ojeras de conocidas prostitutas o tejíanse las piernas desnudas de obscenas estampas. Láminas macabras había donde se mirase; constituían la nota dominante: parcas en atavío nupcial, o vestidas como reinas, o tocadas como damas galantes cuyos mitones daban paso a falangetas mondas que oprimían sangrientas rosas; parcas rígidas en armaduras medioevales; parcas de chambergo, cabalgando negros corceles y embozadas en capas inmensas de vuelos que obscurecían la tierra; la clásica, en fin, envuelta en su túnica, y al hombro 'la guadaña fiera'; y cual si no bastase, un cráneo encima del velador, a guisa de palmatoria, con la caja de fósforos entre los dientes» (I, 416).

the poetic world of Braulio and company, Barrios takes one final opportunity to attack the false world of poetry, especially as it manifests itself in the critics for whom Barrios had no great love: «La crítica, la opinión ajena, me interesa, pero no influye en mi labor sino en la medida mínima en que la visión de un inteligente contribuye a nuestra claridad interna» (*También*, I, 29). This particular critic's contribution to the world of literature is the invention of a new movement called *tropicalismo*: «Todo lo malo, toda literatura que peque por superabundancia de imágenes y adjetivos, la llama "tropical"» (I, 416).

This description of the critic as «un ser árido, un salvaje», as a failed writer, is further impressed upon Luis when he gains employment in the Biblioteca Nacional.[5] Although Eduardo Barrios uses various manifestations of the plastic arts in the early novels as representative of art in general, after the first trilogy he tends to concentrate on literature, and in particular, poetry, as the means of identifying art *(Páginas de un pobre diablo, Gran señor y rajadiablos, Los hombres del hombre)*.[6] At the library, in a suitable ambience, surrounded by poets who have achieved the distinction of publishing a volume of verse, he recalls the advice of papá Juan on art as a prop in life. With great effort he laboriously composes a short story which he finds mediocre. Whilst working on a second one, he listens to the anecdote of another aspiring writer who did all the right things to achieve his goal —he read, studied, analysed as a preparation for writing several short stories, a short novel and a play before coming to the conclusion that he would never become a writer. His work had all the ingredients, but it failed because «no había emoción ni personalidad» (I, 452). The only avenue left to him was to become a good critic: «Pero algo me gritó desde la conciencia que no por esto dejaría de ser un fracasado, que muy fácil resulta criticar cuando se aprende, aunque no se haya podido vencer, y hallé indigno el papel» (I, 452). Impressed and depressed by this story of literary failure, Luis gives up trying to put into practice the advice of papá Juan. Although Barrios returns to this theme of redemption through writing in a suggestive manner at the end of «Páginas de un pobre diablo», it constitutes in a more positive way the substance of Barrios' last novel, *Los hombres del hombre*.

Although music and musicians as such figure little in Barrios' novels in the way that writers and painters do, music is at the root of his fiction. All his prose works are written with the express aim of creating music through words.[7] The same claim can be made for Barrios with regard to

---

[5] Barrios too was a long-time employee of the Biblioteca Nacional of which he rose to become Director.

[6] It is significant that many of Barrios' protagonists are writers who keep a diary or record—Gastón, *el niño*, Fray Lázaro, Adolfo, *el hombre*.

[7] These ideals of «Música y transparencia» (*También* I, 28) will be treated in detail in later sections of this chapter.

poetry. Although Barrios has published novels, short stories and drama, he has never published any poetry, though novels like «El niño que enloqueció de amor», *El hermano asno* and parts of *Los hombres del hombre,* could better be described as *poemas en prosa,* as Gabriela Mistral and others have noted. The only representative figure of the musical world, apart from the antipathetic caricature Chela Garín of *Los hombres del hombre,* a grotesque dilettante in ballet, music and poetry, is Don Manuel María who feels nothing for, and allegedly does not even like, music, according to the musicians themselves. His contribution to the world of art lies in musical statistics: «Se contentaba con ser el registrador de los acontecimientos musicales de Chile. Porque otra de las manías era la estadística, llevaba una crónica de cuantos conciertos se dieran en el país, coleccionando los programas y los billetes y anotando por el sistema de fichas el número de audiciones que cada pieza llevaba» (I, 456). In the harsh contrast that he draws between the real artists, usually the young and struggling, and the *aficionados,* the older pseudo-intellectuals, Barrios reflects in *Un perdido* a view of human nature that is still basically pessimistic and reveals the Naturalistic traits inherited from the first collection. Only the true artist emerges untouched in a corrupt, evil world. Barrios elevates the artist to a higher level, keeping him above the sordid interests of the masses. Even when they do have to associate with prostitutes and the like, they remain insensitive to the spectacle of coarse, disgusting creatures who, under the influence of alcohol, utter obscenities: «Los bohemios permanecían insensibles al espectáculo; apreciaban aquello como tesoro de tipos y escenas utilizables en el arte, y nada más» (I, 517).[8] This objectivity of the artist, which Barrios had already touched on in «Tirana ley» when Gastón remains impervious to the obvious charms of the French model,[9] is another pointer to Barrios' view of not only the artist's objectivity but even of his superiority, moral and intellectual—an implication already advanced in «Tirana ley» and to be repeated in later novels. Though Valverde is a balanced character *(Gran señor y rajadiablos),* it is Charlie's poetic sensibility (in *Los hombres del hombre*) that raises him one rank above Valverde to the level of the artist—the real artist, and not the shallow dilettante.

A good example of the sympathetic artist is Téllez, the sculptor, who

[8] The following passage can hardly be bettered as an example of Naturalistic description: «Era un antro inmundo y rufianesco. Servían el café, los ponches y los licores mujeres horripilantes, a la vez camareras y prostitutas a quienes la hombrada borracha sentaba sobre los muslos y manoseaba en forma tosca y obscena. La mansedumbre servil de aquellas hembras embrutecidas no encontraba para tales tratos sino carcajadas grotescas, gritos y muecas que exhibían dentaduras podridas, con filos que tajaban los labios siempre inflamados por el alcohol» (I, 516).

[9] «... comprendí que mi deleite no había sido el refinado del macho que saborea con la vista la hembra que se le va a entregar, sino el del artista enamorado de la forma que se detiene en apreciaciones de estética. Descubrí que mi alma impresionable y trabajadora había estado atenta a sus encantos y graciosas actitudes como a una lección de arte, que mis deseos permanecían impasibles...» (I, 134).

appealed most to Luis: «Ofrecía Téllez características pintorescas, combativas y un poco estrafalarias; mas al fondo de todos sus actos, aun de los más violentos, sonreía la bondad» (I, 519). It is this basic kindness, goodness, so reminiscent of papá Juan and linked with poetry and Jesus, that strikes a common bond with Luis. It would not be too daring to suggest that in Téllez, this defender of the weak and the poor, whose exploits were legend, Barrios was already groping for, by compensation, the combination of art and strength, the elusive synthesis that Luz wanted to see in Gastón. Téllez represents a youthful, unsubtle attempt by Barrios, the incorrigible sentimentalist, to live out his frustrations, and to combine the superior sensitive qualities of the artist with the desirable strong traits necessary to survive in this hard life.

Un perdido, being Barrios' first full-scale novel, is his most comprehensive statement not only on the role of the artist in society but also on the philosophy of art. The affirmation of papá Juan on the need to cultivate an art, which comes on the second page of the novel, is the key to Luis' salvation or perdition, and is the link between Barrios' metaphysics and aesthetics. Without the vital significance of art as an escape, all the description of the bohemian way of life, the discussion of the artist's position, and his philosophy of life is mere window-dressing and contributes nothing to Barrios' vision of life. As a philosophical novelist, like Baroja and Mallea, Barrios uses discussions, not only in «Tirana ley» and *Un perdido,* to express his point of view—in these two novels, for example, to expostulate on the philosophy of aesthetics.

Luis, almost at the end of his spiritual decline in the closing pages of *Un perdido,* recalls all the people he had known in his life who had suffered the blows of fate. Running through a long list of good souls who suffered, he identifies his grandfather, his grandmother, his mother, his sister, culminating in the poor artists of this world: «los artistas pobres, concibiendo sus obras para sólo sembrar de tumbas sus caminos de hambre» (I, 532). Talent is not enough, as Jorge had tried to convince Gastón in «Tirana ley», without the economic means to further it. For the poor artist in this harsh world, Barrios says, the paths of talent lead but to the grave. Even the fortunate artists cannot be really happy either. If they are successful, triumph does not eliminate sadness, since the successful ones are always seen in better light by their admirers than they are by themselves. The public might appreciate their ability but the true artist suffers the black vision of his failings. Before becoming artists, they believed to be talented certain people who penetrated and conquered everything. Now artists themselves, they do not see themselves in the same light, but merely as limited containers holding very little mystery. When something enters, something else has to go out. Fitted into the context from which it is drawn, this view of the artist's role is an anguished cry from the heart, Purporting to be the opinion of an artist whom Luis overhears in the library, it adds to the overall picture of humanity that Luis, in his final days of despair, has painted. Disillusioned by religion, orthodox and unorthodox, Luis wants to be left alone with the scepticism of the Book of Ecclesiastes and the deterministic view of a cruel, absurd world. The good people, his relatives and his artist friends, have all succumbed to the evils of a hostile world. Even the successful artists, apparently, derived little consolation from their triumphs:

> Ostentadores de lo que sentimos, disimuladores de lo que ignoramos y... comediantes de lo que fingimos... ¡Oh, cuántas, cuántas pequeñeces suman la grandeza! Averigüemos en seguida: ¿Para qué todo este afán? Para obtener la gloria, pompa inflada por el unido soplar de incomprensivos, interesados, celosos o frívolos amantes del renombre que fácilmente se gana vapuleando con mayor o menor destreza, con mayor o menor ingenio, la producción del esfuerzo serio; pompa inflada también por algunos admiradores sinceros cuya veracidad, si tal cual vez se deja reconocer en medio de la grita heterogénea, ya hemos visto a que se reduce: a la ironía, al desconsuelo de comprender que mucho se nos supone, cuando al fondo del vacío de nuestras incapacidades un eco nos repite: «¡Míseros, limitados!» (I, 532)

In spite of the misery and the limitations of the artist, however, there is the spark that lights the darkness: «Sin embargo, de esas ineptitudes nace el ansia de avanzar, razón del crecimiento; y todavía son esos negros vacíos los que hacen que los llenos sean capacidades, tal como los espacios abiertos entre un objeto y otro hacen que los objetos como objetos existan» (I, 532). The important point is that the artist must not demand, as a reward, glory but only the pleasure of beauty which exalts us: «... el arte no debemos exigirle como recompensa la gloria, sino el goce de que la belleza nos exalte» (I, 532). The pleasure, however, comes only during the luminous fever of conception. Afterwards it is converted into work and even torture. Even for the successful artist, life and creation are difficult: «Reconocieron un placer, único intenso y digno de tomarse a favor: el de concebir» (I, 532).

Life, in the Schopenhaureian world of *Un perdido,* is anguished and pessimistic. The only true escape, for the select few, is through the medium of art, itself a difficult but rewarding process. Barrios, influenced both by Schopenhauer's philosophy and aesthetics, does not underestimate the value of art as a vital force. Indeed he goes so far as to elevate the creative process to a rite or ritual, and art itself almost to a religion.

After his description of the bohemian world of *Un perdido,* Barrios does not insert the life of painters, sculptors, musicians and the like into his succeeding novels for the mere sake of philosophical debate or artistic *costumbrismo.* Since *El hermano asno,* the peak of the first period, takes place in a convent, it could not naturally be the proper setting for artistic figures. However, that is not to deny that it contains some of the most beautiful poetry, music and pictorial qualities achieved by Barrios. Though

«Páginas de un pobre diablo», set in an undertaker's parlour, is one of the gloomiest of Barrios' novels, Adolfo, like Lázaro, writes for therapeutic reasons. At the end of the novel he leaves the funeral home, perhaps to escape the hardships of life by means of an artistic career—in this case, writing. In the second trilogy both *Tamarugal* and *Gran señor y rajadiablos,* set in the nitrate regions of the north and the central rural district respectively, lack the «sophistication» of the novels of the city, and hence the awareness of the arts. José Pedro Valverde, however, as a result of his college education, does find some consolation in his reading of the classics, escaping the barbarism through Horace and Ovid. Not till his last novel, *Los hombres del hombre,* does Barrios renew the theme of art, not just as a topic for discussion but as a key to the business of living.

On one level *Los hombres del hombre* is about true art as opposed to sham art—in this case, poetry, though the other arts figure prominently in the novel. Just as Barrios had demonstrated the dangers of abusing emotion and the consequent tragedy thereof, so too with art. On the figure of Chela Garín Barrios has heaped all his contumely for the shallow amateur who uses art for the wrong ends. It is she who persuades Beatriz, the wife, to renew her piano playing, not for pleasure but as a weapon she can use in the battle of the sexes. When Beatriz plays beautifully Débussy's «La fille aux cheveux de lin», recreating for *el hombre* the mood of their courting days, the nostalgia is shattered by the noisy entrance («el gangoso *lará, lará*», II, 1021) of Chela. This caricature of the early liberated woman, divorced, free to lead her own life, is one of the most overdrawn of Barrios' characterisations. Though Barrios had been an advocate of women's emancipation (in his dramas), Chela emerges as a repugnant example of her sex.[10] More important, from the aesthetic point of view, is her contrast with the true poets—Charlie and his sensitive father. Chela is dangerous because of her influence over Beatriz, and, by extension, over Charlie. Just as she had persuaded Beatriz to read *el hombre*'s diary, which had precipitated the marital crisis, so too does she incite the impure motives for Beatriz's piano playing. When Beatriz justifies her practices by the remark «Una debe realizarse», she is merely echoing the chorus of the liberated Chela: «Me realizo. Porque una mujer necesita realizarse» (II, 1021). If not quite as soul-less as the musical statistician of *Un perdido,* she too is a collector of artistic happenings and trivia. The gift of *la mascarilla de Beethoven* and the boasting of having witnessed the dress rehearsal of the ballet are typical and symptomatic of her superficial relationship with the real world of music and ballet. With little talent herself, she directs the new-found

---

[10] «... cuarentona, bien plantada, bonitas piernas, sobre las cuales sus adiposidades se sostienen, para moverse ágiles. Una faja y un sostén muy flojos permiten a sus turgencias esa soltura esa soltura de las gordas deportivas y trotacalles. Sin mirarle la cara, puede que guste; pero encima del cuello con papada y bajo el pelo teñido color caoba, se repantiga su antipatía: ese mentón sumido y esa dentadura saliente» (II, 1022).

career of Beatriz, to help her establish her personality, of course, all the while name-dropping: «Mira, el *touché*, ¿comprendes?, hazlo más breve, a lo Gieseking, a lo Rosita Bernard, con dedo firme pero liviano... Sólo con la mano... Acuérdate de Arrau. Ya nadie toca de muñeca, sino a todo brazo...» (II, 1040). In October 1937, writing for *Las Ultimas Noticias*, Barrios devoted at least two editorials eulogising the musical skills of the aforementioned Rosita Renard and the other Chilean pianist Hugo Fernández.[11] In his treatment of the insufferable Chela, Barrios demonstrates his own familiarity with the world and technique of music, as he had done in the earlier novels with regard to painting.

The rancour of *el hombre* is directed at Chela not only for her excessive influence on Beatriz but also because of her meddling in the life of Charlie. Her preoccupation with the externals of art, like learning formal poetry and insisting on Charlie's taking ballet lessons, is anathema to the father (and Barrios) because of the danger of destroying the boy's love for true art which has nothing to do with learning verses by heart nor attending practices of *Coppelia*. The sensitive child begins to associate drama and poetry with the pieces of recitation imposed by Chela. The duty of the father is to show that poetry is pleasurable and is to be found in natural phenomena like the song of a bird, flowers, sunlight, etc. Only then can he combat the vicious influence of the Chela Garíns of this world, who appear to make up the second public to whom Barrios dedicates the novel. The first and the third group who interest Barrios are those of «la sensibilidad refinada y la conciencia»; and «la frescura y la espontaneidad». The other public which will receive the book is the mediocre: «la indigestión de los semiversados, las ínfulas de la petulancia, la costra erudita de quienes por haber estudiado creen saber, a veces, la hiel de cuantos desearon ser alguien y no lo consiguieron, a menudo también cierto viscoso gris de algunos que mezclan sus odios y sus juicios» (II, 983). It is from pseudo-intellectuals like Chela Garín that real poetry has to be preserved; and in spite of whose efforts the father nurtures the poetic intuition of Cabecita: «... deberé salvar de sus repugnancias a la poesía» (II, 1062-63). As a result of Chela's insistence on recitals and theatrical performances, the innate poetry in Charlie is being driven out by his hatred of Chela and her overbearing ways. It is the aim of the father to save it at all costs. This is not mere art for art's sake, but a manifestation of the metaphysical role that Barrios attributes to art throughout his work, and which he crowns in this, his last novel: «Justo porque Cabecita lleva la poesía adentro, debemos evitar que se le convierta en molestia» (II, 1072). In Charlie's case, his poetic gift is what separates him from the mediocre, the masses, and distinguishes him

---

[11] «Un pianista nuestro», XXXV (2 de octubre, 1937), 4 and «La hazaña pianística de Rosita Renard», XXXV (9 de octubre, 1937), 4.

from the sham artists like Chela. More important, it is the path that Luis and company could not tread in their effort to give meaning to life.

If Chela represents Barrios' second public, the mediocre group of *semiversados,* obviously *el hombre* and Cabecita correspond to the first and third groups. Barrios uses the expression «la sensibilidad afinada» (II, 1001-02) to describe the feelings of *el hombre,* who, as an adult, has already acquired by maturity and experience of life an awareness that he is trying to inculcate in young Charlie who, still in his youth, is all freshness and spontaneity. His father advises him thus: «Anda, vive libre y espontáneo» (II, 1068). With this paternal guidance, as the novel progresses he acquires the consciousness of his own poetic gifts, and gradually refines his innate grasp of the beauty of natural things. Individual events, taken from nature, constitute the core of the lessons from which he draws his learning about life and poetry. If Charlie is different from the musical statistician, from the *tropicalista,* from Chela Garín, in short, from all the impostors of the second public, as Barrios implies, then he has to distinguish between artistic bagatelles (the Beethoven mask, the musical programmes, the poetry notebooks), which are the weapons of the *farsantes,* and true art. External trappings of art are useful, but without the soul of true poetry they have no value.

Just as López in *Un perdido* considered just watching the landscape and distinguishing between the various colours of a sunset to be an integral part of his training, so too does Charlie penetrate to the soul of things, face to face with the world of nature. Barrios uses two simple, elemental examples—the song of a bird and the presence of flowers—to teach the lesson that poetry is not found merely in books or on stage, that art is not just recitations or masks. Arising from the simple childish question as to whether birds exhale or inhale while singing, Charlie after meditation comes to the conclusion that, whatever the method, the notes emerge «tan limpias. Parecen desnuditas» (II, 1065). The father elaborates thus: «No es, a pesar de todo, una voz que se desnuda; más bien una que se viste. La voz del aire, que viene como un misterio, callando, y se va coloreada y vestida de plumas. Hecha poesía» (II, 1065). With the meaningful punch line, the seed is sown without further action or comment on the part of the father. It is significant that Barrios transfers father and son from the city to the country house in order to give *el hombre* the opportunity to show him what makes authentic poetry. It is a retreat not only from the city environment but from the false artistic ambience created by Chela and the other impostors.

The second lesson that *el hombre*/Barrios teaches is centred this time on the flowers which not only give pleasure but are also enviable:

> Porque siendo vivas, siente uno que viven a una inacortable distancia de las gentes, ventaja que yo, y se me ocurre que tú, sabemos apreciar. También nosotros solemos hallarnos lejos. Sólo que la distancia nuestra es, por des-

115

gracia, salvable; de repente, a un grito, a la sacudida que nos dan en un brazo, volvemos de nuestra distancia. ¿No te pasa igual?
—En el colegio...
—En el colegio más a menudo, ¿ves? Sueles entonces sonreír; pero te queda una como tristeza de trizadura, no sabes en qué punto del alma, por estos regresos bruscos. (II, 1066)

Having created a propitious atmosphere, increased the intimacy and identity between himself and his son, the father goes on to make the link between the natural phenomena of the flowers, the emotions of both humans, and the inherent poetry of the situation: «No he perdido esa riqueza, hijo, y la conservo porque algunos poetas me la defienden. Los leo y mi razón confirma que cuanto en sueños se sufre y se ama como en la realidad, y aun ciertas emociones sin objeto, las que más en lo profundo remecen y huellan muchas veces, son poesía» (II, 1066). It bears repeating that emotion, so vital a concept in Barrios' metaphysics (e.g. as a force for good and evil, basis of religion), should have an equally important role to play in his aesthetics. By virtue of the examples of the flowers/emotions, *el hombre* impresses on Cabecita the differences between written/spoken verse and true poetry: «La poesía... no siempre se halla en los versos, y menos en algunos delirios inventados y grandilocuentes o estrafalarios» (II, 1067). By means of this distinction he hopes to show the respect for poetry which may have been damaged in the boy's unfortunate encounters with Chela.

The third lesson in the burgeoning awareness of the sensitive boy's feeling for poetry takes place accidentally, but is a logical corollary of the flower/emotion incident and an extension of the musical poetry lesson of the bird-song episode. If the two previous incidents highlighted the aesthetic qualities of non-verbal poetry, the final episode, significantly on the eve of their departure from the country, completes the circle and reaffirms the value of genuine conventional poetry. Using the expression «la soledad silenciosa», *el hombre* provokes a flash of marvellous recognition in Charlie. Aware now of the importance of feelings or emotions (second lesson), he is struck by the aptness of his father's expression which describes exactly how he has felt in the past, but has never been able to explain or articulate. Now suddenly he sees the essence of his emotions described perfectly in these words—*la soledad silenciosa,* to which he rises when he feels lost and tired in a crowd of people. He had been vaguely aware of the fact that he was different from other boys, but he had never been able to formulate his ideas. Now in a flash, he learns: «Siento mucho tiempo algo y no lo veo. Sabe todo el mundo en el acto lo que le pasa. Yo, no. Me demoro, me demoro. Hasta que un día escucho dos palabras sueltas, en una conversación que nada tiene que hacer con mi asunto, y esas palabras son esa cosa mía. Debo de ser muy tonto. Las cosas que siento parece que no existen bien hasta que les encuentro las palabras» (II, 1067). Conscious of his own sensitivity, he is not fully aware of what his parents, especially his father, had grasped early—that he was a poet. This incident brings about the third stage in the poetic revelation that poetry can be verbal without being mere recital fodder: «Porque las palabras, hijo, ciertas palabras únicas que corresponden, son la verdadera cara de todo eso, de los sentimientos sobre todo, y no están siempre a la mano, ni para ti ni para nadie... Eres un poeta» (II, 1068). When his father uses the magic word, the boy grimaces and makes the obvious association, conjuring up painful memories of Chela, which prompts the father to differentiate between Chela's poetasters and true poets who «hallan su libertad en el espacio último y durante la soledad silenciosa» (II, 1068). What he could have added but did not, for fear of confusing the boy with an excess of adult terminology, was that down amongst the ordinary men the search for the hidden word to express feelings and emotions goes on: «Porque sin el verbo, ya lo enunció el Espíritu, nada nace de verdad» (II, 1068). Charlie, who has discovered the key words to describe perfectly the soul of things, is above the herd. Charlie is a poet. The father's hope is that he has saved the reputation of poetry in the boy's eyes, and that Charlie should go on finding the secret words that speak the language of poetry.

Although Barrios chooses poetry as the manifestation of his artistic ideal in *Los hombres del hombre,* compared to painting in the first novel, he does not abandon the painter's technique which he had learned. Despite the literary preoccupations of the protagonist and his son, Barrios in *Los hombres del hombre,* as one critic has rightly pointed out, «conceives everything in terms of painting—landscapes, still-lifes, portraits—and even employs painting techniques in the elaboration of his pictures».[12] Landscape pictures like the following show Barrios' pictorial training:

> La tarde continúa lindísima. De los cerros enormes parecen bajar los árboles al llano como una muchedumbre que regresara para recogerse. Aun ese rodado de peñas molidas por las heladas a lo largo del tiempo, se tiende suave como delantal gris de su montaña. La transparencia del aire asombra en estas alturas; por ella las enormidades abruptas se funden con la ternura de los verdes y los azules celestes aquietan ranchos, torrentes y caminos. Es un paisaje inmóvil de porcelana, que aun sonaría notas claras si le diéramos con los nudillos. (II, 994)

His portraits range from the Byronic, satanic protagonists of the early short stories of *Del natural,* like Carlos Romero («alto, esbelto, de facciones correctísimas, elegante y distinguido..., sus ojazos castaños y dormidos, de largas pestañas que dábanle una expresión acariciadora, avasallante...» [I, 36]), to the Modernist ideal woman like Luz in «Tirana ley»:

> Tenía los ojos verdes de ágata crisoprasa; las pestañas negras, largas, tendidas y levemente encrespadas en las puntas; las cejas espesas y en arco. Aquellas

---

[12] JOEL C. HANCOCK, «The Purification of Eduardo Barrios' Sensorial Prose», *Hispania,* LVI, No. 1 (March, 1973), 54.

9

pupilas sombreadas hipnotizaban, embebían, como el mar en el crepúsculo. Su
nariz tenía el perfil clásico y puro de los rostros latinos, su boca breve y elás-
tica reunía la frescura de la fresa y el ardor de una sensualidad inconsciente;
y todo este conjunto impecable seducía bajo la sombra de una cabellera castaña
con irisaciones cobrizas, peinada con cierta negligencia artística, y sobre un
cutis perlado, felpudito, de la blancura exangüe de un crisantemo blanco.
(I, 94-95)

The cruel caricature of Chela Garín in *Los hombres del hombre* is a long
way from the fine lines of an Italian Renaissance beauty in the portrait of
María Mercedes in *El hermano asno:* «Pequeñita, con no sé qué de íntimo,
reunido y caricioso en la silueta, y en la carnación, a la vez fina y rolliza,
la tierna morbidez de esas italianas del Renacimiento que el Veronés solía
pintar» (II, 565). Barrios uses caricature a great deal, however (cf. also
Un perdido and *Tamarugal*), as revelatory of hidden truths: «Una cari-
catura sirve para revelar las verdades que se esconden, se revisten y se
disimulan.»[13] Other painting techniques that Barrios uses skilfully are framing, usually by means of doors and windows to focus the reader's attention;
silhouetting, in black and white, and the *chiaroscuro* technique, employed
mostly in dawn and dusk situations. All these pictorial practices are
employed by Barrios to render better in artistic form the poetic dimension.
The whole pictorial process achieves a kind of *transposition d'art* effect in
the novel. By his skilful use of one art, painting, he is able to render in an
aesthetic way the effects of another branch of art, literature, and in particular
poetry.

The final link between the first and the last novel is made in *el hombre's* description of the creative process. In «Tirana ley» Gastón Labarca,
through his love for Luz, his ideal woman, was able to achieve harmony
and happiness in the marriage of his love and art. Luz not only serves as a
physical model and an inspiration for his paintings but is also the source
of strength that gives meaning to his life as well as his art. In other
words, art is conceived in, and nurtured by, love. At the end of his
literary career Barrios repeats the message in *Los hombres del hombre.* In
rationalising his feelings about his son, *el hombre* wonders aloud about
truth, and the difference between understanding and discovery, before
coming to the conclusion that the basis of all artistic discovery is love:

> Reabro, pues, hoy este cuaderno tan abandonado. Anotaré cuanto he visto vivir
> a mi chicuelo en el último tiempo. Debí hacerlo a medida de observar y com-
> prender. ¿Por qué no lo hice? La desconfianza me presentaba cuanto atisbé
> como un conjunto de verdades presuntas. Pero ¿no son presuntas todas las
> verdades? ¿En qué consiste la comprensión, si no en presumir con acierto lo
> que dentro de otro ser sucede? Y entre comprender y descubrir hay poca o

[13] Review «*Hijuna* por Carlos Sepúlveda Layton», *Las Ultimas Noticias,* XXXII
(9 de mayo, 1934), 12.

ninguna diferencia. *Todo está en que nos alumbre el amor.* Entonces acertare-
mos. El novelista, cuando nos describe una vida interior, también así procede:
amándola, descubre la entraña del laberinto, y su figura se levanta y anda, viva
de toda humanidad. Sólo hace falta identificación; y esto, con mi niño, sobra.
(II, 1030; my italics)

Love, then, as Labarca also found out, is the guiding light and the source
of artistic inspiration. This is the message, first and last, of Barrios' work,
which he unfolds, whether he treats of painting, poetry or fiction.

From this coterie of artists—painters, poets, sculptors, musicians, novelists—who pass through the pages of Barrios' novels, it is clear that Barrios
was familiar with the artistic life in its myriad manifestations. From his
skilful use of painting techniques, his easy familiarity with schools and
styles, and his own confessions as to his pictorial aspirations, it is clear
that Barrios was no tyro in the field of plastic arts. In the field of music
he demonstrates a knowledge of piano techniques and their exponents, as
well as an awareness of the finer points of the world of ballet and opera.[14]
Though conversant with these forms of the arts, in the peak of the second
trilogy he chooses poetry as his medium, having already introduced poets
and critics in the first trilogy (e.g. *Un perdido*). Art, however, is no mere
picturesque element in Barrios' work, nor are his artists presented merely
to add colour or eccentric interest. The cultivation of an art, preached by
papá Juan, is a goal to be achieved not for snob value but as a means of
establishing order in one's life, of finding a «faithful companion» which
will make an essentially tragic existence tolerable. Herein lies the link
between Barrios' aesthetics and his metaphysics.

ART AS RELIGION

It is evident, then, that art for Barrios is no mere diversion nor just an
escape from boredom. Given its position in Barrios' philosophy of life, and
his own close identification with Modernism, it is no surprise that Barrios
held art in high esteem, raising it often to the level of a religion. If Barrios
is identified with Modernism from the sensibility point of view—that is,
rooted in the post-Romantic malaise—and shares that movement's enthusiasm
for formal innovations in style, language and technique, in his attitude to art
and the artist he is not far behind the master Darío. In his poetry Darío
often uses religious terminology to describe his feelings toward art which
for the tormented. agnostic Modernist takes the place of religion. When
Darío quotes directly from scripture the words of Christ to describe the
purity of art, he is indicating the extent to which the Modernists relied on

[14] See his editorial «El fenómeno de la ópera», *Las Ultimas Noticias,* XXXV
(16 de septiembre, 1937), 4.

theological concepts and liturgical connotations to denote their evaluation of art not only as an ideal but as a saving grace:

> Vida, luz y verdad: tal triple llama
> produce la interior llama infinita;
> el Arte puro, como Cristo, exclama:
> *Ego sum lux et veritas et vita!*
>
> («Yo soy aquél»)

Barrios holds literature, the literary vocation, and the creative process in the same high esteem. Writing, for him, is a lofty calling, and he is not ashamed to confess his worship at the altar of art: «Escribir es un rito. Debe serlo siempre, aunque se haya convertido en la esencia de nuestro ser, en oficio y ejercicio de todos los días.»[15] This Modernist view of art as religion is reflected in Barrios' terminology. Though, as we have noted, not an orthodox Catholic, Barrios saw the advantages of religion, and especially the wonder and beauty of church liturgy, music and theology. For papá Juan in *Un perdido,* let it be remembered, one of the attractions of religion lay in the poetry of church liturgy and its concomitant emotion, which is the essence of religion, to which he was sensitive in the extreme. A religious service, rather than just a pretext for reciting prayers, was, in what could be termed a compendium of Modernist essentials, «un concierto apacible de gesto, visión, perfume, color y sonido» (I, 256). If art is religion, then undoubtedly the reverse is true. Divinity and poetry have exactly the same meaning for papá Juan, as we have seen. The following passage can be quoted equally in support of aesthetic religion or religious aesthetics:

> Luego, el cuadro refrescaba con su puerilidad: un pequeño altar ante uno de los pilares, túmulo blanco y azul, puro de gasas, lirios y azucenas, deslumbrante de plata, de plata en hojas, en estrellas, en hilos; una imagen suave aureolada de luces; el resto del templo en clara penumbra, que fingía más alta la bóveda, más tranquila la arquitectura; un solo cántico de un único motivo ingenuo que gira, gira y obsesiona, y adormece, como el ejercicio místico de respiración con que los santos se producían la dulce locura del éxtasis; y desde lo alto, la voz poderosa del órgano, presidiendo las emociones, recogiéndolas en sí, como un Dios augusto y benévolo, tonante y manso. (I, 256)

If the powerful voice of the organ booms out like a noble and mighty God, much more typical of Barrios and more in keeping with his Pascalian view of religion is the gentle figure of the Jesus-poet, out of whose Sacred Heart spring goodness and poetry which go much more deeply than justice. Jesus, the kind poet, makes his mark more profoundly than the equitable judge, God the Father. Though «Tirana ley», written at the peak of his

---

[15] «Perfil de Eduardo Barrios» by JORGE ONFRAY BARROS, *Revista Zig-Zag,* XLII, No. 2149 (30 de mayo, 1946), 25-26.

anti-morality, anti-clerical period, could hardly be called a religious novel, Barrios does not hesitate to take advantage of ecclesiastical vocabulary to portray secular, even profane, matters. When Luz, in the opening page, is trying to formulate her admiration of Labarca's artistic and physical qualities, she almost paraphrases Darío's twofold response to the ever-present anguish —*unir carne y alma:* «Entonces, el espíritu y la materia, unidos, caigo en la más excelsa de las comuniones y bendigo la hora en que nos encontramos» (I, 89). Luz, who is both his ideal woman and his artistic muse, inspires Labarca to evoke words like *beatífica, celestial, hierática, sublime, pura* to describe her. Together their love produces an atmosphere illuminated by «una luz beatífica, y tranquila, luz de santuario» (I, 121), which lends to the setting «un brillo religioso».

The whole creative process is, as Barrios describes it, almost a mystical experience, worthy of St Teresa and John of the Cross, whose works he knew so well and quoted so often. The artist has to go through the various stages, almost, of prayer and meditation before the final moment of glory—the act of conception, which is the unique, intense and only worthy pleasure (UP I, 532). The *Zig-Zag* interview continues thus: «El espectáculo y la contemplación de la vida me sugiere un tema: voy pensando un argumento, urdiéndolo *in mente;* veo surgir los personajes, tallados en una sola pieza y fraccionándose, poco a poco, en cien sutiles pormenores psicológicos. No me pongo todavía a llenar, cual un loco, páginas y páginas; espero.» This is only the first stage on the road to illumination. Other processes follow: «Tengo una concepción rápida de la obra. Es como un rayo que ilumina el cerebro, como una corriente de aguas prodigiosas y súbitas que irriga mi sensibilidad.» The analogy with Santa Teresa's four stages of prayer en route to mystical union with God is obvious and not too extravagant or forced. The irrigation stage is not sufficient. The mind (soul) is still not ready for the final act of creation (communion): «Pero no basta: soy miedoso para escribir. Antes de acometer el libro, lo pienso mucho. Horas, días, meses, trazo su arquitectura, medito el plan, vigilo los episodios, paso revista a los detalles. Cuando el proyecto ha madurado, todavía me faltan fuerzas por llevarlo a feliz término. Me pongo a realizarlo con temor, y paulatinamente alzo el vuelo; empiezo con dificultad y, a medida que el tiempo transcurre, la audacia—este desenfado de escribir—acelera mi pluma.» The divine gift of creation, of writing, is something mysterious revealed only to a few. This metaphor of fearfully and slowly *alzando el vuelo*—the final stages of the mystical creative process/levitation—Barrios treats explicitly in *Los hombres del hombre* in the triple lesson of the father to his son, who has the mystical gift of words, hidden words, select words which correspond exactly to the true face of things, i.e. the gift of poetry (II, 1068).

Barrios believed in the inspiration of writers, who suffer the same experiences as mystics. The terminology is not coincidental: «Yo creo en la inspiración de los autores. Hay en ella la misma nobleza, los mismos accidentes fisiológicos que en los éxtasis de las religiones. De repente una luz ciega la mirada y paraliza el gesto. Uno quiere seguir siendo igual y ya no lo es. Lo cotidiano, lo usual de la existencia se pierde; un velo de sombra cubre a nuestros semejantes. El contorno de las cosas se esfuma; las conversaciones ajenas pierden todo valor. Se habla a nuestro lado, se ríe, se sufre y ya no lo sentimos.»

In this important interview, written not in youth but towards the end of his literary life, Barrios summarises succinctly and clearly his religious, almost mystical, attitude to art. It is interesting that Barrios, who had revealed his Schopenhauerian interest in Buddhism, perhaps influenced by the poetry of Amado Nervo, talks of the ecstasy of religions (plural), indicating that mystical or ecstatic experiences are not the sole property of the Catholic religion. There is no doubt, however, that he was well acquainted with the works of the Spanish mystics, whose human traits he also understood and appreciated.

The human condition, tragic in its essence, is at the basis of all art, including Barrios': «Creo que sin estos fenómenos no hay arte. Quien no los ha sufrido no puede crear. Al menos, sin ellos, yo no habría podido componer ni una novela, ni un solo cuento.» Life is a learning process, as suggested by his novels which are the literary manifestation of his spiritual evolution. The second trilogy is a gradually developing counterbalance to the first black trilogy, because in the intervening twenty years Barrios has profited from the lessons of life. Suffering, personal and fictional, which has matured the man and the artist, produces the balance of the second trilogy and, if not optimism, at least a metaphysical outlook which enables him to cope with the inherent tragedy of life.

ARTISTIC TECHNIQUE AND THE CREATIVE PROCESS

Barrios in the aforementioned *Zig-Zag* interview discusses the religious qualities of art and believes in the inspiration of authors. In *Los hombres del hombre,* his last and perhaps most consciously artistic novel, he treats the role of the novelist and his fictional technique in terms of truth, love and beauty (II, 1030), abstract qualities which underscore the Modernist view of art as religion. As Barrios goes on to suggest in various places—to extend the theological imagery—faith (in his own idea) without good works is of little value. As the mystic does not achieve full communion without prayer, fasting and self-discipline, neither does the artist experience the pleasure of creation without effort and sacrifice on his part. All Barrios' artist-figures are successful only when industrious and dedicated to their art. Even the ambivalent Gastón of «Tirana ley» opts for the hard life of

Paris (with the consequent abandonment of Luz) to perfect his talents. López, the painter in *Un perdido,* spends his whole day working, studying, discussing, observing, to the neglect of earning money for food. All of Barrios' aspiring writers from Adolfo to *el hombre* devote a considerable part of their day to putting their thoughts on paper. Though the latter comes to the conclusion that love leads to illumination, like the mystics, he has to do the preparatory hard work to make the soul ready for the moment of communion, of creation.

In the *Zig-Zag* interview, interspersed with the passive terms of receptivity which depict the waiting artist are to be found the concepts denoting the desirability, nay the necessity, of activity. After inspiration, but before execution of the task, long hours, days, months, years are spent in thinking, planning, mapping out the form of the book, working out the plan, watching over the episodes, revising the details. Even then the writer realises, concretises his thoughts slowly and with a certain fearfulness. Any ritual, which writing is for Barrios, implies action, sacrifice and the central participation of the celebrant. Though there is much of the contemplative in Eduardo Barrios, as a preliminary stage of the creative act, the literary end-product cannot be achieved without the act of writing, with all its implied mechanical difficulties, which is the final stage.

The *Zig-Zag* interview was published in 1946, before the appearance of *Gran señor y rajadiablos* (1948) and *Los hombres del hombre* (1950). Ten years later in another interview the same basic approach to writing is revealed, with no attempt to disguise the work processes involved. As well as being a fascinating revelation of the novelist at work, one is struck by the positive tone of the response as to the role of the writer. In reply to the question as to whether he prefers to work from a prearranged, structured, complete plan of the novel to be written, or to allow the novel to take its own free course as it evolves, Barrios answered:

> El primero. Viene a mí una idea que considero digna de desarrollo. *Le doy vueltas* en la cabeza durante días y noches. Creo así, de uno en uno, los principales personajes y los más importantes acontecimientos. *Ordeno* unos y otros en un esquema y no es sino después de todo este *trabajo de preparación,* cuando *me entrego* al desarrollo... Claro que esto sólo versa con lo principal: los personajes secundarios y los incidentes de menor importancia son productos del desarrollo mismo.[16]

The italics, which are all mine, are meant to highlight the positive, active nature of the Barrios creative process.

---

16 HUGO LINDO, «Con un novelista insigne», *Cultura* (El Salvador), No. 8 (marzo-abril, 1956), 10.

DEFINITION OF ART

Eduardo Barrios had positive ideas also on the definition of art and literature which he did not confine to his novels. In his autobiographical work, «También algo de mí» (1923), and in his other writings, especially prologues, editorials and book reviews, he expounded clearly and consistently his artistic theories which he rendered in fictional terms in his novels. The most important statement, though not the only one, of his literary theories is to be found in this autobiographical essay «También algo de mí». Though rather a long passage, the following merits quotation in full as being explanatory and illuminatory of Barrios' view of art. Though published after the appearance of his first trilogy, the theories expressed therein are a true reflection of the kind of fiction written in his first period:

Odio los gestos, las presuntuosas bizarrías con que algunos suelen adornarse de pluma. Odio esto en la vida y en el arte, en *mi* arte. No soy un simple; aspiro a ser un simplificado. Amo la sencillez precisamente porque en ella encuentran la paz los complejos. Y como en la sencillez cabe la multiplicidad, ella es mi norte, mi fin en la depuración.

He definido el arte así: *Es una ficción que sirve para comunicar, no la verdad misma, sino la emoción de la verdad.* Y he dicho sobre mi ideal de estilo: *Música y transparencia,* porque con esto cumplido, las demás virtudes vienen solas.

Acerca de mi definición del arte, no creo necesario insistir. Cuando más, pido fijarse en que digo *comunicar* y no *expresar.* La expresión lisa y llana, por exacta y poderosa que sea, pertenece a la ciencia; comunicar y aun contagiar es misión del artista.

Defino en cambio esas dos palabras sobre el estilo: *Música y transparencia.* Porque yo desearía que al leer mis obras el lector se olvidara de que lee y que recibiera sólo, como directas de la vida y la naturaleza, las sensaciones y las emociones de cuanto quise comunicarle. A esto tiende todo mi esfuerzo de prosista: a la transparencia, para que nada estorbe ni distraiga, y a la música, porque sin ella no hay ondas simpáticas que penetren el corazón. Ya sé que esto resulta lo más difícil, porque las lecturas de nuestro aprendizaje literario, queramos o no, dejan en nosotros taras que nos entorpecen, que llegan a hacernos más fácil un modo difícil de hablar, más fácil que el fácil en realidad por lo simple y espontáneo; pero ello se consigue con un anhelo incesante de honradez y simplificación. El arte es, ¡felizmente!, muy difícil. Lo odioso es esa fácil mentira artística, la simulación de esa «exquisitez» que no pasa de pretensión. Abomino los estilos presuntuosos; son los falsificadores de la propia verdad. Además, este literatismo conduce a la estultez de pretender mostrarse excepcional. El gran error, advirtió Hugo, está en creer «que yo no soy tú». No importa sentir como todos los hombres; antes bien, conviene, para ser universal. La cuestión estriba en ahondar en ese sentir común a todos. He ahí el vigor. Y he ahí por qué es tan vigoroso tratando un tema fuerte como uno delicado. Seamos intensos y nuestra obra será vigorosa siempre, aun cuando usemos ese medio que vulgarmente no se reconoce como vigoroso; el de la sugerencia alada o inapresable. Del resultado, de la resonancia que obtengamos en el espíritu del lector, sabremos cuánto vigor hubo en nuestra obra; no de la índole del tema ni del procedimiento. (I, 28-29)

The hatred of pompous prose and the converse love of simplicity does not mean that Barrios is simple. As one saw in his view of philosophy, Barrios is not a primitive, nor is he naive, as his intuitive conclusions in the field of psychology prove. Simplicity is not a state of passivity or inertia but rather, as we noted in the creative process, a condition towards which one strives. The kind of simplicity towards which Barrios aspires is that achieved by children and, by analogy, those who seek to be like children, i.e. the pure, the innocent and the young at heart. Thus, the two best examples of the desired simplicity are «El niño que enloqueció de amor», and *El hermano asno,* significantly situated in a monastery of Franciscans, who traditionally have been known for their poverty, humility and simplicity.

«El niño que enloqueció de amor», which is Barrios' first novel of the trilogy, is one view of the sought-after simplicity. In this story of a nine-year-old boy who falls in love with an older woman, Barrios achieves the maximum effect of simplicity by having the story narrated in the first person by the child, through the medium of the later much-used diary form. By this technique of the first-person narrative not only does he gain the vital simplicity but he also adds the authenticity of having the story told in childlike language which heightens the tragedy and strengthens the verisimilitude of the novel—the use of diminutives, breathless exclamations, repetitions, the general unpretentious style of an innocent child.

El hermano asno is also a first-person narrative, but by an intellectually superior friar, ex-man of the world who suffers the pangs of pride and lust. It is obviously a more difficult task for Barrios to effect the qualities of simplicity—which he does, however, through the description of the spiritual and natural ambience of the monastery and its surroundings. This probably accounts for the high level of esteem in which *El hermano asno* is held, and makes the simplicity achieved more meritorious. Gabriela Mistral, who praises the form and narrative of the novel, sets Barrios' simplicity apart from that achieved by other great writers, because his lacks artifice and is «una sencillez humana»: «Hay muchas sencilleces: una es la de Garcilaso en las Eglogas; otra es la de Nervo en toda su obra; otra la de Santa Teresa. Tal vez la mejor sea ésta en que se ha abreviado hasta el último límite nuestro Eduardo Barrios; pues la primera es todavía muy retórica, la del mexicano se vuelve a veces blanda y desmadejada, y la de la Santa se ensombrece de conceptismo. Esta es humana y divina a la vez; se parece al surco negro cuando la luz cae sobre él y es tierra y oro conjuntamente.»[17] In this novel, the peak of the first period, Barrios has managed to attain the perfect blend of content and form by successfully utilising the desirable and desired simplicity both as a force and a vehicle. That is to say, in his efforts to convey the feeling and atmosphere of simplicity he makes use of a language that is the essence of simplicity. In this way the style and the

---

[17] Prologue to *Y la vida sigue* (Buenos Aires: Editorial Tor, 1925), p. 12.

effect desired become fused as one, with the force (simplicity) merging into the vehicle (simplicity) and vice versa. This perfect blend of style and content which he initiated in *El niño que enloqueció de amor* and perfected in *El hermano asno,* has not always been understood by Barrios' critics. It may be coincidence that the critics who have best understood the simplicity of Barrios' work have been Chileans. Gabriela Mistral appreciates the poetry of the two novels: «Desaparece el estilo por perfección del estilo, y desaparece el artista» (Prólogo, p. 12). Torres-Ríoseco praises «este estilo breve, sugerente, de una diamantina sencillez»; [18] whilst Silva Castro appreciates the art behind the artlessness that produces the perfect correspondence between *forma* and *fondo:* «Escribió con extrema finura, con pocas imágenes, procurando hallar siempre palabras simples, claras, las que le parecían más adecuadas al plan de perfección en que vivían sus héroes.» [19]

A striving, then, for simplicity, but a refined simplicity which contains in its essence a totality purged of all redundancy, is the aim of Barrios' art. For Barrios the novel is an art, something composed, which has, therefore, to go through a creative process. He does not see himself as a mere copier of nature either in speech or in description. Without the treatment of the artist, this «realism» has no aesthetic value: «Una frase copiada taquigráficamente, esto es, fotografiada, no es una frase creada, y el arte es creación y composición. No quiero ser un novelista Kodak, sino un novelista Goya.» [20] Though written in 1948, these words echo and develop the key definition of art offered in «También algo de mí» of 1923 which constitutes the core of his theory of aesthetics: «[El arte] es una ficción que sirve para *comunicar,* no la verdad misma, sino *la emoción* de la verdad» (I, 28). Barrios goes on to point out that he uses the term *comunicar* rather than *expresar* intentionally to distinguish the creative process from the scientific. *Comunicar,* with its religious connotations, links with the mystical attitude to the ritual of art expressed in the *Zig-Zag* interview. The feeling of communion between author and reader is reinforced by Barrios' elaboration of the idea: «comunicar y aun contagiar es misión del artista». This basically Romantic notion of the God-artist-magus figure communing with his reader dates from nineteenth-century France. Alfred de Vigny in *Stello* (1832) affirms the concept of the poet as a magus and a prophet, a mission that he has received from God: «Je crois fermement

---

[18] *Grandes novelistas de la América Hispana.* Tomo 2: *Los novelistas de la ciudad* (Berkeley: University of California Press, 1949), p. 56.

[19] *Panorama literario de Chile* (Santiago: Ed. Universitaria, 1961), p. 251.

[20] MAGDALENA PETIT, «Entrevista a Eduardo Barrios», *El Imparcial,* XXI (19 de septiembre, 1948), 10. One notes this self-comparison with Goya with whom Barrios has been linked, especially in his use of the grotesque. It is interesting too that Torres-Ríoseco should have compared Barrios' prose in *El hermano asno* with that of Valle-Inclán, whose *esperpentos* have been evoked by Barrios' style, especially in *Los hombres del hombre:* «Ofrece algo del encanto de la prosa de Valle-Inclán» (*Grandes novelistas,* p. 55).

en une vocation ineffable qui m'est donnée...» Victor Hugo in «Fonction du poète» (1839), exhorts his readers thus: «Peuples! Écoutez le poète! / Écoutez le rêveur sacré!» Barrios reinforces the Romantic identification of poet-reader and sense of communion by overtly referring to Hugo in the autobiographical essay: «El gran error, advirtió Hugo, está en creer "que yo no soy tú". No importa sentir como todos los hombres; antes bien, conviene, para ser universal. La cuestión estriba en ahondar en ese sentir común a todos» (I, 28-29). The terminology of the passage impresses on us, as always, the importance of sentiments, the inner feelings intuited by the heart before the brain comes into play—all the stuff of his novels, in fact, as we have seen in the previous chapters. The vital concept of emotion, underlined in Chapter 3 devoted to Barrios' metaphysics, has yet again a key role to play in Barrios' aesthetics. The basis of his art is that it communicates not truth itself but the emotion of truth—a rendering in theoretical terms of a premise already stated in fictional terms years before in *Un perdido* as early as 1918. Barrios' spokesman for his interlinked ideas of emotion/religion/aesthetics, papá Juan, describes the synthesis in terms that predate the autobiographical essay: «La Verdad sería siempre inaccesible, la emoción de ella, no. Y ésta era la Poesía» (I, 256). Absolute truth is inaccesible and cannot be rendered in literary terms. However, the emotion of truth is attainable, and can be rendered or, better, communicated. This communicative process of the emotion of truth Barrios calls poetry, or art. Without the emotion of truth Barrios' three psychological novels would be mere case histories of three «abnormal» characters in need of psychiatric help. Barrios' insistence on the use of the term *comunicar* rather than *expresar* underlines the stress that he puts on communication, i.e. sense of communion, or complete union (in mystic or religious vocabulary). Without the contagious or communicative quality of emotion, the work of art does not exist—it is a mere scientific paper or case study. Thus emotion is the *sine qua non,* the essence, the soul, without which the aesthetic creation fails to soar. One remembers the incident in *Un perdido* when the young librarian-writer narrates to Luis the history of his literary failures. He composed poetry, drama, short stories by the number which proved to be, as the aspiring writer recognised, artistic failures—because they lacked the all-important quality of emotion. This is, however, certainly not autobiographical. Alone, the Chilean critic, affirms: «Barrios es de los pocos autores chilenos que comunican vibración emotiva al lenguaje.»[21] Technical mastery and industriousness, though important in the creative process, cannot compensate for the lack of the all-important emotion.

Before going on to Barrios' stylistic ideal which he also treats in «También algo de mí», it would be useful to look at another source of Barrios'

---

[21] ALONE [HERNÁN DÍAZ ARRIETA], *Panorama de la literatura chilena durante el siglo XX* (Santiago: Nascimento, 1931), p. 80.

literary definition which takes up and reaffirms the thread of communication as the aesthetic function. More than a decade after the first publication of «También algo de mí», Barrios wrote an important prologue to the afore-mentioned work of Hernández Catá, *Sus mejores cuentos* (1936). Again, one passage is of such significance as to merit full reproduction:

> Cuanto dice resulta inevitablemente arte, *porque el arte no es otra cosa que revelación, en su quid radical; y luego, milagro comunicativo en su cumplimiento.* Posee este gran artista una erudición científica excepcional, que se adivina, que él ha transformado de conocimiento en cultura, de alimento en fuerza; y esta cultura, sin remedio, se vuelve arte en él, porque cuanto hay de objetivo en ella se subjetiviza al ser captado por el temperamento creador. No me causaría la menor extrañeza el oír a un hombre de mera ciencia negar la cultura científica de Alfonso Hernández Catá; como no me sorprende el haber leído en Gregorio Marañón, hombre de ciencia y arte a la vez, la afirmación de que Catá asombra por su profundo conocimiento de la psiquiatría y de las neurosis. Y este disfraz de la ciencia es necesario, indispensable al artista. *Su obra ha de hallarse tan saturada de subjetivismo,* que luego en la serenidad suprema de la forma externamente objetiva, *se nos presenta como un espontáneo milagro, como la verdad sencilla de un niño, como la ingenuidad de un simple.* (p. 9; my italics)

One is struck once again by the penchant, in this definition of art, for religious connotation that was later to form the basis of the *Zig-Zag* interview in which Barrios reaffirms the almost sacred function of writing. This notion of revelation, which parallels the illumination of the later interview, is the first step in the creative process. That is to say, truth is at the root of it: «El arte no es otra cosa que revelación, en su *quid radical.*» This important source of definition is a key link in the thesis that there is a close bond between life and art, between metaphysics and aesthetics, as I have tried to demonstrate throughout this work. The second stage in this creative process is the communication of the revealed truth—or better, the emotion of the truth—to the reader. It is this second step, the miraculous identification of reader with author, that achieves the fulfilment of the aesthetic creation: «y luego, milagro comunicativo en su cumplimiento» (p. 9). Without the personal link between artist and reader, the work is sterile. It requires the human emotion, as it were, to fertilise it: «Se confirma que en la realización de su arte pone esa conciencia sin la cual la obra no logra la plenitud estética de comunicación, de suscitar en el lector un goce análogo al del creador.»[22] Without this complementary force of the reader, the work of art fails to get off the ground. To prolong the metaphor, the reader supplies what T. S. Eliot calls «the beating of the other wing», without which the inspired work does not soar to creative heights, does not become poetry. Carlos Magis, in an interesting article on

---

[22] MILTON ROSSEL, «El hombre y su psique en las novelas de Eduardo Barrios», *Atenea*, CXXXIX, No. 389 (1960), p. 189.

fictional technique, describes the process thus: «La obra literaria es un artefacto verbal de carácter artístico cuya motivación y objetivo profundos son la integración anímica entre el autor y sus "interlocutores" ... La obra literaria no debe considerarse una cosa en sí, estética y perfecta, sino un fenómeno: el proceso de comunicación, el nivel profundo, entre alguien que expone su experiencia y alguien que la hace suya.»[23]

Although truth is at the root of the process, true recording of facts by itself is not literature, but some kind of photography or other technical, scientific skill. This is the difference between Barrios and Freud, or Pasteur, or the other scientists whose findings he predated intuitively. Facts by themselves have no literary value. It is the artist's subjective treatment of objective things that transforms knowledge into creative art. Gabriela Mistral sums up this quality of Barrios thus: «Es Barrios un transfigurador de lo cotidiano... Hace el milagro del musgo en las piedras feas. El don poético por excelencia, alzar las cosas en una posición en que el rayo de la belleza las dore, es suyo totalmente.»[24] Barrios' assessment of the composition and technique of Hernández Catá is, of course, the perfect expression of Barrios' own creative process: «Posee este gran artista una erudición científica excepcional, que se adivina, que él ha transformado de conocimiento en cultura, de elemento en fuerza; y esta cultura, sin remedio, se vuelve arte en él, porque cuanto hay de objetivo en ella se subjetiva al ser captado por el temperamento creador» (*Sus mejores cuentos,* p. 9). This disguising of scientific knowledge is absolutely essential to the artist whose work has to be so imbued with subjectivity that in the objective form it is presented to the reader as a spontaneous miracle, the simple truth of a child, as the innocence of a simple person: «Este disfraz de la ciencia es necesario, indispensable al artista. Su obra ha de hallarse tan saturada de subjetivismo, que luego, en la serenidad suprema de la forma externamente objetiva, se nos presenta como *un espontáneo milagro,* como *la verdad sencilla de un niño,* como *la ingenuidad de un simple*» (p. 9; my italics). I have italicised the descriptions of the work of art to highlight the consistency of Barrios' terminology in his effort to define the artistic creation.[25] The concept of the

---

[23] «Novela, realidad y malos entendidos», *Revista de la Universidad de México,* XXV, No. 6 (febrero, 1971), 10-17.

[24] Prologue to *Y la vida sigue,* pp. 12-13. Cf. DONALD FOGELQUIST's view in «Eduardo Barrios, en su etapa actual», *Revista Iberoamericana,* XVIII, No. 35 (febrero-diciembre, 1952), 20: «Tiene el don maravilloso de embellecer la realidad con la magia de la poesía.»

[25] VÁZQUEZ-BIGI has neatly divided the creative process into three levels: «uno primario, totalmente encubierto y difícil de penetrar, de rigurosa observación e intuición objetiva; un segundo plano intermedio, que se transparenta desde fuera, de identificación subjetiva y emocional con el personaje; finalmente y cubriendo por completo a los otros dos, un tercer plano de serenidad y dominio de la materia, de economía y exactitud expresiva, de plasmación de la palabra que infunde realidad al sentimiento» («Los tres planos de la creación artística de Eduardo Barrios», *Revista Iberoamericana,* XXIX, No. 55 [1963], 128).

work of art in terms of truth, simplicity, ingenuousness and childlike innocence dates back to *El niño que enloqueció de amor* (1915) and *El hermano asno* (1922) in fictional terms, and «También algo de mí» (1923) in literary theory, whilst looking forward to *Los hombres del hombre* (1950) in both fictional terms (in the novel) and from the theoretical point of view in the dedication to the various kinds of interested public—those of «la sensibilidad refinada y la conciencia» and those who exude «la frescura y la espontaneidad». If the father represents *la sabiduría* and Charlie *la inocencia,* then perhaps the ideal reader is he who manages to combine both good qualities: «cuando en un lector el sabio y el niño se reúnen, este lector es grande» (II, 983). The story of *Los hombres del hombre* is the mutual impact and the growing identification of father and son through their common sensitivity and the awareness of the value of poetry (in the child) as a force in life. The final words in the last novel refer to poetry and the child. There is for Barrios an important bond between them—[26] not only in the particular example of this novel but in the general simplicity, spontaneity and innocence which is at the root of his art.

Thus, over a period of almost half a century, Barrios has constantly made efforts to define art, in particular his own art, in works as varied as an autobiographical essay, book reviews, interviews, prologues and, of course, his novels which are meant to be the fictional manifestation of his ideas, both philosophical and aesthetic.

STYLE

Although style is also an important preoccupation of Eduardo Barrios, most critics, whilst paying lip service to the notion of Barrios as a stylist, have not generally sought to examine his stylistic qualities. Silva Castro deplores the neglect of this aspect of Barrios' work: «A mí me parece, a propósito, que no se ha estudiado eficaz y hondamente, hasta ahora, el aspecto del estilo, esto es, la elaboración de la forma de Barrios considerada como instrumento de comunicación entre autor y lector, para indicar sobre todo la evolución hacia la sencillez y la transparencia, que se observa en las obras que corren entre *Del natural* (1907) y *El hermano asno* (1922).»[27] The two words that best describe this ideal style are music and transparency (*También* I, 28). Barrios' criterion for the success of this style would be

---

[26] One remembers the discovery of *el hombre* that love (of his child, in this case) is the basis of his art. It is love that puts flesh and blood on fictional creations; it is love that humanises his literary offspring (II, 1030).

[27] *Cuadernos,* No. 78 (1963), 77. NED DAVISON echoes this complaint in «Recapitulaciones», *Sobre Eduardo Barrios y otros* (Albuquerque: Foreign Books, 1966), p. 79: «Por las virtudes estéticas que encierra, su obra admite gran variedad de enfoques críticos, e invita a proseguir un acucioso estudio de sus creaciones. La estilística de Barrios ofrece, por ejemplo, un campo casi virginal.»

the ability, on the part of the reader, to forget that he was reading,[28] and to receive naturally all the sensations and emotions that Barrios wanted to communicate to him. In an interview after the publication of *El hermano asno*, one remembers, Barrios synthesised his literary ideal as wanting to be able to write without words. Since this is not possible, however, Barrios has aimed for a prose style that is transparent and lucid, which does not distract the reader from communing with the author's work, from receiving the desired emotion. Because of our literary tradition, this is a very difficult task, since we have been conditioned to accept the «stylistic» form of writing which ends up by becoming more natural to us than the simple and the spontaneous. Since one cannot write without words, one aims for «lo simple y espontáneo», which can be attained but only with «un anhelo incesante de honradez y simplificación» (*También* I, 28). Barrios insists on this distinction between «simple» and «simplificado», since one can achieve simplicity only by working at being a «simplificado». Simplicity is the end-product of the simplifying process which contributes to the transparency of his prose. His other desideratum, music, is essential to the communicative process because without it «no hay ondas simpáticas que penetren el corazón» (I, 28).[29] This aspiration to simplicity, manifested in *El niño que enloqueció de amor* and especially in *El hermano asno*, runs parallel to his abandonment of the excessively affected style of the immature *Del natural*, much more under the Decadent wing of the Modernist movement, which achieved not the refined exquisiteness of the masters but a poor copy of it: «Lo odioso es esa fácil mentira artística, la simulación de esa "exquisitez" que no pasa de pretensión. Abomino los estilos presuntuosos; son los falsificadores de la propia verdad» (I, 28). This explains his disdain for the *tropicalista* in *Un perdido* and the charlatans like Chela Garín of *Los hombres del hombre*.

Although a successful intuitive in the field of psychology, Barrios was very much the conscious artist in the field of literature. Despite his aspiration to simplicity, he still held the literary vocation in the highest esteem, viewing the creative process in religious terms. This view of art, however, which he defined throughout his work and life, is of little value if it remains in the realm of theory.

---

[28] This is in agreement with Azorín—an aesthetic link, as well as philosophical, with the Generation of '98.

[29] JEFFERSON REA SPELL sees affinities between the literary tendencies of Barrios and the Spanish Modernist writers (Valle-Inclán, Ricardo León, Azorín, etc.) in their common esteem of the pure music of style, in his *Contemporary Spanish American Fiction* (Chapel Hill: University of North Carolina Press, 1944), p. 152.

APPLICATION OF ARTISTIC THEORIES:

The Early Period

That Barrios has generally achieved a synthesis of his literary desiderata is obvious in his novels. Torres-Ríoseco, although not always fully appreciative of the metaphysical qualities of Barrios as a writer, lauds his aesthetic merits, especially in *El hermano asno* which is without doubt the apogee of his early art: «Este estilo breve, sugerente, de una diamantina sencillez, musical sin esfuerzo visible del *Hermano asno,* es el producto de una emoción afinada en largas horas de análisis y expresada por fin con singular maestría» (*Grandes novelistas,* p. 56).

This musical transparency is hinted at in «El niño que enloqueció de amor» whose form and style are a promise of the mature aesthetics of *El hermano asno* and in keeping with the theories expressed in «También algo de mí».[30] The following representative passage is exemplary of the childlike style (repetition, use of diminutives, cataloguing by means of the simple conjunction «y») and the emotive force of the sensations and feelings that Barrios desires to communicate to the reader through the medium of the diary of the sensitive boy:

> ¡Lo que son las cosas! Ahora está viniendo muy seguido. Sale al centro casi todas las mañanas y después viene acá, y cuando yo llego del colegio, a almorzar, me la encuentro *muy sí señora en el cuarto de costura, charla y charla,* mientras mi mamá zurce la ropa de nosotros. No le he podido hablar nada de eso todavía, pero no importa: ¿qué apuro hay? ¿No me va bien así, acaso? Estoy feliz, pero bien, bien feliz. Y por las tardes me subo al departamento de los sirvientes, porque me gusta ese corredor que da a los tejados, al anochecer, y de ahí veo las copas de los árboles que asoman de los patios y oigo las campanas de San Francisco y de otras iglesias más distantes, y las copas de los árboles y las campanadas me parece que flotan en el aire. Por un lado, el cielo se mueve, y van bajando las listas de colores, que unas son como de fuego, y como oro, y rosadas, y verdes, y por el lado de la cordillera, los cerros le ponen color ladrillo primero, y después morados, y el cielo como con *una pena muy suavecita.* Yo pienso entonces en Angélica y a veces me entra una alegría inmensa, y otras veces me da esa *misma pena suavecita* del cielo... Por las mañanas me gusta el patio de las plantas. *Los pajaritos* llegan hasta la misma ventana del comedor. *Conmigo son muy valientes, los caballeros:* yo no me muevo y ellos no se vuelan. ¿Sabrán que los quiero? *Dice la Juana que qué van a saber* y que si no veo que lo que quieren es comerse las migas donde ella sacude el mantel. *El chorrito* de la pila también parece un pájaro a esa

[30] One wonders with Torres-Ríoseco if the novels were written based on his aesthetic theories or if he evolved the theories *after* the publication of the first trilogy: «La forma de esta novela ["El niño que enloqueció de amor"] está de acuerdo con la teoría estilística del autor expresada mucho más tarde [1923], no sabemos si basándose en la observación de su trabajo ya ejecutado o razonando objetivamente sobre el problema» (*Grandes novelistas,* p. 28).

hora, no sé si porque el agua sale como a *saltitos* o si por lo que suena. Todo es fresco a esa hora, como si el patio, lo mismo que las personas, se lavase y se peinase por las mañanas... (I, 156-57; my italics)

Whilst the vocabulary and construction are childlike and make for the desired simplicity, his use of repetition, alliteration, and vocalic sounds («... en el *cu*arto de *co*stura, *ch*arla y *ch*arla») conveys the ingenuous babbling of the innocent youth. Sensitive, with the intuitive art of young Charlie of *Los hombres del hombre,* whom he prefigures, *el niño* conveys the beauties of nature with a simple, crystalline sense of poetry that contrasts with the artificiality that adorned the prose of *Del natural:* «... veo las copas de los árboles que asoman de los patios y oigo las campanas de San Francisco y de otras iglesias más distantes, y las copas de los árboles y las campanadas me parece que flotan en el aire.» Though manifesting the simplicity of the child's mentality, Barrios is still close enough to Modernism to be affected not only by the musicality of the Symbolists but also by the colourism so beloved of Darío and his followers. This is not the oppressive, overwhelming colourism of the Decadent *Del natural,* but rather the spontaneous, fresh use of colours filtered through the creative process of the conscious artist, and rendered with the simplicity of the child-narrator: «Por un lado, el cielo se mueve, y van bajando *las listas de colores,* que unas son como de *fuego,* y como *oro,* y *rosadas,* y *verdes,* y por el lado de la cordillera, los cerros se ponen *color ladrillo* primero, y después *morados,* y el cielo como *con una pena muy suavecita*» (my italics). After the catalogue of colours, *el niño* makes the abrupt reference to his *angustia,* quickly stressing the metaphysical problems that underlie all of Barrios' art, and reminding us that, beyond the aesthetic preoccupations of its transparent and musical style, «El niño que enloqueció de amor» is a tragedy. After the bittersweet involuntary memories of his ideal woman Angélica, symbolically linked with the heavens, he returns to the living beauties of nature, flowers and birds, which are to be the source of Charlie's poetic revelations in *Los hombres del hombre.* He has the same curiosity about natural phenomena as Charlie («¿Sabrán que los quiero?»), the gifts of metaphor and simile, properties of the innate poet («El chorrito de la pila también parece un pájaro a esa hora, no sé si porque el agua sale como a saltitos o si por lo que suena»), but kept spontaneous by his innocent mind and his childish terminology. His diary reflects the same love of nature that is seen in Fray Lázaro's, but is unique in its freshness and spontaneity: «Todo es fresco a esa hora, como si el patio, lo mismo que las personas, se lavase y se peinase por las mañanas.» These moments of lucidity and rejoicing in the beauties of nature become increasingly rare as the tragic element of the novel begins to predominate.

The above passage is a good pointer as to Barrios' progress from the overwriting of his first work and marks the halfway stage, as it were,

10

between the appearance of *Del natural* (1907) and his truly artistic novel *El hermano asno* (1922), which is a sustained effort to achieve the difficult balance of stylistic ideals as defined in his theoretical writings. At least one critic deems Barrios to have attained this synthesis in *El hermano asno*, if not in other novels: «La verdad es que los dos ideales son difíciles de lograr, y que la dificultad sube de punto cuando se les reúne y aparca como Barrios. El análisis del estilo en atención a la transparencia y la música nos permitiría demostrar, tal vez, que las dos virtudes lograron un dinámico equilibrio en *El hermano asno*; que dominó la primera en *El niño que enloqueció de amor*, y que acaso el autor se inclinó demasiado a la segunda, esto es, el afecto musical de la prosa en *Gran señor y rajadiablos*.»[31] This judgment of *El niño que enloqueció de amor* would seem to bear out my assessment of the progression of Barrios' skills between the short novel of the apprentice and the complete balance of the mature artist in *El hermano asno*.

El hermano asno was published in 1922, almost contemporaneous with Güiraldes' lyrical *Xaimaca* (1923) which is the precursor of his great post-Modernist novel *Don Segundo Sombra* (1926). The link with Güiraldes, with whom Barrios has been associated in the minds of several critics,[32] is a pointer to the aesthetic excellence of *El hermano asno*. This post-Modernist strain is reinforced in the prologue to the novel with the reference to the poetry of Amado Nervo who, along with Gabriela Mistral, a long-time admirer of Barrios, constitutes the core of the human, neo-Romantic reaction to the excesses of the Vanguardist tendency in Modernism: «Sobre la primera página de este manuscrito, en una esquina, con una tinta muy aguada y en caracteres diminutos, como si Fray Lázaro lo hubiera querido decir al oído, había estos versos de Nervo:

'¡Oh soñado convento
donde no hubiera dogmas
sino mucho silencio! ...'»

(II, 541)

Nervo too had indulged his tastes for rhythmical innovations and precious images in his youth, but abandoned them later, preferring the simple, concise and intimate expression which characterises the best work of his mature period, i.e. the first two decades of the twentieth century, the period that influenced Barrios' *El hermano asno*. It is this vague religious feeling, mixed with a delicate sensuality and a gentle irony, that pervades the atmosphere of *El hermano asno*. The religious influences on both writers

---

[31] RAÚL SILVA CASTRO, «La obra novelesca de Eduardo Barrios», *Cuadernos*, No. 78 (1963), 77.

[32] DONALD FOGELQUIST, «Eduardo Barrios, en su etapa actual», *Revista Iberoamericana*, XVIII, No. 35 (febrero-diciembre, 1952), 20; and CARLOS HAMILTON, «La novelística de Eduardo Barrios», *Cuadernos Americanos*, LXXXV, No. 1 (enero-febrero, 1956), 289.

are similar: Thomas à Kempis *(Un perdido)*, San Juan de la Cruz, Buddha *(Un perdido)*. Nervo's mocking distrust of reason and knowledge, with the corresponding trust in intuition, is the essence of Barrios' whole fiction. Nervo's constant wavering between faith and doubt, the spirit and the flesh, his flirtation with Christian and non-Christian religions and their manifestations—mysticism and pantheism—are all the stuff of Barrios' work. *El hermano asno* is the best example of this (post-)Modernist (depending on one's view of the dating of the demise of the movement) writer's influence on Barrios. The opening quotation of Nervo unleashes a whole catalogue of ideas which characterise the novel and strengthen the bonds between Barrios and the Modernist movement, especially the last stages as represented by Nervo.

Barrios uses his favourite diary technique, this time in the form of a found manuscript, but with the subtle twist of mixing the auditory with the visual to give the effect of the reader's half-hearing (?) the written word. This technique of mixing the senses to produce an aesthetic effect was also favoured by Modernists like Nájera and Darío. In «La serenata de Schubert», for example, Nájera tries to convey in poetic terms the musical effect of a serenade by Schubert. In «De blanco» he strives for the visual effect of colour but in verse form, whilst Darío's «Sinfonía en gris mayor» is a *transposition d'art* in musical/painting terms. Casal, in his two sonnets on Prometheus and Salome, «Museo Ideal», creates the Parnassian effect of a Gauthieresque type of poetry by attempting to render the visual sensation, in poetic terms, of these two portraits by the painter Gustave Moreau. Barrios, who had learned well from his Modernist masters, never abandoned this aesthetic belief in the correspondence of the senses. Güiraldes, to whom one constantly makes comparisons, was writing in the same year: «Me parece que estoy oyendo el sol... ¿Se puede oír el sol?»[33]

This modernist delight in the senses, which in the first novel *Del natural*, was rendered almost exclusively in sexual terms, in *El hermano asno* is refined but is no less intense in its portrayal, in almost Baudelairean terms, of this correspondence of the senses. This preoccupation with sensationism is expressed (in non-sexual terms) in the opening pages, setting the mood of the novel: «Hay olor a tierra que se moja, a retoños que se refrescan...» (II, 542). «La mañana está fresca, centelleante y pura, como la voz de un pájaro. He abierto mi ventana y mis puertas de par en par, y entran olores jóvenes que aspiro hasta el fondo de mis entrañas» (II, 545). By cataloguing the descriptions, Fray Lázaro brings all the senses into play to create a sensational hymn to the beauties of nature, still pure and fresh («Todo entraba nuevo por mis sentidos limpios y ávidos», II, 546) that almost reaches the heights of Nervo's pantheism: «Y el sol resbala su tibieza entre mis dedos, la derrama por mis facciones inmóviles, pasa a través de mis

---

[33] *Xaimaca* (Buenos Aires: Losada, 1944 edition), p. 121. See also pp. 14, 21.

párpados y toma posesión de mis venas como una divinidad del bienestar»
(II, 546). This strong pagan joy in the senses, characterised by Modernism,
is tempered only by the fraternal Franciscan attitude to the sun, ancient
source of life and worthy of worship: «Yo quisiera estar hoy allí desnudo
bajo el sol, vestido sólo de juventud... ¡Bendito humano sol, suave y ro-
busto, que haces brotar el lirio en torno a la fuente y le encrespas de ardor
los pétalos!» (II, 607). Even when the sensual does appear to be breaking
through the surface, it is moderated and refined into the crystalline prose
that is consistent with his desire for musical transparency, e.g. in his
description of the beautiful young girl, the temptress María Mercedes: «Aquel
óvalo puro y prolongado en punta de almendra; aquel mismo pelo, broncí-
neo y a ondas, y su misma garganta, suave, alta y llena, rítmica en los movi-
mientos; y aun el color de nardo y las cálidas ojeras que envuelven los ojos
pesados de pestañas» (II, 546). There is no doubt that this is a sensuous
description, but the limpid prose, with its *esdrújulos,* alliterative plosives,
and liquid sounds, purges the passage of the concupiscence typical of the
early *Del natural* and gives the prose a feeling of *sensualidad suave.*

The introductory verses of Nervo, taken from his poem «El convento»,
provide a useful point of departure for an aesthetic study of the novel
and its relation with Modernism, especially in that movement's later stages.
The role of the convent itself is a significant one in Barrios' philosophy of
life. As Ned Davison has pointed out (*Eduardo Barrios,* p. 140), the convent,
like *el rincón* of *el niño,* is a sanctuary to which his tormented protagonist
can flee to find peace—an extension of *el castillo interior* of Rodó, the
key Modernist prose writer. The country house to which *el hombre* and
his son escape from the city and its false artists is also a place of refuge.
The haven of the monastery, «donde no hubiera dogma», underlines the
anti-rationalism of Barrios, especially in the field of religion, where he
echoes, as we have seen in Chapter 2, the Pascalian point of view. This
central baroque struggle between heart and head is reflected in the anguished
torment of Fray Lázaro whose intellectual pride prevents him from achieving the Franciscan simplicity required by his order. Outside of the religious
field too, simplicity is the key, being the essence of poetry, granted only
to the select few like Charlie. Nervo's poems «Simplicitas» and «El poeta
niño» are self-explanatory, pointing the obvious parallels between the two
writers.

If Nervo's second line highlights another theme of the novel from the
religious and philosophical point of view («se burlaba... de la razón y de
la ciencia, confiando sólo en la intuición»),[34] the third line indicates a very
important feature of the novel, evident not only in Nervo but later Modernists
like Enrique González Martínez (who earned the reputation of wringing the

---

[34] CARLOS GARCÍA PRADA, *Poetas modernistas hispanoamericanos* (Madrid: Ed. Cultura Hispánica, 1956), p. 194.

swan's neck), viz. quietism. After the peak of Modernist anguish in writers like Silva and Darío, Nervo and González Martínez sought to find a solution to the enigma of life and a meaning for existence by way of a more spiritual philosophy which was a vague mixture of Christianity and Buddhism, mysticism and pantheism, in which the human, animal and natural were to achieve a kind of super-terrestrial harmony with the spiritual, in its broadest sense. Nervo's «Expectación» illustrates the hope and the waiting, mixed with the quietist confidence of union with the supernatural:

> Siento que algo solemne se aproxima, y me hallo todo trémulo; mi alma de pavor llena está. Que se cumpla el Destino, que Dios dicte su fallo. Mientras yo, de rodillas, oro, *espero* y *me callo,* para oír la palabra que el Abismo dirá...

Apart from highlighting the quietist philosophy of Nervo, this poem is an interesting example of the religious/pagan ambivalence and the contradictory Romantic synthesis of *Dios/Destino/Abismo.* «Espacio y tiempo», based on a quotation of Santa Teresa, is a fairy-tale adaptation of mystical doctrine in which the soul becomes an enchanted princess. «El castaño no sabe», a hymn to the mysteries of the universe and nature, ends with typical theosophist terminology, reminiscent of Barrios' «El Teósofo» in *Un perdido:*

> [los versos], como el árbol, la espiga, el sol, la rosa cumplieron ya, prestando su expresión armoniosa a la Inefable Esencia, que es, ha sido y será!

It is in the title and refrain of «Callemos...», however, that Nervo urges the virtue of silence, by means of which we may penetrate the mysteries of the universe:

> En el callar hay posibilidades
> sin límite...

González Martínez develops this quietism of Nervo, imposing even more pantheistic overtones. If «Psalle et Sile» underlines the silence («No turbar el silencio de la vida, / ésa es la ley...»), then «Busca en todas las cosas» points to the solution of the enigma of life to be found in nature:

> Busca en todas las cosas el oculto sentido;
> lo sabrás cuando logres comprender su lenguaje;
> cuando escuches el alma colosal del paisaje
> y los ayes lanzados por el árbol herido...

The mood and meaning of these quietist poems were not lost on Eduardo Barrios, and they illustrate just how much *El hermano asno* is in the quietist tradition of these later Modernists. González Martínez's «Viento sagrado» exudes the Franciscan spirit of Barrios' novel not only aesthetically but theologically:

Hará que los humanos,
en solemne perdón, unan las manos
y el hermano conozca a sus hermanos.

This quotation resumes the whole struggle of the intellectually-proud Fray Lázaro who cannot come down to the level of his fellow-monks. Fray Rufino's simplicity, saintliness, and ability to commune with God's most lowly creatures, the animals, is reflected in these verses of González Martínez:

no cejará en su vuelo
hasta lograr unir, en un consuelo
inefable, la tierra con el cielo;

hasta que el hombre, en celestial arrobo,
hable a las aves y convenza al lobo;
hasta que deje impreso
en las llagas de Lázaro su beso;
hasta que sepa darse, en ardorosas
ofrendas, a los hombres y a las cosas,
y en su lecho de espinas sienta rosas;
hasta que la escondida
entraña, vuelta manantial de vida,
sangre de caridad como una herida...

These lines, which sum up the anguished struggle of Fray Lázaro and Fray Rufino, constitute a simple gloss on a complex novel.

If quietism is one of the keynotes of the novel, as suggested by Nervo's prologue, it is Barrios' subtle use of this feature that raises the novel to its deserved position. Rather than presenting a mere series of quietist descriptions, Barrios heightens the effect of the quietism by fusing it with the metaphysical (to highlight the anguish of the protagonist) and rendering it in terms of the aesthetic (so that *forma* and *fondo* become one). That Barrios sets out to convey the effect of silence, after the manner of Nervo and González Martínez, is evident:

El silencio que hay ahora en ellos [los claustros] no es fácil definirlo. Es una quietud externa y una agitación interior. Oprime, intranquiliza. Los pasos resuenan demasiado; dan tumbos sus ecos por las galerías. Ya no acompañan los cuadros; lúgubres, suelen parecer una amenaza entre las sombras. Los patios, como agrandados, no amparan; impulsan a correr hasta la celda, para sentir la protección de las cuatro paredes reunidas y la compañía de las cosas familiares.
    ¡Y cómo crece el misterio en los jardines agrestes! Este misterio de la vida recóndita, que penetra, frío, y muerde las entrañas. (II, 558)

On its most superficial level, the descriptive, the passage depicts the emptiness of monastery cloisters and the corresponding silence that one associates with the monastic life. On this plane it is an effective portrayal of the religious scene. *El hermano asno,* however, as we have seen, is more than a novel of ecclestiastical *costumbrismo,* and Barrios is no mere painter of religious manners. As a commentator on life, Barrios is suggesting that beneath the surface of the *quietud externa* there is to be found an *agitación interior,* symptomatic of the anguish of the protagonist and indicative of the inherent tragic elements to be developed in the novel. The too noisy footsteps echoing in the galleries conjure up images of vaults and death. Even the portraits seem gloomy, constituting a threat in the shadows. This Romantic concept of an inimical force mirroring the soul of the hero is a far cry from the expectant optimism of Nervo and González Martínez, whose quietism Barrios knew, appreciated and imitated on suitable occasions. This passage early in the novel depicts the threatening silence to convey the troubled soul of Lázaro. This is a good example of Barrios' use of the atmosphere to create by just a few pregnant words *(lúgubres, amenaza, sombra)* the mood of the novel. The final paragraph takes up the theme of the mystery of nature and the hidden life, but it is a life that penetrates and gnaws at one's entrails. This pessimistic view of life is a reminder that, though Barrios profited from the colourism, quietism and musicality of the Modernists, he never departed from his basically Romantic premise that life is tragic. If Barrios is a stylist, he never allows his stylistic excellence to run away from the philosophical content. In fact, it is the perfect marriage of the content and the form, as we see so often in Barrios, that produces his best prose. It is only when he places his aesthetics perfectly at the service of his metaphysics that he hits the mark, as in *El hermano asno.*

In another passage from the same section he renews the theme of silence, this time coupled with its melancholy sister, solitude:

> Y en todas partes silencio y soledad.
>
> Sólo en las pinturas quedan formas humanas: rostros orantes y contemplativos, imágenes de monjes que inmovilizan sobre la tela el fervor atormentado o la paz seráfica. Allá, un cielo turbulento, una cruz borrosa, unos miembros lívidos y unas llagas oscuras. Más lejos, en trofeo, los instrumentos del martirio: la lanza, la escala y la caña con la esponja de hiel y vinagre. Donde se mire, lienzos, lienzos en profusión, antiguos lienzos de mano cándida, que representan un milagro y tienen, tras los personajes principales del cuadro, una multitud que presencia, pintada sin relieve y amontonándose en una perspectiva equivocada. Y todo entre tonos que fueron brillantes e ingenuos y son hoy púrpuras opacas, negros cenicientos, blancos de rancia cera. (II, 558)

In this skilfully blended passage of art, nature and religion, Barrios achieves the overall aesthetic effect of silent loneliness/lonely silence to underscore the reality of Fray Lázaro's mental suffering. The paintings contain the only human beings present, the monks, immobilised on the canvas in poses of *fervor atormentado* or *paz seráfica,* symbolising the Rufino/Lázaro contrast, and highlighting Lázaro's spiritual dilemma. Nature reflects not only the mood of Fray Lázaro but also of the captive monks, in the turbulent sky, which also manifests, in true Symbolist nuance, the religious outward signs of the convent—a cross (albeit *borrosa*), Christ's limbs (albeit *lívidos*) and the wounds (albeit *oscuras*). The natural religious imagery, seen as through a glass darkly, leads on to the concrete instruments of the Crucifixion, the lance, the reed, and the vinegar-soaked sponge. The whole sky is a miraculous profusion of canvases in varying colours depicting the Calvary scene, but now in colours of dark purple, ashen black and off-white. This passage is a supreme indication of Barrios' ability to take the post-Modernist theme of quietism and to graft on, or, better still, infuse, his own underlying anguish by means of art (the paintings), nature (the sky, the clouds, etc.) and religion (the cross, the reed, the lance, the sponge) to create the desired effect of silence and solitude that would convey the mood of Fray Lázaro, the tone of the novel, and Barrios' version of the world consistent with his philosophical findings.

Fray Lázaro, like Barrios, however, was capable of escaping occasionally from this cold, empty silence, especially via the garden, the orchard or even the church, all of which at various times provide him with a quietist haven, far from «esta vacuidad helada, envolvente y angustiadora» (II, 558). The sun-drenched choir, for example, presents a colourful contrast with the dark cloisters, though filled with the same silence:

> El sol, un sol caliente de atardecer, caía tendido por el vitral policromo, y nuestros sayales castaños se teñían de reflejos violetas, anaranjados, azules. Yo sentía el color sobre mi brazo, sobre mi nuca. Los frailes, en fila delante de la baranda, permanecíamos inmóviles, saturados de unción. Poco a poco, nuestros pechos habíanse ido vaciando de conciencia, aligerándose en una dulzura que nos elevaba. Allá, abajo, lejos, desde la tarima del altar mayor, el humo del incensario, puesto ante el Santísimo, empinábase quieto, delgado, recto hasta lo alto; empinábanse las llamas de los cirios, y nuestros cuerpos, ingrávidos, diríase que adelgazados, como las llamas de los cirios y como el humo votivo, empinábanse también hacia Dios. Era todo una oración armónica, que subía en el grave recogimiento del templo cerrado, inmenso y hueco, lleno de silencio, de penumbra y de santidad. (II, 559)

The sun, filtered through the stained-glass windows, plays strange tricks with the brown habits of the monks, producing shades of violet, orange and blue, in contrast with the blacks and greys of the outside cloisters. In this setting the trappings of religion are the joyful candles and incense, whose smoke even rises quietly, whilst the flames of the candles burn brightly. The overall effect is one of a harmonious prayer rising to God, within the confines of the closed (compared to the open cloisters), immense, hollow choir of the church, peopled by happy human beings (cf. the loneliness of the cloisters). If this scene is also one of silence, it is a holy silence. In this passage Barrios again demonstrates his feeling for, if not religion, at least the poetry of the liturgy and the underlying emotion which is essential to worship, and which equates divinity with poetry.

In this parallel passage Barrios makes use of nature (the sun), art (the stained-glass windows, the architecture of the choir) and religion (the candles, robes, incense, etc.) to produce a result that is totally aesthetic, creates the desired mood of quietism, and prepares for a metaphysical crisis in the passage that follows:

> La columna de humo, ya en la altura, se torcía en ancha comba, para venir hacia el coro atravesando el vacío. Una golondrina se había metido en la nave y cortaba en vuelos violentos la senda de humo, para ir a chocar desatentada contra las filas de canes retorcidos que sostienen la gran techumbre plana de la iglesia. (II, 559-60)

The swallow, which disturbs the peace and tranquility of the scene, is a symbol of the return of Lázaro's past life in the guise of María Mercedes, the sister of his ex-fiancée.[35] Once again Barrios demonstrates that he is no mere picture-painter, rather that he utilises his aesthetics to prepare the way for the tragedy which constitutes the heart of the novel. The disturbing, half-glimpsed vision of the girl becomes reality and acts as the catalyst that is to initiate not only the spiritual evolution of Fray Lázaro and Fray Rufino, but also to set in motion the events that produce the climax which brings about the tragic conclusion of the novel. The setting is idyllic: «Hace una tarde luminosa. En el cielo, muy azul y muy lejano, vagaba la luna, esa blanquísima luna diurna, delgada, transparente e incompleta, como una hostia desgastada» (II, 563). This is an excellent example of Barrios' stated desire to write without words, to create a simple, transparent prose. As in all his best work, he links the mood to the prose, creating the atmosphere and the effect through the language, which is used both as the vehicle and the force. The language used *(luminosa, lejano, vagaba, blanquísima, delgada, transparente, incompleta)* is so true in its essence that it can be used to describe the natural setting, the mood, even the prose itself. It is the perfect blend of form and content that one cannot separate. Each of the words is the perfect, the only, vehicle for rendering the effect that Barrios is trying to attain. The form becomes, in fact, *is* the content; the vehicle *is* the force in a total fusion of the external and the internal. Carlos Magis has tried to express this phenomenon thus: «la distinción entre "fondo" y "forma", o sea entre "verbalización" y contenido es falsa—e inoperante—, ya que la obra literaria es—como ya lo vio la Estilística—un todo en el cual el "modo de experiencia" y el "modo de expresión" (verbalización y contenido) funcionan estrechamente interrelacionados y determinándose mutuamente» (p. 10). The brightness of the afternoon combined with the blueness of the sky and the distance of the burgeoning white moon, slender, transparent, not fully mature, sets the tone. The unusual image of

---

[35] Cf. the same technique in «El niño que enloqueció de amor», with *el niño's* thoughts of Angélica (I, 156-57).

the young moon as a half-consumed host conjures up memories of Chateaubriand's inverted analogy of forest trees looking like cathedral pillars. That Barrios should have selected the liturgical image of the host is surprising but entirely fitting, reminding us of the monastic setting and indeed bringing us back to the religious reality in what appears to be profane prose. The female figure of the moon (as opposed to the male sun) in pagan mythology [36] is associated with Diana the huntress, Venus the goddess of love, and looks forward to the appearance of the temptress, María Mercedes: «¡Ah!, y allá, sobre la trasera de una casa, en un corredor alto con baranda, completando el conjunto de la pampa vacía, de la palmera y del cielo, se divisaba una muchacha. Su traje blanco flameaba. Y era una visión leve, leve y diáfana, como la luna en el día» (II, 563). The brightness of the day and the whiteness of the moon are accentuated by the whiteness of her dress. The word *flameaba* is pregnant with ambiguity in that it suggests both the beginnings of sensuality flaring up in Mario/Lázaro as well as the provocative flapping or fluttering of the girl's skirt. The transparent brightness of the day is strengthened by the vision of the girl, and her light and diaphanous qualities which link her to the moon with its similar qualities. Thus we have the double set of images of the moon and the host, and the moon and the girl; therefore, by extension, the daring image of the adolescent, blooming girl likened to the partly-consumed host—with all the corollaries relating to body and consummation, and the changeable application of adjectives to describe the moon, the girl, and the host.[37] The two passages, with the images to be drawn by inference, are skilfully linked by a parallel, contrasting adjectivisation *(luna diurna/luna en el día; transparente/diáfana; blanco/blanquísima)* that heightens the effect of whiteness and transparency not only of the three images but of the whole atmosphere of the scene, the tone of the passage, and the youth of the girl,[38] played out against the contrasting

[36] Cf. a similar Mayan legend which is the basis of Asturias' *Mulata de tal*.

[37] This daring ambiguity of religious/secular imagery is reminiscent of the mystical poetry of San Juan de la Cruz, whose work Barrios admired, especially the possible profane interpretation of poems like «Canciones entre el Alma y el Esposo», the tone of which is passionate and physical. See *Spanish Lyrics of the Golden Age*, ed. P. D. TETTERBORN (London: Bell, 1952), p. 36.

[38] See R. O. JONES' introduction to his *Poems of Góngora* (Cambridge: Cambridge University Press, 1966), p. 9, for an illuminating discussion of an analogous technique in Góngora, that Barrios would have known and appreciated: «his intensified use of the commonplace similes... to create out of them a poetic language of his own». This characteristic, coupled with his ability for compression that leads to interchangeability, is at the root of Góngora's mastery of imagery. In both writers the particular is merged in the generic, the universal. What Professor Jones has said of Góngora can be applied equally to Barrios: «He seems in his "generic" imagery to be attempting to capture the essence that lies behind the particular.»
On one occasion (I, 620) Fray Rufino is described as «tan espontáneo y comunicativo, tan diáfano en su simplicidad de niño», a quotation that reinforces my point that Barrios' essential adjectivisation (e.g. *transparente, espontáneo, diáfano*, etc.) can be applied to the concrete, the abstract, mood, atmosphere, prose, language, quality,

Modernist blue of the sky, with the titillating effect of the *flameante* skirt and the nascent sexuality (still refined) which her presence provokes in Mario/Lázaro (II, 564).

This suggestion of sensuality provoked by the Romantic vision becomes slightly more pronounced in their next meeting, though again the tone is still diaphanous: « ¡Qué niña es! ¡Y qué bien se veía! Tan *clara,* tan *diáfana,* de pie tras la baranda; tan *fina* y *ligera* sobre el muro pesado y áspero. Con aquellas ropas de verano, contra el cielo *fulgurante* de *luz,* ponía un *destello* rosa en el aire. Hablaba, y su voz también era un *destello.* Y eran pequeños *destellos blancos* los *jazmines* que desde la mata miraban a la altura» (II, 567; my italics). His awareness of the summer clothes, the image of the rose (long a symbol of love, youth and beauty from Catullus to Ronsard) and the exotic jasmine flower create the atmosphere whereby nature, if not the girl, is charged with a kind of sparkling and glinting (*fulgurante de luz,* the repetition of *destello*). Although Lázaro rejects these new feelings provoked by the girl, the process of self-deception seems to be well under way: « ¡Oh, todo el azul del cielo se va tiñendo de rosa! » (II, 574). Self-delusion is linked to self-analysis in Fray Lázaro's case, and the rest of the novel is the history of his self-inflicted torture and the physical manifestations of insomnia. This insomnia of Lázaro, caused by «el murciélago del remordimiento» (II, 608), serves to highlight the tranquility and quietness of the rest of the convent, buried in a soporific haze: «*Duerme* todo el Convento; *duermen* los monjes, las bóvedas y la fronda; *duermen* la iglesia y los jardines, y el pozo y la campana; *duerme* la tierra, y en estas noches de otoño, cuando ya con el crepúsculo la bruma se levanta, *duerme* también el cielo. Apenas en algún crucero, entre dos patios *dormidos, vela el ojo amarillo de una lámpara;* pero aun su mirada es *un sopor,* reflejo que sobre un marco desdorado *se aletarga* y *se apaga* de *la tiniebla* de una tela antigua» (II, 608; my italics). Barrios creates the quietist effect in this passage by his emphasis on sleep and the repetition of the verb *dormir* in its various forms. Part of the effect is produced by the reversed order of Barrios' catalogue. Rather than listing the single sleeping objects and building up to the climax of the whole convent sleeping, Barrios states the whole, then lists the parts, beginning with the men and ascending all the way to the heavens. This is the tranquil, Wordsworthian side of Romantic nature as opposed to the tormented, Byronic side, as depicted in the cloister scene. He underlines the hazy, sleepy atmosphere by reference to autumn («season of mists...»), *la bruma* and *el crepúsculo.* As the black dot on the white canvas heightens the overall effect of white,

---

so that the words, rather than just becoming vehicles of expression, acquire a mystical force and become part of the effect rather than merely the instrument. Hence his repetition of these key adjectives like «transparent» or «diaphanous» which may seem rare qualifiers of an abstract quality like simplicity—or of a person.

so too does Barrios place, between *dos patios dormidos,* the yellow eye of a lamp which can muster up no more than a drowsy look, a mere reflection on a tarnished gold frame, before fading in its lethargy and being extinguished against the darkness of the black canvas of night.[39]

Having used the visual (the single weak beam of the lamp) to highlight the quietness of the dark night of the convent, Barrios, so tuned in to the senses, now utilises the auditory to reinforce the same atmosphere: «el reloj del campanario dio la una. La campanada única pasó a través de la niebla, por sobre los tejados, como un alma, y como otra alma que penara inmóvil flotaba la torre entre la bruma que luces de la calle emblanquecían» (II, 608). The single stroke of the clock tower, like the single beam of light, heightens the silence, before fading into the fog. Barrios' rare but authentic image of the sound of the bell making its way like a soul through the fog, whilst another spirit, the motionless tower, floats hazily in the mist rendered white by the street lamps, makes the whole scene vaguely spiritual, in terms appropriate to the convent setting.

Well aware of the aesthetic attributes of the senses, Barrios closes the scene with the olfactory, to add to the visual and auditory: «palpita la oscuridad, entibia el aire, se hacen más medrosos los sonidos. Y sobre todo predominan los olores. La sala que fue de los terceros y hoy hemos llenado con los trastos en desuso, a cada ráfaga evoca las vitelas miniadas de los viejos salterios polvorientos, y facistoles, arcas y credencias penetrados de aceite y de polillas, y brocados deshechos que el hilo de oro oxida... En la noche este perfume oprime» (II, 608).

In his desire to convey the quietness of the convent setting and the tranquil atmosphere fitting to the novelesque background, Barrios does not hesitate to use and reuse certain situations and expressions. Since his aim is to purge his prose of pretentiousness and seek the essential simplicity, corresponding to the monastic life, that would produce the desired effect of writing without words, Barrios is not averse to utilising frequently key concepts or words to convey, for example, silence or transparency, so vital to his prose. Since it is the final impact that he wishes to attain, his prose becomes the effect. As we have seen, if the end product is sleep, then Barrios will use forms of the verbs, adjectives, synonyms and images to convey the soporific atmosphere of a drowsy evening in a sleepy convent. He adopts the same technique to render the effect of whiteness. In his search for clarity and simplicity he frequently resorts to *transparente, diáfano* and such words that describe the ethereal quality not only of his prose but of the persons, moods, and abstracts that he wishes to depict. The following passage, with the essential words italicised, is a good example of the desired effect:

---

[39] This is a good example of Barrios' artistic technique borrowed from painting, as discussed in the first part of this chapter.

Además, esta tarde *clara* de domingo el invierno parece detenido. Sólo en el aire una *transparencia azul* y un *blando bienestar* en el *silencio.* Y conforme el Convento se ha ido *aquietando,* ha empezado a bajar sobre mi corazón la piedad de Dios y a encender mi ternura por el hermano conturbado. (II, 619)

The clearness and the silence of the day are achieved by the clarity and simplicity of the cumulative effect of the language which reinforces the feeling of quietude and the diaphanous quality of the natural phenomena selected. As always in Barrios, the aesthetic effect created does not exist for its own sake, but is closely bound to, and prepares the way for, the metaphysical crisis that follows—the mental break-up of the saintly Fray Rufino, whose sin of pride, as the Capuchin vision points out, has to be expiated. That Fray Rufino uses as the instrument of his self-debasement the sin of lust, concretised in the girl María Mercedes, the source of Fray Lázaro's problems, is the stuff of Barrios' skilful psychological development.

In the closing pages of the novel when the two strands of the evolution of Fray Lázaro and Fray Rufino come together and fuse in the attempted rape of the girl and Fray Lázaro's acceptance of the blame, the monastery still sleeps on in tranquil fashion: «*Dormía* el monasterio y arriba el espacio tremolaba como el interior de una campana *en reposo.* Una campana inmensa, *de azul* y *de noche.* La iglesia estampaba su lomo negro sobre el cielo estrellado. Me fui quedando poco a poco *inmóvil, suspenso.* Y los *sueños* han venido, *calladamente,* por los senderos *invisibles* de la noche *callada*» (II, 625; my italics). The familiar allusion to sleep, night, quiet, silence and the recurrence of the bell motif (this time *una campana en reposo*), the motionlessness of the protagonist, all contribute to the sense of stillness, coupled with expectation. Once again Barrios paints a beautiful quietist scene, beautiful in itself but significant for its preparatory function in leaving the way open for a vital statement on the importance of emotion in life. In this case the arrivals are, logically, the nocturnal children, the silent dreams coming along the invisible paths of the still night. Like truth, and religion, the dreams themselves cannot be retained. However, when the images of the dreams depart, we are left with the emotion of them: «al irse, nos dejan siempre su emoción. Se ha desvaído toda imagen, pero la emoción permanece» (II, 625). It is significant that Barrios should have used his final quietist scene as a means of underlying the importance of emotion in life. As Barrios bluntly states «¿Y algo hay que sea más que la emoción?» (II, 625).

If *El hermano asno* is, as Gabriela Mistral puts it, «el libro de prosa más nítida y suave que se haya escrito en Chile» (Prologue, p. 12), Barrios has not sacrificed his content to form. *El hermano asno* is, as I have tried to illustrate, the exemplary novel of aesthetics put to the service of metaphysics. Rather than striving after the exotic and the rare, Barrios has sought a language, devoid of ostentation and stridency, that matches the tone and mood of his novel. If simplicity, music, and transparency are the keynotes of his theory, the prose of El hermano asno is the living example of it. Gabriela Mistral had a clear view of what Barrios was trying to achieve:

> Una prosa como la hoja larga del helecho, flexible, exquisita y suave. Repulsión por lo brillante y lo ruidoso del lenguaje. El lenguaje común, pero depurado de la escoria y podado de todo exceso. Una especie de franciscanismo artístico. En la frase, breve siempre, se recoge el paisaje o un estado de alma íntegra y ardientemente. El arte se esfuma. *La transparencia de la palabra es tal, que hace olvidar la palabra.* Así el cristal límpido de la ilusión de su inexistencia y se cree mirar directamente, cuando se mira a través de él. *Desaparece el estilo por perfección del estilo. Y desaparece el artista.* (Prologue, p. 12; my italics)

Mistral grasped perfectly, and expressed even more adequately than Barrios himself, his aesthetic aims realised so clearly in El hermano asno. Maeterlinck and Carlyle have praised silence. Barrios has made of it not only a virtue but also a quality so alive that it becomes audible in this novel. The following passage is perhaps an extreme example of Barrios' technique of rendering the purity of spirit by purity of language, but the mixture of key concepts/words of clarity, freshness, fineness and transparency, the smooth sensations rendered alliteratively by means of a whole series of liquid [s]s, produces a rare union of vehicle and force:

> Esto es la felicidad, Señor, una *limpieza* de fuera y dentro, y sentir el alma *fresca y transparente,* hecha *un cristal* muy *fino* al cual llegan *suavemente sensaciones suaves,* semejantes a *seres* simpáticos que se nos aparecen sin que los esperemos y con el rostro sonriente y *claro.* (II, 545; my italics)

The conscious and careful selection of words like *limpieza, transparente, cristal* and *fino* indicates the hard-earned simplicity for which Barrios strove to produce the desired crystalline prose. The repetitive litany of [s] sounds which may seem excessive and forced in other writers is Barrios' attempt to produce the overall musical effect, pleasant to the ear if not to the eye. Barrios was too much of an artist not to have been aware of the possible visual anomaly of the passage. However, his desire for the total euphonious effect overrides any formal considerations. If his language is limpid and musical, creating the spiritual, poetic effect desired, it will have melted into the substance of the prose to the extent that form and content will be indistinguishable.

This blurring, fusing, melting technique that Barrios borrowed from the Symbolists via the Modernists, is an effect that he aims for not only in the complete picture (the force) but also in the language, the use of colours, etc. (the vehicle)—hence his delight in times of day like *crepúsculo, atardecer, amanecer,* his use of *bruma, neblina,* his tendency to filter scenes through clouds, dust, his fondness for words like *borroso, oscuro, lívido* (as applied to the sky, for example, II, 558), and his feeling for mixed colours, especially black and white which produce grey and charcoal *(gris, ceniciento)*. The following passage, which looks at first glance like a typical Modernist hymn to colourism, never emerges out of the shadows of black, white and brown:

> Sobre la tierra *parda,* lucían el color de la mula *blanca,* el sayal *castaño* y el perro *negro; borrábase* el pollino *ceniciento,* y tres nubes de *polvo* iban estelando el aire... Permanecí hasta que hubo fresco y las *sombras* de las casas, tendidas ya sobre todo el solar, se *confundieron* con el velo del *crepúsculo.* (II, 576-77; my italics)

Sandwiched between the dark, brownish-greyish earth and the dust clouds, anything of even minimum colour (white, black, brown) is soon obliterated *(borrábase, se confundieron)* by growing dusk.

These colours, however, need not always be depressing. Depending on the mood of the protagonist and the natural phenomena, which are usually linked, the muted colours can have a soothing effect. In the following passage, for example, neither the convent nor Fray Lázaro is at all gloomy despite the rain:

> Yo miro por mi ventana el patio enorme y los claustros *sombríos.* Una luz *cenicienta* lo *suaviza* todo: *el verde frío* de los arbustos, *el tono* de las pinturas y *el oro* envejecido de sus marcos. Aun *el castaño* de los sayales *se vela suavemente de gris.* (II, 605; my italics)

Using basically the same dark colours *(ceniciento, gris, castaño),* Barrios gives them a soothing quality *(suaviza, suavemente)* which softens the usually bright green (here depicted as *verde frío*) and gold (here *oro envejecido*) and gives an overall effect of softness and tranquility.

The same so-called drab colours can be used also to produce an impression of simplicity. In the following passage one can see how Barrios takes the blacks, whites and greys to create not just the effect of simplicity but simplicity itself—in all the senses that Barrios desired: the Franciscan simplicity of poverty, obedience and chastity, reflected in the austerity of the cell. This is achieved by using simple words. The linguistic simplicity creates a spirit of simplicity (apart from the religious) and a tone, mood and atmosphere that bespeak simplicity. All three melt into one, making it difficult to ascertain where the linguistic, religious and ambiental begin. In brief, Barrios creates the essence of simplicity:

> Es *pura* mi celda, grata su *austeridad* monacal. Un cuarto *alargado* y *alto, blanco* y *negro.* Cuatro muros *de cal sin un cuadro,* siete *vigas desnudas,* y *el enladrillado,* que los años han puesto *gris.* Sobre *la blancura* de la pared pende a mi cabecera la cruz de *pino, negra* y *sin efigie,* y con ella mi palma bendita, mi rama de olivo y mi *cirio* de la buena *muerte.* (II, 601-02)

In this beautifully stark passage Barrios achieves the maximum of effect with the technique almost of a painter's black and white sketch. As in his description of the sleeping monastery, he opens with the general description of his cell (pure and austere), before listing the particular details. Architecturally also, simplicity is the keynote—high and long, black and white. The cell is elemental in its construction, wood and stone, with the beams bare and the bricks turned grey by time. The whitewashed walls are highlighted by the black of the cross (also wooden) which does not even have a figure of the crucified Christ. The sparseness of decoration is heightened by the underlining of the lack of pictures *(sin un cuadro)* on the walls and the lack of a figure on the crucifix *(sin efigie)*. This technique of pointing out the absence of pictures and figures highlights the even barer appearance of the cell, when the impression on the reader is already total starkness and austerity. The painting is rounded out by the triple manifestation of the religious office—the blessed palm, the olive branch and the candle. Lest the reader be carried away with Romantic notions of escapism in the monastery cell, Barrios reminds us with a parting shot that the candle is for death, albeit the happy one that Fray Lázaro craves. As always, Barrios returns not only to the objective of the religious vocation in this novel but to the business of life itself which inevitably ends in death.

Religion, for Barrios, is not always gloomy nor are his monastic colours always muted, as we observed in the passage describing the sun-filled choir (II, 559). One of the attractions for Barrios of the church is the beauty of the liturgy, architecture, and music. In several passages of *El hermano asno,* and throughout his fiction (for example, *Un perdido*), he describes the beauties of religion with an almost Modernist élan, in the sense that he praised the aesthetic side of religion, the beauty of the ceremony, the symbolism and the poetry of the liturgy, with its basic underlying emotion. In passages like the following Barrios does for religion what Darío did for aesthetics, but in reverse. He elevates religion to the level of art:

> Y está hermosísima la iglesia, Señor. Les hubiera gustado. Hinchada de música y de incienso, trémula de lirios y de gente. El altar mayor, su retablo hasta arriba, y ante él todo el estado, fulguran de luces, raso blanco y orfebrería de oro. Los oficiantes parecen joyas enormes que rutilan: se hunden sus cabezas entre los indumentos rígidos e incandescentes, que bajan en pliegues acampa-nados; giran sus siluetas cónicas, y a cada giro fosforecen mil carbunclos sobre el tisú. (II, 617-18)

By means of the trappings of religion (music, incense, flowers, etc.) and the emotion of the congregation, Barrios composes a harmonious hymn which rises like the incense and the music to the heavens. The high altar is positively aglow with lights, gleaming with gold of the most intricate handiwork. Even the celebrants in their brilliant robes appear like jewels glittering in bright array. Seldom have the Modernists themselves equalled this literary *Te Deum,* with its incandescent, phosphorescent images, its exquisite jewellery and finely crafted materials, its gleaming golds and whites, its beautiful liturgical poetry—a tribute to the colourist and musical canons that Barrios learned from his Modernist mentors, both early (Darío and his followers) and later (Nervo and González Martínez).

There is no doubt that *El hermano asno,* to prolong the Modernist metaphor, is the gem of Barrios' work. In this novel, as in no other, he has achieved the perfect blend of form and content, symbolised in his search for the elusive combination of music, transparency and simplicity. It is in the effective use of these qualities, both as vehicle and force, that he managed, as Gabriela Mistral so admirably states it, to attain the perfection of style which makes style disappear. In simple and crystalline prose he has written a quietist novel which has its roots in later Modernism and perhaps even further back in Spanish mysticism. Barrios, of course, had many spiritual fathers as he was wont to confess, but *El hermano asno* is truly a beautifully-conceived, original novel [40] which reaches the heights of poetic tragedy: «El autor... ha grabado hondamente un fuerte poema humano y eterno, en que sus emociones de amor iluminado y sus terrores religiosos ultraterrenos se conjugaron para dar a la novela el temblor de un poema y la sombría fatalidad de una tragedia clásica» (Hamilton, p. 286). Without doubt one can say that *El hermano asno* is the aesthetic peak of Barrios' first creative period. With hindsight one can add that he never again achieved this perfect co-ordination of all the parts that go to make up a great work of art.

The Later Period

After a silence of twenty years Eduardo Barrios took the first faltering steps of a return towards the literary life in 1944 with the publication of *Tamarugal,* which, as we have seen, had little artistic merit, though it is important from the metaphysical point of view, being the first attempt of Barrios to formulate his new outlook on life. *Gran señor y rajadiablos,* which developed the shift in sensibility hinted at in *Tamarugal,* was a huge best-seller, more on account of its popular creole elements than for its aesthetic qualities.

That is not to say that *Gran señor y rajadiablos* is totally devoid of fine writing or stylistic prose. One cannot agree, however, with Donald Fogelquist in his description of the novel: «En *Gran señor y rajadiablos,* como en los

---

[40] In the plagiarism controversy already mentioned, FERNANDO SANTIVÁN, without reference to *La Rosa de Grenade* of JEAN RAMEAU, which is generally cited as the source of Barrios' «plagiarism», feels that Barrios may have borrowed to some extent: «Creo que Barrios tomó el "tono" de una hermosa novelita poemática [*Le Visage émérveillé*] de la condesa Matthieu de Noailles... Pero el "tono" nada más, como quien dice, el tono que el director de orquesta ofrece a los músicos antes de empezar una audición» («Eduardo Barrios en su tiempo», *Atenea,* CLIV, No. 404, 94).

demás libros de Barrios, la maestría artística está en el estilo mismo. Pocos escritores hispanoamericanos manejan la prosa como él. Combina la sencillez con una gran sensibilidad poética. Las metáforas son aptas, naturales, hermosas. Barrios nunca se esfuerza por conseguir una originalidad estrambótica; nunca sacrifica lo natural por lo extravagante.»[41] Although all of his laudatory remarks describe perfectly *El hermano asno,* it seems to me that he is remiss in seeking to include *Gran señor y rajadiablos* in his all-embracing eulogy. In fact, most of the positive affirmations with regard to Barrios' prose style are the very qualities that are lacking in the later novel. Fogelquist's error is in trying to superimpose on the novel the unequalled intimate lyricism, the poetic sensibility of *El hermano asno* (and parts of *El niño que enloqueció de amor* and *Los hombres del hombre*). Of course, Barrios has hit on several felicitous expressions to convey the beauties of rustic Chile and the country life. One admires with Fogelquist pictures of the night «agazapada bajo los árboles», and a ranch which in the sleepy atmosphere of late afternoon «bostezaba humo». Barrios even carries over the beautiful, muted scenes of gathering dusk, so well painted in *El hermano asno:* «Como el crepúsculo ha empezado a envolver ya en su misterio todas las cosas, ellos no piensan desmontar. Permanecen un rato mudos. Los ha ido cogiendo el encanto de las malvas que suavizan el tronar de las aguas» (II, 45). This, like many others, is a beautifully written passage, but it is no more than that. It lacks the spirit of the rural epic that he is trying to convey. There is no finer example of poetic prose than this symphony in blue, a colourist *tour de force,* polished and reworked to produce a veritable jewel:

> Están azules los cielos y los espejos de los charcos, los pinos y los cristales de la casa, y aun allá, sobre las praderas mojadas, hasta nítidas lejanías, el azul barniza todo verde y penetra los humos tenues que suben de los ranchos. Azul canta la flauta de los pájaros, azules llegan los grititos de las niñas desde el interior. Si hablase ahora ella, también azul sería su voz. Azules se vuelven sus pensamientos. Su alma toda se tiñe de azul. Y cuando la campana llamando a misa la despierta, le parece que se desparraman los sones por el aire cual si se desgranase un rosario de cuentas azules. (II, 882-83)

This is an exquisite piece of fine writing, paradoxically closer to Modernism at its peak than anything in the first trilogy, in which all the senses are synthesised to produce a masterly *transposition d'art,* blending nature with religion to produce a miraculous manifestation of a rare moment of spiritual beauty. As one critic has shrewdly observed, however, Barrios had polished a little too hard: «Barrios en *Gran señor y rajadiablos* ha repujado la prosa con disciplina de orfebre, puliendo, retocando, enriqueciendo el vocabulario, buscando expresiones nuevas, con una preocupación consciente por huir de lo vulgar y repetido. Nueva demostración de su "voluntad de estilo".

---

[41] «Eduardo Barrios, en su etapa actual», p. 20.

No siempre da la sensación de naturalidad y fluidez, pues se advierten, de cuando en cuando, huellas de la lima, y de pronto las frases se retuercen perdiendo ese ritmo natural de la respiración que pedía Flaubert para el estilo.»[42] In spite of Barrios' claim to hate «los estilos presuntuosos», he may have, on this occasion, sacrificed the natural for the extravagant. Although there are passages of great beauty in this novel, which one can enjoy as little poems in prose,[43] the novel fails because they are just that—little poems within a prosaic mass, which do not blend with the total effect of the novel. Barrios has failed to produce what he achieved in *El hermano asno*, i.e. the happy union of content and form. The sporadic Modernist outbursts within the framework of a nineteenth-century novel of the land in no way match the essential simplicity of *El hermano asno*. In his superimposition rather than infusion of style into content, Barrios fails to achieve the felicitous blend of music and transparency. Too many of the beautifully-written passages, though imbued with musical qualities, suffer from an obvious displacement, an opacity, and a despiritualisation. Barrios may have attained the musical effect, but to the detriment of the complementary clarity. Notes without soul, colour without spirit, do not make for artistic masterpieces. The novel fails because, dare one say it, it lacks emotion. Though studded with gems of poetic prose, *Gran señor y rajadiablos* cannot be termed aesthetically satisfying. It does, however, stand, in the second period, in relation to *Los hombres del hombre* as *El niño que enloqueció de amor* does to *El hermano asno*, both from the metaphysical and artistic point of view.

From the metaphysical perspective, as we have seen, *Los hombres del hombre*, rather than adding a great deal to *Gran señor y rajadiablos*, recapitulates, resumes and refines the point of view expressed in the previous novel. What signifies an advance is not merely the overt theme of poetry as a vital value but also Barrios' aesthetic treatment, his more psychologically penetrating characterisation of the sensitive protagonists, and, not least, his concern with style that reaches the apogee of the first period, *El hermano asno*. Though one cannot place *Los hombres del hombre* above *El hermano asno*, one can sympathise with the critic who perhaps overstates the case in an effort to rehabilitate a neglected novel: «Si en *El hermano asno* logró ingerir poesía en el conjunto poemático, con *Los hombres del hombre* consigue aún más. No se fuerza en ningún instante la narración,

---

[42] MILTON ROSSEL, «El hombre y su psique en las novelas de Eduardo Barrios», *Atenea*, CXXXIX, No. 389 (1960), p. 205.

[43] «Por el camino pasan gentes hablando, con los ecos extraños que tienen las voces dentro de la niebla. Se alejan y no se sabe qué gris errabundo queda palpitando entre los demás grises. Los minutos andan lentos. Hasta que el sol, por muy fugaz instante, dora los filos de muros y cornisas, deslíe un poco de púrpura indecisa en el frontis de la capillita. Súbito, se apaga, cual si hubiera plegado el párpado y enfría todos los matices del cuadro» (II, 881).

no se hace gala de escribir bien, y es ello el mayor mérito, precisamente por lo milagroso de la prosa.»[44] Though it does not reach the heights of *El hermano asno*, *Los hombres del hombre* is a finely written novel and significant as Barrios' last work and therefore his final word. Though writers are not always the best judges of their own work,[45] Barrios appeared to favour *Los hombres del hombre* as the most mature expression of his art.[46] Apart from being the definitive restatement and culmination of the themes of the previous novels, it is also the artistic peak with regard to style and language: «The highly aesthetic orientation of the descriptive language of his writing—which critics concur in identifying as the most salient feature of his work—also finds a logical conclusion in *Los hombres del hombre*.»[47]

It seems to me, however, that Hancock overstates the appreciation of the linguistic and stylistic qualities of Barrios' work by the critics—certainly in the case of *Los hombres del hombre*, in which too many fail to detect, beyond the facade of the psychological mastery, not only the aesthetic treatment but the metaphysical role of art as symbolised in the poetry of Charlie. Apart from Hancock in particular and Davison, the only other critic to have demonstrated a keen awareness of the linguistic and stylistic value of the novel was Vernacci in his review immediately after publication: «la manera de escribir de Eduardo Barrios... ha alcanzado una perfección, una claridad, una exactitud, que considero cima para el cultivador de las letras» (p. 81). Barrios, even during his quiet period of the 1930s, took advantage of the book reviews and editorials he was writing for Chilean newspapers to develop and concretise the literary theories expressed in «También algo de mí» and elsewhere. Taking as his criteria the oft-repeated triple desiderata of music, clarity and simplicity, his journalistic writings betray the same preoccupation with the purity of language and expression. His love of simplicity and good taste swayed him towards Castilian writers like the mystics of the Golden Age and the prose writers of the Generation of '98: «Suele faltar en nuestras prosas esa nobleza lingüística, que entre los peninsulares marca irremediablemente, hoy como ayer, su huella de sandalia frailuna o de chapín palaciego.»[48] This affinity

---

[44] ENRIQUE RUIZ VERNACCI, «Una gran novela americana—*Los hombres del hombre*», *Repertorio Americano*, XLVII, No. 6 (15 de mayo, 1951), 83.

[45] One remembers Barrios' violent defence of his weak novel *Tamarugal* against the attacks of the critic, Alone.

[46] See [RICARDO LATCHAM?], «Eduardo Barrios, académico», *La Nación*, XXXVII (23 de junio, 1953), 2.

[47] JOEL C. HANCOCK, «The Purification of Eduardo Barrios' Sensorial Prose», *Hispania*, LVI, No. 1 (March, 1973), 51.

[48] «*El hombre en la montaña* por Edgardo Garrido Merino», *Las Ultimas Noticias*, XXXII (23 de mayo, 1934), 12. Ruiz Vernacci reaffirms this debt to Castilian: «Es que ha ahondado en el idioma, ha encontrado esa elegancia del castellano sencilla-mente seductora... Construye la frase con una gentil sobriedad, sin alarde de purismo, con prurito de exactitud que enamora» (p. 83).

with Peninsular writers has not gone unnoticed by Torres-Ríoseco who cites Barrios' familiarity with «la rica prosa de Fray Luis de Granada, Santa Teresa y Fray Luis de León» (*Grandes novelistas,* p. 56), a relationship that has not been unfruitful: «parece que el autor, después de haber entrado en la floresta de los místicos españoles, ha salido de ella perfumado de humildad y de fervor místico, de amor por los seres y por las cosas» (p. 55). Barrios' affinity with the metaphysical crisis of the '98 Generation has already been noted. Jefferson Rea Spell, also acknowledging his debt to the Spanish mystics, goes on to affirm, as we have observed, the literary tendencies which he shares with the Spanish Modernists, Ricardo León and Valle-Inclán, attaching more importance to the pure music of style. Torres-Ríoseco also draws a parallel with Valle-Inclán whose prose, he feels, does not match up to the simple, crystalline prose of *Los hombres del hombre.* According to Ruiz Vernacci, «Valle-Inclán se hincha un tanto. Barrios, jamás. Barrios posee riqueza de léxico, construye con singular prestancia, saborea el idioma. Esta manera de escribir de nuestro autor es difícilmente igualable. No denota esfuerzo. Y existe el esfuerzo. A esta diafinidad no se llega porque sí» (p. 83). Hence the admiration for works composed of pure sounds and classical simplicity and his recommendation of the use of language modulated with Castilian intonation. His own novels, especially *El hermano asno* and *Los hombres del hombre,* are but the practical application of these canons expressed in his own theoretical writings and in his newspaper articles. His almost religious attitude to the literary vocation, his devotion to his craft, and his affection for language and style prevented the mature artist from consciously allowing his fiction to deviate from the paths of good taste and to degenerate into pornography or artificial mannerism, which are by definition and practice the converse of simplification and simplicity: «Tengamos presente que cultura es simplificación, sencillez máxima, ponderación, jamás amaneramiento... la persona culta adquiere estilo, no manera.»[49]

This distaste for cultivated mannerisms and false art is at the root of *Los hombres del hombre,* a novel about true poetry, freshly and spontaneously expressed. Developed thus, poetry can be more than just an expression of beautiful sentiments in fine language. In this last novel poetry is for Barrios the path of art which man can follow to escape the anguish of life. Apart from its metaphysical force, however, poetry, and in Barrios' case, poetic prose, is a vehicle for communicating the emotion of truth. That this should be done simply, clearly and musically was the point of his oft-quoted definition. Twenty years later he expressed in similar terms his aesthetic convictions which are the basis of his best literature, exemplified by the

---

[49] «Demasiados amaneramientos», *La Nación,* XXXVI (30 de diciembre, 1952), 4. Written in 1952, this could well be an oblique attack on the «excesses» of the first examples of *la nueva novela* with which Barrios had little sympathy.

pristine prose of *Los hombres del hombre:* «El adorno lírico es adjetivo en cuanto adorno, pero en cuanto lirismo de ley es arte, porque tiende a la mayor expresividad, al encanto comunicativo. Entonces es flecha directa sobre la sensibilidad. Esto se consigue, además, con la música.»[50]

Los hombres del hombre, written in the diary form favoured by Barrios, is the perfect medium for revealing not only the inner thoughts of *el hombre* and his various egos but also the artistic temperament of the narrator, all clothed in metaphorical, poetic language. The diary technique, which renders best the aesthetic revelation of the protagonist's psyche, offers also the escape from his anguish by providing him with an outlet for his emotional problems. In this sense *Los hombres del hombre* represents the final example of the fusion or the inseparability of content and form that one finds in *El hermano asno,* but which is lacking in other works where he employs the same diary technique («Tirana ley»), and even in the relatively successful «Páginas de un pobre diablo».

The awareness of *Los hombres del hombre* not only as an aesthetic novel but as a novel about aesthetics is manifested in the opening dedication to the literary public. Advertisements, however, do not make the novel. Nor does the revelation that the protagonist is a writer, who finds escape from his spiritual malaise in writing («Escribiré, pues. Sin la disciplina de los renglones a nada llegaría», II, 990), automatically raise the novel to the level of good literature. Without the inspiration (in its etymological as well as literary sense) of an aesthetic Holy Spirit, the mass of material remains but that—a mass of material, lacking the spiritual totality which comes only with the fusion (not superimposition) of this matter with the quintessential form. In the following passage, already quoted as an example of Barrios' landscaping skills, which could have been aptly excerpted from the monastic ambience of *El hermano asno,* the rural scenario of *Gran señor y rajadiablos* (but less convincingly for the reasons stated in my treatment of, for example, the «symphony in blue») melts into the spiritual state of the protagonist and the whole tone of the novel:

> La tarde continúa lindísima. De los cerros enormes parecen bajar los árboles al llano como una muchedumbre que regresara para recogerse. Aun ese rodado de peñas molidas por las heladas a lo largo del tiempo, se tiende suave como delantal gris de su montaña. La transparencia del aire asombra en estas alturas; por ella las enormidades abruptas se funden con la ternura de los verdes y los azules celestes aquietan ranchos, torrentes y caminos. Es un paisaje inmóvil de porcelana, que aun sonaría notas claras si le diéramos con los nudillos. (II, 994)

The description of the beauty of the evening serves as a perfect background not only for the physical realities of the deceptively still, almost immobile,

---

[50] MANUEL VEGA, «Eduardo Barrios en la intimidad», *Revista Zig-Zag,* XL, No. 2070 (24 de noviembre, 1944), 39.

trees which descend from the mountains to the plain, but also for the spiritual atmosphere. Even the rocks, smooth through centuries of being weather-beaten, stretch out, but gently «como delantal gris de su montaña». This is not the aggressive, stormy nature of the Romantics. There is a softness, a gentleness, more consistent with the Modernist view of nature: «Es un paisaje inmóvil de porcelana.» The multiple ambiguity of the vehicle-force transparency which describes not only the air but also the method and the effect (stylistic and natural) of what Barrios is trying to achieve, coupled with the fusion/confusion of the mountains melting into the tenderness (with all its spiritual and emotional implications) of the greens and heavenly blues, creates an overall impression of quietism equal to the best of *El hermano asno*. The silence and stillness of the motionless porcelain landscape is so intense that if one were to rap it with one's knuckles, it would give out clear, distinct notes. Barrios has rarely written a passage of more potent beauty, characterised by quietism, colour, transparency and music, yet ripe with pregnant nuance, expressive of the correspondence between the senses—truly «un silencio de música recién callada».

This doctrine of sensationism, which Barrios inherited from the Modernists, became, as Hancock so rightly saw, «an integral part of Barrios' narrative style and was a constant element. He strove to incite the sensual perceptions, either individually or simultaneously. The use of synesthetic descriptions, where objects are endowed with sensory qualities ordinarily not attributed to them was another technique Barrios employed to stir the senses» («The Purification...», p. 53)—a device evidenced already in *El hermano asno*. The following passage is a veritable breviary of sensations, transcending even the most impressive natural descriptions of *El hermano asno*. Barrios (and occasionally Güiraldes, especially in *Xaimaca*) is the first novelist since Larreta in *La gloria de don Ramiro* (1908) to realise the importance of sensationism, which Ned Davison has called «the cultivation of materials and devices for the purpose of defining and evoking sensations»: [51]

> Salí de Chile una de las postreras mañanas de abril. En las alamedas quemaban la hojarasca barrida, una bruma tenue mezclábase a los humos que ascendían de las piras, y ambos grises, confundidos, enroscábanse a los árboles, para subir después a velar más el azul del cielo. Olía todo el barrio no sé si a niebla, si a ceniza, si a paz o si a melancolía. Y he vuelto a mi tierra cuando han reflorecido los cerezos de parques y jardines, cuando las ráfagas, en vez de hojas muertas, echan a volar pétalos rosados por el aire y cuando los álamos se prenden ya los primeros moños verdes. Y ahora, ya en mi aislado caserón desde anoche, uno ha sido levantarme, salir al patio y aparecérseme de súbito

---

[51] *The Concept of Modernism in Hispanic Criticism* (Boulder, Colorado: Pruett Press, 1966), p. 37.

el peral todo blanco de flores. Los cinco sentidos se refunden. Huele a gérmenes
y a sol, a cantos, a colores, a leches y a niñez. (II, 1008-09)

This spring morning description has all the characteristics of hazy blend-
ings which produce even more fusion/confusion—all against the blue of
the sky: «una *bruma tenue mezclábase* a los *humos* que ascendían de las
piras, y ambos *grises, confundidos, enroscábanse* a los árboles» (my italics).
Taking the fog, which might at least be conceived in terms of the visual
(if not too precise), Barrios goes on to render it in terms of the olfactory,
in a litany that goes from hardly concrete to spiritually abstract: «Olía
todo el barrio no sé si a *niebla*, si a *ceniza*, si a *paz* o si a *melancolía*» (my
italics). Conceptually, formally and linguistically, the sentence has a Gon-
goristic ring/odour (?) to it, with its cumulative catalogue in reverse going
from the concrete to the abstract.[52] The impression of the beauty of the
morning is vividly expressed in the rapidly changing visual images of the
pink petals, the green tops of the poplars, and the white blossoms of the
pear trees. These images are not, however, limited to the particular senses
of touch, taste, sight, hearing and smell. In one last welter of sensorial prose,
all five senses come together in a perfect, overwhelming correspondence:
«Los cinco sentidos se refunden. Huele a gérmenes y a sol, a cantos, a
colores, a leches y a niñez.»

Max Henríquez Ureña, in his celebrated *Breve historia del modernismo*,
quotes Valle-Inclán's affirmation that the exploration of sensationism is one
of the most important features of Modernism: «La condición característica
de todo el arte moderno, y muy particularmente de la literatura, es una
tendencia a refinar las sensaciones y acrecentarlas en el número y en la
intensidad.»[53] Baudelaire, for whom smell equals not only sound but colour,
can write:

> O! Métamorphose mystique
> de tous mes sens fondus en un
> son haleine fait la musique,
> comme sa voix fait le parfum...

Valle-Inclán, whose influence on Barrios we have already suggested, giving
special importance to impressionism which manifests itself by means of
synaesthesis, defines the synesthetic imagery of Baudelaire, Rimbaud, D'Annunzio thus: «Esta analogía y equivalencia de las sensaciones es lo que

---

[52] Cf. for example, the 1582 sonnet «Mientras por competir con tu cabello» on the
transience of youth and beauty which, like all earthly things, are changed «en tierra,
en humo, en polvo, en sombra, en nada». This sentiment is re-echoed by Sor Juana
(sonnet beginning «Este que ves, engaño colorido...») in her equally nihilistic
baroque cry from the heart on the ephemerality of beauty: «es cadáver, es polvo,
es sombra, es nada».

[53] México: Fondo de Cultura Económica, 1962, 2nd ed., p. 168.

constituye el "modernismo" en literatura.»[54] Barrios' prose, especially in this last novel, is the living embodiment of this fusion of the senses, and of his debt to his Modernist masters.

This fusion of the senses, portrayed with such intensity, is a rare moment of miraculous beauty in literature as in life. Not many of Barrios' passages of sensorial prose come close to it. However, his feeling for nuance, the hidden, the suggested, the half-heard, the half-seen, developed in *El hermano asno,* is perfected in the acceptable poetic prose of the writer-protagonist: «Mi alma estaba en paz, el niño conmigo, no hablábamos casi. Diríase que se había enrarecido la mañana y pasaba por mi pecho como el aire pasa por una caña verde» (II, 1035-36). In the rarefied atmosphere of a beautiful morning, nature mirrors the peace and quiet he feels within his soul, as he walks with his son—of equal poetic temperament, one remembers, and the sole moral support of his disturbed father. The regularly broken prose prolongs, not only by semantics but also by rhythm, the quietist mood established in the previous passage: «Anduvimos, vagamos, lentos, en silencio, cual si nos hubiéramos propuesto sólo recibir el ambiente unidos» (II, 1036). The sense of mystical communion between father and son, and between both and the ambience, infuses a spiritual quality into the already quietist scene. When the silence is broken, it is not brutal but in keeping with the mood: «En los parques vienen *de lejos pedacitos de voz.* No importa qué digan, cabalmente su valor está en que *no se entienden,* en que son *fragmentos* de un todo cuyo sentido nos place imaginar a gusto de mil maneras, ya remecedoras, y sedantes» (my italics). The voices that break the silence are heard in the distance. In fact, they are scarcely voices but *pedacitos de voz.* The use of the diminutive, combined with the inaudible quality of the partial voices, highlights the distance, whilst the inaccessibility of these sounds enhances their attraction making them part of a mysterious harmonious whole whose anonymity provokes the imagination to more pleasing creative action. The link between the invisible mouths and the secret ears strengthens the auditory mystery and intensifies the pantheistic quality of the scene: «Salen de *bocas invisibles* que parece tener la brisa y se cuelan por *oídos secretos* formados de atmósfera. Un tímpano hay sin duda enfrente de cada *laringe misteriosa*» (II, 1036; my italics).

The intuitive poet in the boy wants to sustain the spell of the half-heard sounds, to continue to expose the mystery of these auditory glimpses (!) to his imagination, the fantasy world being more attractive than the world of reality. This, however, is not to be. As the vague buzzing of sounds is translated into syllables, and syllables into words, the boy's anxiety increases. As the spirit which inhabits the park becomes concrete and

[54] This article was originally published in *La Ilustración Española y Americana* (22 de febrero, 1902).

physical, and the invisible mouths are transformed into human beings, the spell is broken—to the boy's chagrin:

> Y Cabecita... se inquieta. Percibe de repente un sonido y vuelve la cara, buscándolo. ¿Está del otro lado de la espesura? Voló en una ráfaga, soltó dos sílabas y ahora se ha cortado. Poco después, la misma voz acaso, disloca otra palabra en dirección opuesta, y calla también, y se oculta. El siente cómo ese algo queda palpitando entonces en el parque; no atiende a las demás cosas ya: son concretas. Prefiere apresar, retener aquella trunca sensación cuya permanencia resulta dulce desconocer. Ocurre alguna vez que se aparecen de pronto, por entre unos arbustos, las personas que hablaban, y a la vera de Cabecita pasan, y le rompen el encanto. Lo cual le duele. (II, 1036)

Although the wonder of silence is broken for the moment, Cabecita has learned to retain, and will perfect, because of his poetic gifts, if not these moments themselves at least the emotion of them. Like his father, long trained by experience, he will be able to conjure up and relive «sus instantes y sus silencios activos». Although the father sees in the incident the seeds of the proof he needs for closer identification with his son, and therefore for paternal identity, it is also an important lesson for Charlie on his road to poetic revelation. Though no lesson is spelled out explicitly, nor words exchanged between teacher and pupil, this quiet moment prefigures the bird-song incident (II, 1065), the flowers-emotion lesson (II, 1066), and the phenomenon of silent solitude (II, 1067), which all serve to point out Charlie's poetic bent.

The link between the metaphysical (search for identity, paternity) and the aesthetic (quietism, sensationism) is underlined the following night, again through the medium of Nature, when *el hombre* receives explicit proof of his fatherhood:

> Me parece que mi *espíritu* se tiende sobre la noche *tibia* y abierta. Viene desde la calle, por *el aire quieto, el eco* de las herraduras de un caballo que marcha sobre la calzada. Sin duda ronda un carabinero. Cantan *algunos* gallos, *muy lejos;* el nuestro responde, sobresaltándome. Luego, *el silencio,* que por lo absoluto es como un vacío, en el cual entra entonces para llenarlo *esa melancolía inmotivada y suave* por la cual, en las noches frescas que siguen a un día caluroso, nuestra sensibilidad se acuna y quisiera dormirnos vestidos encima del primer sofá solitario. (II, 1036-37; my italics)

In the quiet air of the mild night to which *el hombre*'s soul seems to stretch out, the only sounds are the echoes of a horse's shoes on the roadway, the suggestion that a policeman (unheard) might be on his beat, and the crowing (in the distance) of a few cocks. The vagueness and the distance of these sounds is merely highlighted by the single, startling reply of the narrator's cock (close by, in the foreground). This shocking interruption serves only to intensify the ensuing silence «que por lo absoluto es como un vacío». Into the vacuum created by the silence that vague, gentle melancholy, by which one's sensibility is rocked to sleep, insinuates itself for no reason. Having created the quietist mood aesthetically, *el hombre* then deduces, even recomposes, the affinity that exists between him and his son—«su vivir sensorial paralelo al mío»—which is the basis of the recognition of his paternity.

To put to the test his newly-won feelings of paternity, *el hombre* discusses with Charlie his own childhood memories of a similar bedroom with a similar skylight window. Together, almost as one spirit, they reconstruct the sounds, sights, and smells of the previous night, heightened through the prism or the filter of the little window: «Aquel techo no era entonces sino el cuadrito luminoso proyectado por el tragaluz, espejo gastado y medio ciego donde apenas había un presentimiento de las formas de la calle nocturna. Pero asistía yo en cambio a otro desfile, que también interesa mucho: el de los sonidos» (II, 1038). Given the visual inadequacies because of the window *(espejo gastado y medio ciego)*, one has to compensate with feelings *(presentimientos)* of the nocturnal shapes. However, by use of the auditory, one recuperates the missing forms: «En vez de figura, pues, pasan ecos diminutos, recortados también como siluetas. Todo toma el tono y el color de la noche y las notas chispean lo mismo que las estrellas. Uno ve los ecos, más que los oye. Se mueven, huyen, se detienen... Todo en sonido, pero en su dibujo exacto» (II, 1038). In a series of synaesthetic images, miniature echoes are drawn in outline like silhouettes. This notion of a synthesis of the arts, which was mainly inspired by the theories of Wagner and popularised by Baudelaire, is an aspect of the interrelation of the artistic media much used by Barrios. The fusion of aesthetic and psychological sensations, as developed by Swedenborg's *correspondances,* with its mystical implications, has left its mark on the work of Barrios, especially in *El hermano asno* and *Los hombres del hombre.* When Barrios talks here of the tone and colour of the night, he is blending gradations of colour and sound to create an artistic, sensorial effect reminiscent of D'Annunzio, cited by Max Henríquez Ureña in his history of Modernism: «canta la nota verde d'un bel limone inflore»; or René Ghil who, in his doctrine of «l'instrumentation verbale», attributes not only colourist but musical value to the vowels and consonants: «A, claironne vainqueur en rouge flamboiement.» It is this equivalence of the senses that constitutes at least the formal side of Modernism. When Barrios summarises the recreated scene («Todo en sonidos, pero en su dibujo exacto»), he characterises perfectly the synthesis not only of the senses (auditory and visual) but also of the implicit arts (sketching, painting, music, etc.) which go to form the total effect of poetic prose. Having reconstructed the events of the past night, and in so doing assured himself of the strong bond between himself and his son, *el hombre* permits the evoked past to take its normal course of action, to evaporate into the silence, and sleep beneath the poetic magic of its words. Totally convinced of his fatherhood, brought closer to his son by dreams and metaphor, the stuff of poetry, the father, in true Barrios fashion, is overwhelmed by emotion.

If we needed further proof of his artistic mastery after *El hermano asno, Los hombres del hombre* provides another example of Barrios' skill in writing beautiful prose to fit the matter treated. Although this last novel cannot match *El hermano asno* for overall beauty, spirituality and simplicity of style, there can be little doubt that Barrios' refinement of the sensorial and poetic prose, in keeping with the characterisation of the two protagonists and the theme of the metaphysical role of poetry in life, has elevated *Los hombres del hombre* if not to the top rank of Barrios' work at least to the position of the most artistic, though not the most popular, of Barrios' second period. Aesthetically and metaphysically, therefore, *Los hombres del hombre* is a fitting conclusion to a fictional corpus that generally tries to convey, in a style and language worthy of the content, something of the tragic sentiment of life.

CONCLUSION

Given his metaphysical concern and the high level of his artistic achievement, it is still a fact that Eduardo Barrios has not been wholly appreciated by the critics. The older generation (Torres-Ríoseco, Silva Castro, Milton Rossel, et al.) who devoted much of their effort to making Barrios' reputation known outside of Chile, were not always totally cognizant of Barrios' aims nor of his artistic attainments. Also, Barrios was only one of many literary figures studied by these pioneer scholars who, in their preoccupation with labels and movements, often failed to see beyond the regionalist or the continental. Even the best critics of the late 1950s and 1960s (Davison and Vázquez-Bigi), who produced such fine work on Barrios, have tended on the whole to concentrate on the psychological values in Barrios' work. More recently Joel C. Hancock has highlighted some of the artistic qualities of Barrios, but mostly through his study of one novel, *Los hombres del hombre*.[1] Apart from the excellent theses of these three scholars, there have been only three full-length studies devoted to Barrios: Orlando and Ramírez's little handbook of limited critical value, *Eduardo Barrios: Obras. Estilo. Técnica;*[2] Ned Davison's useful *Eduardo Barrios* which goes beyond his thesis findings but is limited by the Twayne format and intent; and Mariano Morínigo's *Eduardo Barrios, novelista,* a rehash of his university seminar course, which lives up to the claim of the Introduction: «No pretendo decir aquí nada nuevo acerca de un escritor que ha sido suficientemente comentado y estudiado por la crítica chilena e hispanoamericana.»[3] Though not totally neglected by literary criticism, Barrios' work has not always been best served by well-meaning writers who, because of their limited perspective, have seen fit to concentrate on individual

---

[1] «Compositional Modes of Eduardo Barrios' *Los hombres del hombre* with an Appended Bibliography of his Uncollected Prose», unpublished Ph. D. thesis, University of New Mexico, 1970, plus the articles already cited. We are indebted to Hancock for his useful bibliography of book reviews, newspaper articles, etc. written by Barrios, and I am grateful for copies of some of the *crónicas* which he made available to me.

[2] Santiago de Chile: Editorial del Pacífico, 1960, 121 pp.

[3] Universidad Nacional de Tucumán, Tucumán, 1971, p. 7. This work has been harshly reviewed by VÁZQUEZ-BIGI in *Revista Iberoamericana*, XL, No. 86 (enero-mayo, 1974), 200-04.

aspects of Barrios' works (usually the psychological, regionalist, and the social) without having an overall view of the author's work.[4]

This failure to appreciate, based on a lack of understanding, is responsible for the generally held opinion that Barrios is an «unfashionable» writer, especially in these days of the (post-) «boom» of the modern novel. Barrios has contributed to this impression of being old-fashioned or even anachronistic in the themes, motifs, and ideas treated in his novels. His reputation as a *novelista del sentimiento*,[5] whose antirational outlook prevails throughout his fiction, would seem to place him more in the nineteenth century alongside novelists like Flaubert, with whose notions of *l'éducation sentimentale* he has often been identified. If Romanticism is at the root of his metaphysics, then Modernism, more than any other movement, influences his aesthetics. This combination of Romanticism and Modernism,[6] which are, of course, not unrelated, as the moving forces in his art, has tended to paint the picture of an out-of-step sentimentalist or realist, depending on the novel treated, dealing with nineteenth-century problems, using twentieth-century techniques, e.g. in *El hermano asno*. Barrios' later sallies into the (apparent) world of *criollismo* (*Tamarugal* and *Gran señor y rajadiablos*) have strengthened this impression of anachronism amongst some critics who have not been able to penetrate beyond the regionalist plane of these novels which are, in reality, developments of his metaphysical vision. Critics tend to talk of *El hermano asno* and *Gran señor y rajadiablos* in the same breath (though one was written in youth [1922] and the other in old age [1948]), without an awareness of the effect of a twenty-six year gap on the man, the philosopher, and the artist. Because Barrios is a self-confessed admirer of traditional novelists like Rivera, Gallegos and Gálvez,[7] all generally regarded as *passés* and primitive in the sophisticated world of the new novel, the tendency has been to view his novels in terms of the old labels. In this way, Barrios is considered either as

---

[4] It is interesting to note the number of single articles on Barrios by writers who have neither seen below the surface nor pursued their findings.

[5] Cf., for example, GUILLERMO COTTO-THORNER, «Eduardo Barrios: novelista del sentimiento», *Hispania*, XXXIV, No. 3 (August, 1951), 271-72.

[6] Barrios' affinities with Valle-Inclán, the Generation of '98, and Modernism have already been noted. JOSÉ F. MONTESINOS, in his article «Modernismo, esperpentismo o las dos evasiones», makes the link and draws the pattern which would encompass a spirit like Barrios: «el grupo del 98 trató de hallar en los abuelos lo que no encontraba en los padres. Por ello volvía los ojos al romanticismo; de aquí que gran parte de los temas fuesen románticos, que lo fuera en cierto modo la motivación estética de las obras, y, siempre, la actitud vital. Son curiosas las huellas que todo esto deja en el vocabulario; palabras como "emoción", "emotivo", "sentimental", "sensibilidad" recurren con prodigiosa frecuencia, y una de las que más a menudo se documenta en todos, y muy particularmente en el Valle-Inclán de todas las épocas, es justamente "romántico"» (*Revista de Occidente*, Nos. 44-45 [noviembre-diciembre, 1966], 147).

[7] BERNARD DULSEY, «A Visit with Eduardo Barrios», *Modern Language Journal*, XLIII (November, 1959), 349.

a novelist of the land like Rivera and Gallegos, with the emphasis on *Gran señor y rajadiablos* as being exemplary of that genre, or a novelist of the city like Gálvez, with the corresponding stress on *Un perdido* and its importance as a social document. In reality, he is closer to contemporaries (of the older generation) like Mallea, for example, in his view of the novel as a vehicle of ideas, and Juan Carlos Onetti in his attitude to writing as an escape. With both he shares a concern for man's situation in a basically pessimistic world. His novels represent an attempt to give some meaning to an absurd life in which the human condition is one of existential unhappiness.

As Barrios had indicated his admiration for three unfashionable Latin American writers rather than the prestigiously popular Joyce, Faulkner, or Virginia Woolf, so too his aesthetic tastes would render him odd by today's standards. Apart from his acknowledged debt to Modernism, his respect for the language of the Spanish mystics and the pure prose writers of Spanish Modernism is a far cry from the linguistic innovations and verbal experiments that fill the pages of Cortázar's *Rayuela* and its successors.

Conservative in politics, sober in religion, and traditional in art, his ideals of transparency and simplicity, with purity of language and style, are out of step with modern writers. His aim of writing clearly, his striving for simplicity and the desire not to confuse would, apparently, place him diametrically opposite to the ambiguity of the games and puzzles that constitute the core, if not the essence, of typical modern novelists like Cortázar, Severo Sarduy and Cabrera Infante. This emphasis on euphony and purity of language would separate him from a Vargas Llosa: «No admite la novela [*Los hombres del hombre*] la dureza, la cacofonía, el continuo eufemismo por no hallar la palabra justa. Tampoco admite la grosería, ese alarde por reproducir palabras escatalógicas o francamente pornográficas» (Ruiz Vernacci, p. 83). Manuel Pedro González, the fanatical arch-critic of the new novel, perhaps describes best the differences between the traditional novel à la Barrios and the contemporary novel—and comes out in favour of the old:

> Una buena novela es—o debe ser—siempre una obra de arte. Si no conmueve nuestro espíritu ni nos invita a meditar, ni estimula nuestra sensibilidad literaria y nuestro interés, entonces su lectura se hace ingrata y el diálogo tácito, o la comunicación entre autor y lector se inhibe. El fin de la novela no es necesaria ni únicamente entretener, pero es uno de sus objetivos importantes. Hacer de la novela un rompecabezas o crucigrama que debe descifrarse como una adivinanza, es prostituirla y rebajarla al rango de los juegos frívolos y pueriles.[8]

---

[8] «Impresión de *La ciudad y los perros*», in *Coloquio sobre la novela hispanoamericana* (México: Fondo de Cultura Económica, Ed. Tezontle, 1967), p. 106.

Though himself concerned with the essence of language and its utility, nay its necessity, in the composition of the artistic unity of the novel, Barrios was out of sympathy with the literary revolutionaries and the linguistic terrorists amongst the younger novelists whom he labelled *estrafalarios* for their disregard of the correctness of the dictionary and the niceties of Spanish grammar. When Barrios complains: «No se ocupan de su forma», he is implying an attitude to language that deviates from the traditional. Both Barrios and the new novelists are concerned about linguistic renovation, but in different ways which are both revolutionary. Whilst Barrios tries to refine language to the degree that he would like to write without words, to *create* the effect with the vehicle, Cortázar and company are trying to *destroy* all that is conventional both in life and in language, to combat the absurd by means of the absurd, through the instrument of *el lenguaje destructor*. As a protest against the traditional, «el escritor tiene que incendiar el lenguaje, acabar con las formas coaguladas e ir todavía más allá, poner en duda la posibilidad de que este lenguaje esté todavía en contacto con lo que pretende mentar. No ya las palabras en sí, porque eso importa menos, sino la estructura total de una lengua, de un discurso».[9] By his death in 1963 Barrios was spared the fruits of these theories manifested in the extreme linguistic gymnastics of *Paradiso*, *Tres tristes tigres*, *Cobra* and other formidable examples of the new novel.

Barrios, however, was not against experimentation as such, nor against the revivification and the flexibilisation of language, which constituted one aspect of Modernism that attracted him so strongly to that movement. What Barrios would have objected to in the new novel would be the mere imitation of the Joycean technique, for example, which becomes a pastiche, a poor copy, because it lacks the spirit, or better, as Barrios would have expressed it, the emotion of Joyce, or Huxley, or Woolf, or Faulkner, all of whose techniques the new novelists follow. To return to the argument of Chapter 4, formal and linguistic innovations which do not complement and reflect the material treated, are mere decoration: «The best form is that which makes the most of the subject... The well-made book is the book in which the subject and the form coincide and are indistinguishable —the book in which the matter is all used up in the form, in which the form expresses all the matter» (Lubbock, p. 40).

Barrios, whose own aesthetics was rooted in this fusion of the form and content, and whose political opinions were violently anticommunist, would have agreed, if only once, with György Lukács, the Marxist critic, who, referring to Eastern European writers, states:

Los descubrimientos formales son importantes y deben ser aplicados; pero el factor decisivo es siempre el valor artístico... Mas, cuando los medios artís-

[9] *Rayuela*, 2nd ed. (Buenos Aires: Editorial Sudamericana, 1969), p. 509.

ticos y técnicos se vuelven el fin absoluto, entonces se pierde su verdadera importancia, y volvemos de nuevo al arte unidimensional... Semejantes experimentos son simplemente un «bluff pour épater le bourgeois». No tienen valor alguno..., en mi opinión, mucho de lo que hoy se considera nuevo y se piensa que tendrá una repercusión acabará en la fosa común a la vuelta de quince años.[10]

Without sharing the pessimistic opinions of Manuel Pedro González, on whose criticism I have commented elsewhere,[11] I should offer a word of warning to those critics who would pull down the whole framework of the past in their exuberance to praise the merits (often deserved) of the «boom» novels of the present, without casting a thought to the future.[12]

The irony of this relationship between Barrios and the new novelists —his scorn for their lack of regard for formal grammar and language, their contempt for him and his fellow-traditionalists as primitives—is that, on more careful examination, there is a closer link than both would be prepared to admit. Despite the mutual dislike and distrust, both in technique and theme, Barrios anticipates (often by a long stretch) the so-called new novelists.

One of the features of contemporary fiction, e.g. *Pedro Páramo, La casa verde, La muerte de Artemio Cruz,* amongst others, is the fragmentary nature of the work, caused by geographical and temporal dislocation, which demands organisational participation on the part of the reader. This role of the reader as participant discussed in Chapter 4, is touched on in an interesting article by Hernán Vidal, «El modo narrativo en *El hermano asno* de Eduardo Barrios»,[13] the narrative mode being the relations established in the triple link: *narrador-mundo, narrador-receptor, receptor-mundo.* By his sporadic use of the diary technique, Fray Lázaro's narrative is delivered

[10] Interview with A. J. LIEHM in *Unión* (La Habana), reproduced in *Coloquio,* p. 100.

[11] Review article of *Coloquio sobre la novela hispanoamericana, Erasmus,* Vol. 22, No. 6 (March, 1970), 301-06: «In spite of the partial validity of much of his reasoning, González talks too much and too long about his own reputation as an idolbreaker... As a critic González writes like a naturalist, and the realistic validity of his criticism is vitiated by his vitriolic attacks. The pity is that so much of what he says... has some basis, but, buried beneath the all-embracing deprecation, it escapes highlighting» (304-05).

[12] DONALD SHAW has expressed the same concern in his «Baroja y Mallea: Algunos puntos de contacto», *Actas del Tercer Congreso Internacional de Hispanistas,* México, 1970, pp. 851-52: «Quisiera concluir con una advertencia a los críticos que, como vemos en las páginas de *Nuevo mundo* [sic] y en libros tan importantes como *Los nuestros* de Harss y *Coloquio sobre la novela hispanoamericana* por Schulman, Alegría y otros, ensalzan la nueva novela hispanoamericana elogiando (a mi modo de ver con poca perspectiva crítica) la ingeniosidad técnica y el afán de renovación del idioma de los novelistas de *la nouvelle vague.*»

[13] *Revista Hispánica Moderna,* XXXIII, Nos. 3-4 (julio-octubre, 1967), 241-49. For a very recent treatment of narrative technique in Barrios' fiction, see also ALBERTO RÁBAGO, «Técnica narrativa en *El hermano asno* y *Los hombres del hombre*», *Revista Canadiense de Estudios Hispánicos,* III, No. 2 (Invierno, 1979), 121-36.

with so much temporal fragmentation that the reader has to collaborate actively to fill the gaps and reorganise the material in order to render in meaningful terms the world described: «... es precisamente el receptor foráneo quien convierte a la obra en narración, reordenando el mundo presentado» (p. 249). This function of creating order, a common feature of contemporary fiction, has, Vidal suggests, its antecedent in the Barrios novel (written in 1922). This is hardly different from the role envisaged by Iván Schulman for readers of the new literature: «el lector tendrá un papel trascendente en unión con el creador» (*Coloquio*, p. 32). Vidal concludes thus: «Todo esto nos lleva a afirmar que aunque la gran tendencia al cambio en la novela hispanoamericana se produjo, en su corriente principal, hacia la década 1930-40, *El hermano asno* de Eduardo Barrios representa un definido preludio» (p. 249).

Closer to the new novel in time is *Los hombres del hombre* (1950) which was actually published after the appearance of many of these new novels.[14] Though within the period, but not consciously of the spirit, of the new novel, *Los hombres del hombre,* because it too is a diary-novel, is interesting from the architectural point of view. Made up of thirty-eight distinct fragments smoothly incorporated to form a total view, both the totality and the sections are aesthetic entities: «The fragments have an autonomous dimension: each one embodies a complete and comprehensive meaning and idea, and can be read by itself. Proof of this condition is the fact that the reader could easily skip around in his reading of the episodes and still be able to follow the events and the meaning» (Hancock thesis, p. 42). The fragmentary nature of the novel, which facilitates an easy and comprehensible interchangeability, prefigures the best of Cortázar, especially his key novel *Rayuela,* in this sense, and could be interpreted in the tradition of what Umberto Eco calls «la poética de la forma abierta», though it in no way presents the difficulties faced by Cortázar's accomplice readers.

In *Los hombres del hombre* too, Barrios' most daring use of the multiple personality, initiated in *El hermano asno* (Mario/Fray Lázaro), reaches its peak in the presentation of the multifaceted *yo.* This technique of the double personality, of two men in every man, so favoured by Borges («Los teólogos», «La forma de la espada», «Tema del traidor y del héroe»), and by Cortázar in *Rayuela* (Horacio/Traveller, La Maga/Talita) and also in his short stories, links Barrios to a group of writers with whom he had little in common.[15] The fact that Barrios had probably borrowed the idea

[14] For example, YÁÑEZ's *Al filo del agua,* SÁBATO's *El túnel,* plus various novels of Asturias, Carpentier, Mallea and Onetti.

[15] Also, the recent flirtation of modern writers with Zen Buddhism, which Cortázar confesses to have inspired much of his work (LUIS HARSS, *Los nuestros* [Buenos Aires: Ed. Sudamericana, 1969], pp. 218-20). Borges too reflects this interest, e.g. in «Las ruinas circulares» which embodies the Buddhist belief in the world as the

from Unamuno *(Tres novelas ejemplares y un prólogo)* and that it had been used by writers as early as Robert Louis Stevenson in 1886 *(The Strange Case of Dr. Jekyll and Mr. Hyde)* tends to depreciate somewhat the novelty of a technique much vaunted by the new novelists. The diary form, especially in analytical novels like *El hermano asno* and *Los hombres del hombre,* also facilitates the greater use of the interior monologue, so readily linked with the stream of consciousness technique, used successfully as early as 1947 by Agustín Yáñez in *Al filo del agua. El hombre's* conversations with his various *yos,* and their discussions with each other independent of *el hombre,* in a way anticipates the complex exchanges of the various levels of the subconscious («si él soy yo... si tú fue él») portrayed in Carlos Fuentes' *La muerte de Artemio Cruz,* for example.[16]

Fuentes, because of his experience in writing for the cinema, probably uses best, despite Manuel Pedro González's harsh criticism of *La región más transparente* as a poor copy of Dos Passos' *Manhattan Transfer,* the cinematographic technique, whose close-ups, flashbacks, flashforwards, etc. have become indispensable ingredients of the contemporary novel. Barrios, who had used artistic techniques borrowed from painting, music, sculpture, or any medium that served his art, did not shy away from films. In fact during his so-called quiet period of the 1930s, when he devoted himself to writing reviews and editorials, he dedicates at least five editorials in *Las Ultimas Noticias* (between 1935-37) to criticism on the cinema, ranging from eulogies of actors (Tito Guizar and Charlie Chaplin) to humorous articles on film stars («De Sara Bernard [*sic*] a Clark Gable»), whilst seriously deploring the lack of good criticism on films («La crítica ausente»). His training as a painter had taught him the value of framing (by means of doors and windows), silhouetting (by means of light and darkness)—cinematographic techniques that he did not hesitate to employ. *El hombre,* the cultured protagonist of the novel, in his formative artistic discussions with his son, actually uses the image of the cinema to express childhood memories which he hopes will serve to bring his son closer to him: «Pues te decía que me vino a la memoria mi pieza de la infancia, con su tragaluz y su techo, gracias a las cuales presenciaba yo, *como en un cine borroso,* todo reducido a siluetas diminutas y mal recortadas, hechas como con ligeros tiznes, cuanto pasaba por la calle» (II, 1037; my italics). As Joel Hancock rightly points out: «His vision is cinematographic and slightly out of focus

---

dream of Someone. The trend re-echoes a similar fashion amongst the later Modernists via Schopenhauer, taken up, as I have demonstrated in Chapter 2, by Barrios, especially in *Un perdido.*

For an interesting discussion of the double personality theme, see ROBERT ROGERS, *The Double in Literature* (Detroit: Wayne State University Press, 1970), especially the summary in Chapter IX, pp. 172-74.

[16] 3rd ed. Fondo de Cultura Económica, Colección Popular, 1967, p. 315. Valéry, of course, much earlier, was saying «Je est un autre».

at that. The street objects are portrayed as minute silhouettes suggesting the effect of fuzzy charcoal drawings. The skylight, through which the scene is viewed, functions as a screen or frame.»[17]

Though not wholly in sympathy with all the formal innovations of the new novelists, Eduardo Barrios was too much of an artist not to be affected by the new ideas. Though generally regarded as traditional, with all the pejorative connotations of that label, *El hermano asno* and especially *Los hombres del hombre,* despite the protestation of both parties, prefigure, if not reflect, some of the technical innovations characteristic of the younger novelists.

One of the main criticisms of Barrios has been his inability or reluctance to move out of the nineteenth century in which his sensibilities are rooted. With Romanticism as his point of departure, Barrios has consistently treated themes that some would label today as «quaintly old-fashioned». The whole conception of Barrios as a *novelista del corazón,* in whose fiction the important value is emotion which often leads to tragedy, points the way to his themes—madness through love, degeneration through excessive sentimentality, saintliness and sexuality, would hardly be considered sophisticated themes by today's standards. Also, his only foray into the rural novel *(Gran señor y rajadiablos)* was a eulogy of nineteenth-century values (after the fashion of *Don Segundo Sombra*). If *El niño que enloqueció de amor, Un perdido* and *El hermano asno* seem a little dated to us now, a closer look at the themes of madness, dipsomania and emotional instability would place Barrios in a line of writers that goes back to Quiroga and Rivera, is in the same tradition as Roberto Arlt and Eduardo Mallea, and looks forward to the novels of Cortázar and José Donoso. Apart from Cortázar, amongst the contemporaries, it is perhaps with Donoso, also Chilean, that he has closest affinities. José Donoso has lately gained some fame for his portrayal of the decadence, corruption, and moral collapse of the Chilean upper/middle classes. In *Coronación, Este domingo* and *El lugar sin límites,* for example, Donoso has taken over Barrios' «old-fashioned» themes of drunkenness, madness, prostitution, to paint an even more depressing picture of Chilean society. More recently his *El obsceno pájaro de la noche* contains a greater and more varied parade of abnormal characters than Barrios could muster in a lifetime of fiction. These, however, are only the modern manifestations of a phenomenon that dates from the beginning of the century and of which Barrios is a part. The whole question of the moral relaxation of the upper/middle class was treated by Orrego Luco and Edwards Bello, both contemporaries of Barrios.[18] If *Un perdido,* Barrios'

---

[17] «The Purification of Eduardo Barrios' Sensorial Prose», *Hispania*, LVI, No. 1 (March, 1973), 56.
[18] See ARNOLD CHAPMAN, «Perspectiva de la novela de la ciudad en Chile», *La novela iberoamericana* (Albuquerque: University of New Mexico Press, 1952), pp. 193-

best example of the theory of degneration which implies the transmission of atavistic defects, has probably more to do with upper-middle than upper class, the lessons are not lost. Although the *perdido* type and the underlying principle of hereditary degeneration are rooted in the work of Darwin, Spencer and Mendel, rendered in fictional terms by Zola who had a great influence in Latin America,[19] the ground has been well prepared by Barrios and his contemporaries for Donoso, whose efforts at psychological sketches, according to the gloomy Manuel Pedro González, must fall short of Barrios' best characterisations: «Más que retratos dan la impresión de caricaturas» («La novela hispanoamericana en el contexto de la internacional», *Coloquio*, p. 67).

What is obvious, then, is that the so-called outdated themes of Barrios (madness, drunkenness and prostitution, etc.), part of a stage in the development of the urban novel, especially as they apply to the upper/middle classes of Chilean society in the first quarter of this century, have been adopted (and adapted) by Donoso and others, if clothed in new forms and expounded by means of more modern techniques.

In *Un perdido*, generally regarded as his most primitive and most developed expression of *la educación sentimental*, Eduardo Barrios treats the theme not only of military college life but also the awakening of youthful sexuality, which are generally regarded as the salient features of Vargas Llosa's *succès de scandale*, *La ciudad y los perros*. Almost half a century's difference in publication dates helps to explain the difference in form and technique and the explicit descriptions in the latter work of a multiplicity of sexual activities ranging from mass masturbation to bestiality and sodomy. The former is hinted at (as a solitary sin) vaguely and tastefully in «El niño que enloqueció de amor» (I, 161), whilst the latter, which in all its manifestations is glorified in Lezama Lima's *Paradiso*, a veritable hymn to homosexuality, never appears in Barrios. Nowhere in *Un perdido* do the scenes describing youthful sexuality reach the heights (?) overtly expressed in *La ciudad y los perros*. Manuel Pedro González, always the devil's advocate against the «boom» novelists, who is totally unappreciative of Vargas Llosa's contribution to fiction, actually draws the comparison between him and Barrios, to Barrios' advantage, pointing out that not only was the theme not new but also implying that Vargas Llosa's treatment of it was weak, and certainly inferior to Barrios'.

Though out of sympathy with the «re-forms» of the new novelists, Barrios shared their concerns about the human situation—hence the links between Barrios and the absurd of Cortázar, otherwise two unlikely bed-

212. Though hardly about the Chilean upper class, *El roto* (1920) of Edwards Bello is a classic example of the whole theme of moral degeneration.

19 Also, the theories of Freud and Jung, so important in the formation of contemporary fiction, were rendered in fictional terms in Barrios' first trilogy some sixty years ago.

fellows. The bond is less tenuous in the situation of Barrios alongside other novelists of the city like Mallea, Onetti and Sábato, from the «civilised» River Plate region, who are not only encompassed by the all-embracing new novel tag but also by generation overlap into the preceding era and sit more comfortably alongside Barrios. Aside from their common preoccupation with the problems of existence, their use of conventional form, narrative and language put them in the same line as Barrios. Various analogies with Mallea and Sábato have already been drawn. In the absurd world, where man is forced to live out his existentialist unhappiness, there are several ways of escape. In Chapter 3 we noted the importance of writing as an evasion, not only for the author Barrios, but also for his fictional creations like Charlie in *Los hombres del hombre*. Fernando Aínsa has observed the same phenomenon as a characteristic of the novels of Juan Carlos Onetti: «Tiene que existir una salida y para Onetti y sus personajes existe: escribir.»[20] As both Cortázar and Sábato, according to their own admission, wrote to purge themselves of their ghosts, which links their metaphysics with their aesthetics,[21] Onetti, like Barrios, communicates through his fiction in order to solve his own problems: «Desdoblándose en sus personajes el autor resuelve sus conflictos. Los seres hipostáticos que van naciendo de su pluma son transferencias, disyuntivas, roturas en el engranaje... La vida de sus personajes es la suya travestida.»[22] Harss, discussing the later work of Cortázar, actually makes the important link which is the core of this study: «lo estético y lo metafísico se persiguen ensañadamente hasta encontrarse en *Rayuela*» (p. 279). It is only through artistic creation, as Barrios affirms in his last novel, that one can achieve liberation from the metaphysical problems. Emir Rodríguez Monegal sums it up thus: «No sólo es cierto que la liberación de la rutina y de la desvalorización del alma sólo llega cuando nos enfrentamos con la verdad de nosotros mismos, nos despojamos de inhibiciones y compromisos, aventamos malentendidos..., la liberación puede llegarnos por la creación, por las fuerzas que libera el creador al rehacer el mundo, al descubrir con asombro su poder y la riqueza de la vida.»[23]

Though Barrios is closer to his River Plate contemporaries (Mallea, Onetti, Sábato) in temperament, his work is also co-terminous with that of his peers Asturias (Guatemala) and Carpentier (Caribbean), more representative of the Indian and negro component of the Latin American whole. It is rather ironic that Asturias and Carpentier, whose education was basically

[20] «Onetti: un outsider resignado», *Cuadernos Hispanoamericanos*, LXXXI, No. 243 (marzo, 1970), 637.
[21] Cf. CORTÁZAR's short stories like «Casa tomada» y «Carta a una señorita en París» and SÁBATO's *El escritor y sus fantasmas* (Buenos Aires: Aguilar, 1967).
[22] LUIS HARSS, *Los nuestros* (Buenos Aires: Ed. Sudamericana, 1969), p. 234.
[23] «Juan Carlos Onetti y la novela rioplatense», *Número*, 3, 13-14 (mayo-junio, 1951), 186.

European (French), should be the forerunners of the magical realism school whose roots are in the native myths and legends of their respective regions. Barrios, who was very proud of his European heritage (Swedish, Spanish, French and German), has commented on several occasions on the «positive» European, as opposed to the Indian, contribution to the culture of Latin America. In an interview with Donald Fogelquist, for example, he makes the contrast: «No sentía ser de ascendencia enteramente europea... pues en su opinión la contribución del europeo a la cultura había sido mucho más notable que la del indio. Reflexioné que esta convicción era natural en Barrios, siendo chileno, pues su país ha sido siempre uno de los más europeos o "europeizados" de América y nunca vio florecer en su suelo ninguna civilización prehistórica muy adelantada.»[24] Barrios, conservative in politics, apparently forgetful of the Araucanian tradition immortalised by Ercilla and others, seems to have carried his reactionary views into the question of race. Unappreciative of the Indian contribution to culture which is the basis of Ciro Alegría's *El mundo es ancho y ajeno,* he has scant respect for the Indian novel of social protest of the thirties, like Icaza's *Huasipungo* which he considered a disgrace to the Spanish language for its coarseness and lack of propriety. Nor was he impressed by the literary worth of the Indian myths, inspiration of many modern novels. What Asturias has done with the Mayan legends of Guatemala, Carpentier with the Afro-Cuban, and even Fuentes with Aztec mythology,[25] has weighed little with Barrios. Not that Barrios is unappreciative of the value of myth. Since his background is unashamedly European and Christian, he shows this particular bent by continuing to use non-American mythology. His real novelty, however, is the fact that he used myth at all, long before the advocates of the new narrative of language and myth, like Faulkner and Kafka, had sounded the clarion call that so many Latin American novelists were to heed from the late forties onwards. These disciples, in the creation of the new narrative, have, according to Fuentes, turned again to the primal roots of all literary expression, viz. poetry and myth, in their search for a narrative that may no longer portray the realism of the traditional novel, but is no less real for its mythical basis.[26] When this crisis in the novel was precipitating a rethinking of the direction of the

---

[24] «Una visita a Eduardo Barrios», *Cuadernos Americanos,* CXVI, No. 3 (1961), 235. This is an explicit development of what he hinted at in another interview with Bernard Dulsey (see note 7): «He spoke of the *indio* of Chile and of Peru and of Bolivia but much of what he said here was off the record» (p. 349).

[25] Especially his first book of stories, *Los días enmascarados* (1954), which contains his best story «Chac Mool», about the Aztec god of rain. This treatment of mythology is refined in *La región más transparente* to a more subtle influence of Mexico's aboriginal past, characterised in the semi-mythical figure of Ixca Cienfuegos.

[26] *La nueva novela hispanoamericana* (México: Mortiz, 1969), p. 19. Cf. what has been called «la realidad objetiva» and «la realidad imaginaria» in *Pedro Páramo,* for example.

genre, as well as a revision and a substitution of myths more in keeping with the modern sensibility,[27] Barrios was already writing his last two novels, *Gran señor y rajadiablos* (1948) and *Los hombres del hombre* (1950), having already, almost three decades before in *El hermano asno* (1922), narrated the oldest myth of all, universal in its application, «the myth of the fall of innocence as traced from the thirteenth to the twentieth century, both in the adapted episodes and in the persons of the protagonists».[28] What is significant, and no less ironic, is that *El hermano asno*, ostensibly a psychological novel with a religious setting, indebted to sources as widely disparate as St. Francis and Freud, should, by the reliving and the retelling of the eternal myth of man's fall from innocence, a key concept in Christian «mytheology», foreshadow the new novel: «*Essential to myth is not truth, but the "emotion of the truth"* in the retelling of constant and recurring human dramas, whether reinacted by Prometheus and Pandora, Adam and Eve, or two obscure Chilean monks. *El hermano asno* reflects the solitude and terror that has always accompanied man when he faces his existence for the first time, unaided and unprotected, after knowledge has destroyed his childhood beliefs. Barrios has also made it clear that this is also modern man's existential despair: the certainty that he must now be, in whole or in part, his own God» (Brown, pp. 329-30; my italics). With this reiteration of the indispensability of «la emoción de la verdad» (*También* I, 28) as a requisite of myth, Barrios links not only aesthetics, but one of its ingredients, mythology, to the whole business of living and existence (in all times)—metaphysics.

Though far from the magical realism of Asturias and Carpentier, and distant from the Mayan and Aztec legends that have nurtured the new novels, Barrios' use of myth, albeit Western/Christian, is destined to achieve the same end as the tortured fiction of today—to portray «una ontología y una metafísica de la condición humana».[29] If it has been proved that Barrios, by means of philosophical insight, garnered through experience and study, has written metaphysical novels that are about life, then Mark Schorer's definition of a myth as a «large controlling image that gives philosophic meaning to the facts of ordinary life»,[30] surely applies as aptly to Barrios in *El hermano asno* as to the exponents of the new novel whom he predates by a quarter of a century.

If one were excessively pessimistic, one might say with Manuel Pedro

---

[27] JUAN LOVELUCK, «Crisis y renovación en la novela de Hispanoamérica», *Coloquio*, p. 123.

[28] JAMES W. BROWN, «*El hermano asno* from *Fioretti* through Freud», *Symposium*, XXV, No. 4 (Winter, 1971), 328.

[29] IBER H. VERDUGO, «Perspectivas de la actual novela hispanoamericana», *Mundo Nuevo*, 28 (octubre, 1968), 82-83.

[30] *The Study of Literature: A Handbook of Critical Essays and Terms* (Boston: Little, Brown, 1960), p. 315.

González that no good fiction has been written in Latin America (or North America) since 1945—a corollary of Ortega y Gasset's sombre forecast of the death of the novel due to the lack of new themes, and the exacting demands of the public for *más nuevos,* of better quality: «creo que el género novela, si no está irremediablemente agotado, se halla, de cierto, en su período último y padece una tal penuria de temas posibles, que el escritor necesita compensada con la exquisita calidad de los demás ingredientes necesarios para integrar un cuerpo de novela».[31] A more positive interpretation, however, might be that, if the new novel, which reflects so many of Barrios' themes and techniques, is not stagnant, then Barrios, as in the field of psychology, was ahead of his time and foreshadowed the best qualities of the new novel. The form and the ideas expressed, especially in *El hermano asno* and *Los hombres del hombre,* place Barrios among the contemporary figures of Fuentes, Cortázar, Onetti, Mallea, Asturias, Rulfo —to the chagrin of both sides, no doubt. The use of indigenous mythology to portray contemporary reality is but one method used by the new novelists to replace the narcissistic attitudes of the earlier novelists with an outer-looking perspective that sees Latin American culture not as a self-contained unit but something with universal values that have meaning for all men.

It is this universalism, which transcends frontiers and epochs, that raises Barrios above the regionalists, though being Chilean he uses the American backgrounds he knows. It is not, however, the northern pampa, nor the central valleys, nor the urban areas of Chile that matter, but the human dramas played out against these backgrounds. In this sense his novels are not only about Chilean life [32] but life in general and the metaphysical problems that constitute the human condition—the problems of birth and death, man's efforts to support the essential anguish of existence, which thus provide significance to an otherwise absurd world. Barrios' literary reputation has generally rested on his skills as a psychological novelist, whose ability to analyse character has been praised in almost scientific or medical terms. Analysis and psychological values, however, are secondary to a view of life which is a prerequisite of any serious fictional creation. This metaphysical outlook which pervades his novels, although rooted in the pessimism of the Romantic discovery, developed and matured over the years as it was nurtured by his own findings and sufferings in the philosophical field. Barrios, however, was a writer whose sacred task, he believed, was to articulate his findings in artistic fashion. If Romanticism was his metaphysical point of departure, he never forgot the aesthetic canons

---

[31] «Ideas sobre la novela», *Obras completas,* Tomo III (1917-25) [Madrid: Revista de Occidente, 1962], p. 390.

[32] «Opino que es un error considerar al regionalismo como el rasgo distintivo de la novela hispanoamericana» (FERNANDO ALEGRÍA, «Estilos de novelar o estilos de vivir», *Coloquio,* p. 139).

preached by his Modernist masters. For many, the cause of Barrios' reputation has generally been two-fold, resting on a Stendhalian gift for analytical psychology, which sits oddly alongside an exaggerated evaluation of the regionalist and social elements of his work. More important, however, and surely herein lies Barrios' true merit, is his concern for «man's estate» which lifts him above the mere regionalist: «Con Eduardo Barrios la novela americana logra un valor de universalidad.»[33] To have commented on, and offered solutions to, man's vital problems makes Barrios a serious metaphysical novelist. To have done so aesthetically in a form wholly consistent with the content renders Eduardo Barrios a great artist.

[33] MILTON ROSSEL, «El hombre y su psique en las novelas de Eduardo Barrios», *Atenea*, CXXXIX, No. 389 (1960), p. 207.

BIBLIOGRAPHY

I. Works by Eduardo Barrios

Barrios, Eduardo: *Obras completas.* 2 vols., intro. Milton Rossel. Santiago de Chile: Zig-Zag, 1962.
— «Ahora ante Guizar». *Las Ultimas Noticias,* XXXV (14 de octubre, 1937), 4.
— «Baldomero Lillo». *La Revista Chilena,* XX (1923), 416.
— «*Balmaceda: político romántico,* por Luis Enrique Delano». *Las Ultimas Noticias,* XXXV (7 de julio, 1937), 5.
— «La crítica ausente». *Las Ultimas Noticias,* XXXV (14 de julio, 1937), 3.
— «Demasiados amaneramientos». *La Nación,* XXXVI (30 de diciembre, 1952), 4.
— «De Sara Bernard [*sic*] a Clark Gable». *Las Ultimas Noticias,* XXXII (11 de octubre, 1935), 4.
— «El fenómeno de la ópera». *Las Ultimas Noticias,* XXXV (16 de septiembre, 1937), 4.
— «*Hijuna,* por Carlos Sepúlveda Layton». *Las Ultimas Noticias,* XXXII (9 de mayo, 1934), 12.
— «La hazaña pianística de Rosita Renard». *Las Ultimas Noticias,* XXXV (9 de octubre, 1937), 4.
— «*El hombre en la montaña,* por Edgardo Garrido Merino». *Las Ultimas Noticias,* XXXII (23 de mayo, 1934), 12.
— «Mirando a Chaplin». *Las Ultimas Noticias,* XXXIV (20 de junio, 1936), 4, 14.
— «Un pianista nuestro». *Las Ultimas Noticias,* XXXV (2 de octubre, 1937), 4.
— Prólogo a *Sus mejores cuentos* de Alfonso Hernández Catá. Santiago: Nascimento, 1936, pp. 7-15.
— «*Romances americanos,* por José María Souviron». *Las Ultimas Noticias,* XXXV (30 de junio, 1937), 6.
— «La saturación literaria». *Atenea,* No. 1 (abril, 1924), rpt. in CLIV, No. 404 (abril-junio, 1964), 69-74.
— *Teatro escogido: Vivir. Lo que niega la vida. Por el decoro.* Prólogo de Domingo Melfi Demarco. Santiago: Zig-Zag, 1947.
— «Viejo cinematógrafo». *Las Ultimas Noticias,* XXXIV (13 de febrero, 1936), 4.

II. Critical Works Concerning Barrios

Anadón, José: «Una carta de Gabriela Mistral sobre *Desolación*». *Hispamérica,* No. 19 (abril, 1978), 27-42.
— «Epistolario entre Gabriela Mistral y Eduardo Barrios». *Cuadernos Americanos,* CCX, No. 2 (marzo-abril, 1977), 228-35.
— «Gabriela Mistral comenta una novela de Barrios». *Quaderni Ibero-Americani,* VII, Nos. 51-52 (junio-diciembre 1978-junio 1979), 171-75.

175

ANDERSON, ROBERT ROLAND: «The Doctrine of Quietism in *El hermano asno*». *Hispania*, LVIII, No. 4 (December, 1975), 874-83.

BENBOW, JERRY L.: «Grotesque Elements in Eduardo Barrios». *Hispania*, LI, No. 1 (March, 1968), 86-91.

BENTE, THOMAS O.: «La contraposición de *El hermano asno* de Eduardo Barrios; un estudio de polaridades complementarias». *Cuadernos Americanos*, CC, No. 3 (mayo-junio, 1975), 239-47.

BROWN, JAMES W.: «*El hermano asno* from *Fioretti* through Freud». *Symposium*, XXV, No. 4 (Winter, 1971), 321-32.

CARROL, EDWARD LEROY: «Eduardo Barrios as a Literary Artist». Unpublished M. A. diss. University of Texas, Austin, 1939.

CLUFF, RUSSELL M.: «Eduardo Barrios y la novela de iniciación». *Kentucky Romance Quarterly*, XXVIII, No. 1 (1981), 37-51.

COTTO-THORNER, GUILLERMO: «Eduardo Barrios: novelista del sentimiento». *Hispania*, XXXIV, No. 3 (August, 1951), 271-72.

DAVISON, NED J.: *The Concept of Modernism in Hispanic Criticism*. Boulder, Colorado: Pruett Press, 1966.

— «Conflict and Identity in *El hermano asno*». *Hispania*, XLII, No. 4 (December, 1959), 498-501.

— «The Dramatic Works of Eduardo Barrios». *Hispania*, XLI, No. 1 (March, 1958), 60-63.

— *Eduardo Barrios*. New York: Twayne, 1970.

— «Psychological Values in the Works of Eduardo Barrios». Unpublished doctoral diss. University of California, Los Angeles, 1957.

— «The Significance of *Del natural* in the Fiction of Eduardo Barrios». *Hispania*, XLIV, No. 1 (March, 1961), 27-33.

— *Sobre Eduardo Barrios y otros: estudios y crónicas*. Albuquerque: Foreign Books, 1966.

DECKER, DONALD M.: «Eduardo Barrios Talks about his Novels». *Hispania*, XLV, No. 2 (May, 1962), 254-58.

Diccionario de la literatura latinoamericana: Chile. Ed. Armando Correia Pacheco. Washington: Unión Panamericana, 1958, pp. 16-18.

DINAMARCA, SALVADOR: «*Tamarugal*». *Revista Iberoamericana*, X, No. 19 (noviembre, 1945), 172-76.

DONOSO, ARMANDO: *La otra América*. Madrid: Calpe, 1925, pp. 153-80.

DULSEY, BERNARD: «A Visit with Eduardo Barrios». *Modern Language Journal*, XLIII (November, 1959), 349.

«Eduardo Barrios Hudtwalcker...». *Boletín del Instituto de Literatura Chilena*, II, No. 3 (1962), 14-24.

EMETH, OMER (EMILIO VAISSE): *Estudios críticos de literatura chilena*. Santiago: Nascimento, 1940, pp. 49-63.

FOGELQUIST, DONALD: «Eduardo Barrios, en su etapa actual». *Revista Iberoamericana*, XVIII, No. 35 (febrero-diciembre, 1952), 13-26.

— «Una visita a Eduardo Barrios». *Cuadernos Americanos*, CXVI, No. 3 (mayo-junio, 1961), 234-39.

GALAOS, JOSÉ ANTONIO: «Eduardo Barrios. Novelista autobiográfico». *Cuadernos Hispanoamericanos*, LVI, No. 166 (octubre, 1963), 160-74.

GÁLVEZ, MANUEL: «Prólogo a *Un perdido*». Madrid: Espasa-Calpe, 1926, pp. 9-13; rpt. Santiago: Zig-Zag, 1965, pp. 7-9.

HAMILTON, CARLOS D.: «La novelística de Eduardo Barrios». *Cuadernos Americanos*, LXXXV, No. 1 (enero-febrero, 1956), 280-92.

HANCOCK, JOEL C.: «Compositional Modes of Eduardo Barrios' *Los hombres del hombre* with an Appended Bibliography of his Uncollected Prose». Unpublished doctoral diss. University of New Mexico, 1970.

— «El diario como medio de estructura en *Los hombres del hombre* de Eduardo Barrios». *Hispanófila*, No. 49 (September, 1973), 1-9.

— «The Journalistic Writings of Eduardo Barrios». *Hispania*, LIX, No. 4 (December, 1976), 835-43.

— «The Purification of Eduardo Barrios' Sensorial Prose». *Hispania*, LVI, No. 1 (March, 1973), 51-59.

KELLY, JOHN R.: «Name Symbolism in Barrios' *El hermano asno*». *Romance Notes*, XIII, No. 1 (Autumn, 1971-72), 48-53.

[¿LATCHAM, RICARDO?] «Eduardo Barrios, académico». *La Nación*, XXXVII (23 de junio, 1953), 2.

— «*Páginas de un pobre diablo*». *La Revista Católica*, XLVI (1924), 226-28.

LINDO, HUGO: «Con un novelista insigne». *Cultura*, No. 8 (marzo-abril, 1956), 7-10.

LOZADA, ALFREDO: «Humillarse y servir: El espíritu franciscano en *El hermano asno* de Eduardo Barrios», in *Estudios críticos*. Buenos Aires: El Cid Editor, 1978, pp. 7-66.

LOZANO, CARLOS: «Paralelismos entre Flaubert y Eduardo Barrios». *Revista Iberoamericana*, XXIV, No. 47 (enero-junio, 1959), 105-16.

LUISI, LUISA: *A través de libros y de autores*. Buenos Aires: Nuestra América, 1925, pp. 195-216.

MARTÍNEZ DACOSTA, SILVIA: *Dos ensayos literarios: sobre Eduardo Barrios y José Donoso*. Miami: Ediciones Universal, 1976.

MISTRAL, GABRIELA [LUCILA GODOY ALCAYAGA]: Prólogo a *Y la vida sigue*. Buenos Aires: Tor, 1925, pp. 11-15.

MONGUIÓ, LUIS: «Sobre un milagro en Meléndez, Palma y Barrios», in *Estudios sobre literatura hispanoamericana y española*. México: Andrea, 1958, pp. 115-30.

MONTERDE, FRANCISCO: «*Los hombres del hombre*». *Revista Iberoamericana*, XVII, No. 33 (febrero-julio, 1951), 134-36.

MORÍNIGO, MARIANO: *Eduardo Barrios, novelista*. Tucumán: Universidad Nacional de Tucumán, 1971.

OBERDOERFFER, MARIANNE: «Eduardo Barrios, Chilean Novelist». Unpublished M. A. diss. Columbia University, New York, 1955.

ONFRAY BARROS, JORGE: «Perfil de Eduardo Barrios». *Revista Zig-Zag*, XLII, No. 2149 (30 de mayo, 1946), 25-26.

ORLANDI, JULIO, y ALEJANDRO RAMÍREZ: *Eduardo Barrios: Obras. Estilo. Técnica.* Santiago: Editorial del Pacífico, 1960.

PERALTA, JAIME: «La novelística de Eduardo Barrios». *Cuadernos Hispanoamericanos*, LVIII, No. 173 (mayo, 1964), 357-67.

PETIT, MAGDALENA: «Entrevista a Eduardo Barrios». *El Imparcial*, XXI (19 de septiembre, 1948), 10.

RÁBAGO, ALBERTO: «Técnica narrativa en *El hermano asno* y *Los hombres del hombre*». *Revista Canadiense de Estudios Hispánicos*, III, No. 2 (Invierno, 1979), 121-36.

RAMÍREZ, MANUEL D.: «Some Notes on the Prose Style of Eduardo Barrios». *Romance Notes*, IX, No. 1 (Autumn, 1966-67), 40-48.

ROSSEL, MILTON: «Eduardo Barrios». *Atenea*, CLII (1964), 3-5.

— «El hombre y su psique en las novelas de Eduardo Barrios». *Atenea*, CXXXIX, No. 389 (julio-septiembre, 1960), 182-207; rpt. in *Cien años de la novela chilena*. Santiago: Universitaria, 1961.

— «Un novelista psicólogo: Eduardo Barrios». *Atenea*, LIX, No. 175 (enero, 1940), 5-16.

JOHN WALKER

Ruiz Vernacci, Enrique: «Una gran novela americana: *Los hombres del hombre*». *Repertorio Americano*, XLVII, No. 1126 (15 de mayo, 1951), 81-83.

Sánchez, Porfirio: «Aspectos quijotescos del *Niño que enloqueció de amor*». *Romance Notes*, XII, No. 1 (Autumn, 1970-71), 55-61.

Santiván, Fernando: «Eduardo Barrios y su tiempo». *Atenea*, CLIV, No. 404 (abril-junio, 1964), 75-79.

Silva Castro, Raúl: *Creadores chilenos de personajes novelescos*. Santiago: Biblioteca de Alta Cultura, n.d., pp. 157-76.

— «Eduardo Barrios (1884-1963)». *Revista Iberoamericana*, XXX, No. 58 (julio-diciembre, 1964), 239-60.

— «La obra novelesca de Eduardo Barrios». *Cuadernos*, No. 78 (1963), 76-82.

— *Panorama de la novela chilena (1843-1954)*. México: Fondo de Cultura Económica, 1955, pp. 117-31.

— *Panorama literario de Chile*. Santiago: Universitaria, 1961, pp. 248-56.

Spell, Jefferson Rea: *Contemporary Spanish American Fiction*. Chapel Hill: University of North Carolina Press, 1944, pp. 135-52.

— «Eduardo Barrios, novelista psicológico de Chile». *Atenea*, LXXXIX, No. 274 (abril, 1948), 34-48.

— «*Tamarugal*». *Revista Iberoamericana*, XIV, No. 27 (junio, 1948), 142-43.

Stephens, Doris T.: «The Emergence of the Primary Self in Eduardo Barrios' *Los hombres del hombre*». *Romance Notes*, XXI, No. 3 (Spring, 1980-81), 293-97.

Torres-Ríoseco, Arturo: *Ensayos sobre literatura latinoamericana*. Segunda serie. Berkeley: University of California Press, 1958, pp. 191-94.

— *Grandes novelistas de la América Hispana*. Tomo 2: *Los novelistas de la ciudad*. Berkeley: University of California Press, 1949, pp. 21-57.

Vázquez-Bigi, Angel Manuel: «Los conflictos psíquicos y religiosos de *El hermano asno*» (I). *Cuadernos Hispanoamericanos*, LXXIII, No. 219 (marzo, 1968), 456-76; (II), LXXIV, No. 220 (abril, 1968), 120-45.

— «*Eduardo Barrios, novelista*, por Mariano Morínigo». *Revista Iberoamericana*, XL, No. 86 (enero-mayo, 1974), 200-04.

— «El tipo sicológico en Eduardo Barrios y correspondencias en las letras europeas». *Revista Iberoamericana*, XXIV, No. 48 (julio-diciembre, 1959), 265-96.

— «Los tres planos de la creación artística de Eduardo Barrios». *Revista Iberoamericana*, XXIX, No. 55 (enero-junio, 1963), 125-37.

— «La verdad sicológica en Eduardo Barrios». Unpublished doctoral diss. University of Minnesota, 1962.

Vega, Manuel: «Eduardo Barrios en la intimidad». *Revista Zig-Zag*, XL, No. 2070 (24 de noviembre, 1944), 39.

Vidal, Hernán: «El modo narrativo en *El hermano asno* de Eduardo Barrios». *Revista Hispánica Moderna*, XXXIII, Nos. 3-4 (julio-octubre, 1967), 241-49.

Walker, John: «The Aesthetic and Metaphysical Function of Liturgy in the Work of Eduardo Barrios». *Mosaic*, XII, No. 2 (Winter, 1979), 147-59.

— «Anacronismo y novedad en la obra de Eduardo Barrios». *Cuadernos Americanos*, CCXXXVI, No. 3 (mayo-junio, 1981), 192-207.

— «The Case of Eduardo Barrios: A Literary Paradox». *International Fiction Review*, Vol. 3, No. 2 (July, 1976), 107-12.

— «Echoes of Pascal in the Works of Eduardo Barrios». *The Romanic Review*, XLVI, No. 4 (December, 1970), 256-63.

— «La evolución metafísica de Eduardo Barrios a través de sus novelas». *Actas del Congreso VI de la Asociación Internacional de Hispanistas* (Toronto, 1980), pp. 769-72.

— «*Gran señor y rajadiablos*: A Shift in Sensibility». *Bulletin of Hispanic Studies*, XLIX, No. 3 (July, 1972), 278-88.

— «*Los hombres del hombre:* Barrios' Final Comment». *The American Hispanist,* III, No. 20 (October, 1977), 14-18.
— «*Páginas de un pobre diablo:* The Light in the Darkness». *Ibero-Amerikanisches Archiv,* No. 1 (January, 1977), 29-36.
— «Schopenhauer and Nietzsche in the Work of Eduardo Barrios». *Revista Canadiense de Estudios Hispánicos,* III, No. 1 (Autumn, 1977), 39-53.
— «*Tamarugal*—Barrios' Neglected Link Novel». *Revista de Estudios Hispánicos,* VIII, No. 3 (octubre, 1974), 345-55.
— «The Theme of *civilización y barbarie* in *Gran señor y rajadiablos*». *Hispanófila,* No. 42 (1971), 57-67.
WELLMAN, DONNA SUE: «Héroes y heroínas de Eduardo Barrios». Unpublished M. A. diss. UNAM, México, 1957.

III. OTHER WORKS CONSULTED

AIKEN, HENRY D.: *The Age of Ideology: The Nineteenth Century Philosophers.* New York: New American Library, 1956.
AÍNSA, FERNANDO: «Onetti: un outsider resignado». *Cuadernos Hispanoamericanos,* LXXXI, No. 243 (marzo, 1970), 612-38.
— *Las trampas de Onetti.* Montevideo: Alfa, 1970.
ALEGRÍA, CIRO: *El mundo es ancho y ajeno.* Buenos Aires: Losada, 1961.
— «Notas sobre el personaje en la novela hispanoamericana», in *La novela iberoamericana.* Albuquerque: University of New Mexico Press, 1952, pp. 49-58.
ALEGRÍA, FERNANDO: *Breve historia de la novela hispanoamericana.* México: Andrea, 1959.
— «Una clasificación de la novela hispanoamericana», in *La novela iberoamericana.* Albuquerque: University of New Mexico Press, 1952, pp. 61-75.
— *Las fronteras del realismo.* Santiago: Zig-Zag, 1962.
— *Literatura y revolución.* México: Fondo de Cultura Económica, 1970.
ALONE [HERNÁN DÍAZ ARRIETA]: *Panorama de literatura chilena durante el siglo XX.* Santiago: Nascimento, 1931.
— *Historia personal de la literatura chilena.* Santiago: Zig-Zag, 1954.
AMES, VAN METER: *Aesthetics of the Novel.* Chicago: University of Chicago Press, 1928.
ANDERSON IMBERT, ENRIQUE: *La crítica literaria contemporánea.* Buenos Aires: Guré, 1957.
— *Historia de la literatura hispanoamericana.* 2 vols. México: Fondo de Cultura Económica, 1966.
ASTURIAS, MIGUEL ANGEL: *Mulata de tal.* Buenos Aires: Losada, 1963.
ATWOOD, MARGARET: *Survival: A Thematic Guide to Canadian Literature.* Toronto: Anansi, 1972.
AZORÍN [JOSÉ MARTÍNEZ RUIZ]: *Antonio Azorín,* in *Obras completas,* Vol. III. Madrid: Rafael Caro Raggio, 1920.
— *La voluntad.* Madrid: Castalia, 1972.
AZUELA, MARIANO: *Los de abajo.* México: Fondo de Cultura Económica, 1960.
BAQUERO GOYANES, MARIANO: *Proceso de la novela actual.* Madrid: Rialp, 1963.
— *¿Qué es la novela?* Buenos Aires: Columba, 1961.
BARBAGELATA, HUGO D. *La novela y el cuento en Hispanoamérica.* Montevideo: Enrique Miguez, 1947.
BARNET, SYLVAN, et al.: *The Study of Literature: A Handbook of Critical Essays and Terms.* Boston: Little, Brown, 1960.

BAROJA Y NESSI, PÍO: *La lucha por la vida (La busca, Mala hierba, Aurora roja)* from *Obras completas,* Vol. I. Madrid: Biblioteca Nueva, 1946.
— *El mundo es ansí.* Ed. D. L. Shaw. Oxford: Pergamon, 1970.
BART, B. F.: «Aesthetic Distance in *Madame Bovary*». *PMLA,* LXIX, No. 5 (December, 1954), 1112-26.
BEACH, JOSEPH WARREN: *The Twentieth Century Novel: Studies in Technique.* New York: Century, 1932.
BEAUVOIR, SIMONE DE: «Littérature et métaphysique». *Les Temps Modernes,* I, No. 7 (1946), 1153-63.
BENTLEY, PHYLLIS: *Some Observations on the Art of Narrative.* London: Home and Van Thal, 1946.
BLANCO FOMBONA, RUFINO: *El hombre de hierro.* Madrid: Ed. Americana, n. d.
BONET, CARMELO M.: *En torno a la estética literaria.* Buenos Aires: Nova, 1959.
BOOTH, WAYNE C.: *The Rhetoric of Fiction.* Chicago: University of Chicago Press, 1961.
BROWN, E. K.: «The Problem of a Canadian Literature», in *On Canadian Poetry.* Toronto: Ryerson Press, 1943, rpt. in *Masks of Fiction: Canadian Critics on Canadian Prose.* Toronto: McClelland and Stewart, 1961, pp. 40-52.
CABRERA INFANTE, GUILLERMO: *Tres tristes tigres.* Barcelona: Seix Barral, 1965.
CAMBACERES, EUGENIO: *Sin rumbo.* 2nd ed. Buenos Aires: Plus Ultra, 1968.
CARY, JOYCE: *Art and Reality: Ways of the Creative Process.* New York: Harper, 1958.
CEJADOR Y FRAUCA, JULIO: *Historia de la lengua y literatura castellana.* Tomo XII. Madrid: Revista de Archivos, Bibliotecas y Museos, 1920.
CHAPMAN, ARNOLD: «Observations on the *Roto* in Chilean Fiction». *Hispania,* XXXII, No. 3 (August, 1949), 309-14.
— «The *Perdido* as a Type in some Spanish-American Novels». *PMLA,* LXX, No. 1 (March, 1955), 19-36.
— «Perspectiva de la novela de la ciudad en Chile», from *La novela iberoamericana.* Albuquerque: University of New Mexico Press, 1952, pp. 193-212.
CISNEROS, LUIS BENJAMÍN: *Amor de niño* from *Obras completas.* Lima: Gil, 1939.
CONSTANT, BENJAMIN: *Adolphe.* London: Dent, n. d.
COOK, ALBERT SPAULDING: *The Meaning of Fiction.* Detroit: Wayne State University Press, 1960.
CORTÁZAR, JULIO: *Rayuela.* 10th ed. Buenos Aires: Sudamericana, 1969.
CORVALÁN, OCTAVIO: *El postmodernismo.* New York: Las Américas, 1961.
CRAWFORD, W. REX: *A Century of Latin American Thought.* Revd. ed. Cambridge, Mass.: Harvard U. P., 1961.
DARÍO, RUBÉN: *Azul.* 14th ed. Madrid: Espasa-Calpe, 1966.
— *Sus mejores poemas.* 2nd ed. revd. Selección de Eduardo Barrios y Roberto Meza Fuentes. Santiago: Nascimento, 1929.
DEL RÍO, ANGEL: *Historia de la literatura española.* 2 vols. Revd. ed. New York: Holt, Rinehart and Winston, 1963.
DE VOTO, BERNARD AUGUSTINE: *The World of Fiction.* Boston: Houghton Mifflin, 1950.
DONOSO, JOSÉ: *Coronación.* Barcelona: Seix Barral, 1968.
— *Este domingo.* México: Joaquín Mortiz, 1968.
— *El lugar sin límites.* México: Joaquín Mortiz, 1966.
— *Los mejores cuentos de José Donoso.* Santiago: Zig-Zag, 1965.
— *El obsceno pájaro de la noche.* Barcelona: Seix Barral, 1970.
EDEL, LEON: *The Psychological Novel 1900-50.* Philadelphia: Lippincott, 1955.
EDWARDS BELLO, JOAQUÍN: *El roto.* Santiago: Universitaria, 1968.
— *Recuerdos de un cuarto de siglo.* Santiago: Zig-Zag, 1966.

Existentialism from Dostoevsky to Sartre. Ed. Walter Kaufmann. Cleveland: Meridian Books, 1956.

FEIN, JOHN M.: *Modernismo in Chilean Literature: The Second Period*. Durham, North Carolina: Duke U. P., 1965.

FLAUBERT, GUSTAVE: *L'Education sentimentale*. Paris: Henri Béziat, n. d.

— *Madame Bovary*. Edinburgh: Nelson, 1948.

FORSTER, E. M.: *Aspects of the Novel*. London: Edward Arnold, 1927.

FRANCO, JEAN: *An Introduction to Spanish American Literature*. Cambridge: Cambridge U. P., 1969.

— *Spanish American Literature Since Independence*. London: Ernest Benn, 1973.

FREEDMAN, RALPH: *The Lyrical Novel*. Princeton: Princeton U. P., 1963.

FRIEDMAN, MELVIN: *Streams of Consciousness: A Study in Literary Methods*. New Haven: Yale U. P., 1955.

FRYE, NORTHROP: *Anatomy of Criticism: Four Essays*. Princeton: Princeton U. P., 1957.

FUENTES, CARLOS: *Los días enmascarados*. México: Andrea, 1954.

— *La muerte de Artemio Cruz*. 3rd ed. México: Fondo de Cultura Económica, 1967.

— *La región más transparente*. México: Fondo de Cultura Económica, 1968.

— *La nueva novela latinoamericana*. México: Joaquín Mortiz, 1969.

GALLEGOS, RÓMULO: *Doña Bárbara*. 16th ed. Buenos Aires: Espasa-Calpe, 1958.

GÁLVEZ, MANUEL: *El mal metafísico*. 3rd ed. Buenos Aires: Espasa-Calpe, 1962.

GAMBOA, FEDERICO: *Novelas de Federico Gamboa*. México: Fondo de Cultura Económica, 1965.

GANIVET, ANGEL: *Idearium español*. Madrid: Librería General de Victoriano Suárez, 1923.

GARCÍA GAMES, JULIA: *Como los he visto...* Santiago: Nascimento, 1930.

GARDINER, PATRICK: *Schopenhauer*. Harmondsworth, Middlesex: Penguin, 1963.

GERTEL, ZUNILDA: *La novela hispanoamericana contemporánea*. Buenos Aires: Columba, 1970.

GÓMEZ GIL, ORLANDO: *Historia crítica de la literatura hispanoamericana*. New York: Holt, Rinehart and Winston, 1968.

GRAÇA ARANHA, JOSÉ PEREIRA DA: *Chanaan*. Río de Janeiro: Briguiet, 1943.

GÜIRALDES, RICARDO: *Don Segundo Sombra*. 18th ed. Buenos Aires: Losada, 1960.

— *Raucho*, in *Obras completas*. Buenos Aires: Emecé, 1962.

— *Xaimaca*. Buenos Aires: Losada, 1944.

GUTIÉRREZ GIRARDOT, RAFAEL: «Literatura y sociedad en Hispanoamérica». *Cuadernos Hispanoamericanos*, LXXV, Nos. 224-25 (agosto-septiembre, 1968), 579-94.

HARSS, LUIS: *Los nuestros*. Buenos Aires: Sudamericana, 1969.

HENRÍQUEZ UREÑA, MAX: *Breve historia del modernismo*. 2nd ed. México: Fondo de Cultura Económica, 1962.

HERNÁNDEZ, JOSÉ: *Martín Fierro*. 7th ed. Buenos Aires: Espasa-Calpe, 1946.

HESSE, HERMANN: *Steppenwolf*. Trans. Basil Creighton, revd. Walter Sorell. New York: Modern Library, 1963.

HUERTAS-JOURDA, JOSÉ: *The Existentialism of Miguel de Unamuno*. University of Florida Monographs, No. 13, 1963.

HUMPHREY, ROBERT: *Stream of Consciousness in the Modern Novel*. Berkeley: University of California Press, 1954.

ICAZA, JORGE: *Huasipungo*. 3rd ed. Buenos Aires: Losada, 1965.

ILIE, PAUL: «Nietzsche in Spain 1890-1910». *PMLA*, LXXIX, No. 1 (March, 1964), 80-96.

ISAACS, JORGE: *María*. 6th ed. Buenos Aires: Sopena, 1957.

JASPERS, KARL: *Nietzsche: An Introduction to the Understanding of his Philosophical*

13

Activity. Trans. Charles F. Wallraff and Frederick J. Schmitz. Tucson: University of Arizona Press, 1965.

KAELIN, EUGENE F.: *An Existentialist Aesthetic.* Madison: University of Wisconsin Press, 1962.

KAUFMANN, WALTER: «Friedrich Nietzsche». *Encyclopaedia Britannica.* London: Benton, 1965.

— *Nietzsche: Philosopher, Psychologist, Anti-Christ.* 3rd ed. revd. and enlgd. Princeton: Princeton U. P., 1968.

KERN, EDITH: *Existentialist Thought and Fictional Technique.* New Haven: Yale U. P., 1970.

KERRIGAN, ANTHONY: «Borges/Unamuno», in *Prose for Borges.* Evanston: Northwestern U. P., 1972, pp. 238-55.

LARRETA, ENRIQUE: *La gloria de Don Ramiro.* Buenos Aires: Espasa, 1941.

LATCHAM, RICARDO: *Carnet crítico.* Montevideo: Alfa, 1962.

— *Antología.* Santiago: Zig-Zag, 1965.

LEOCADIO GARASA, DELFÍN: *Los géneros literarios.* Buenos Aires: Columba, 1969.

LESSER, SIMON O.: *Fiction and the Unconscious.* New York: Vintage, 1957.

LEZAMA LIMA, JOSÉ: *Paradiso.* México: Era, 1968.

LILLO, BALDOMERO: *Sub sole.* 11th ed. Santiago: Nascimento, 1969.

— *Sub terra.* 5th ed. Santiago: Nascimento, 1952.

The Little Flowers of St. Francis. Trans. T. Okey. London: Dent, 1910.

LIZARDI, JOSÉ JOAQUÍN FERNÁNDEZ DE: *El periquillo sarniento.* 2nd ed. ampl. México: Porrúa, 1959.

LÓPEZ-MORILLAS, JUAN: «Unamuno and Pascal: Notes on the Concept of Agony». *PMLA*, LXV, No. 6 (December, 1950), 998-1010.

LOVELUCK, JUAN: «Crisis y renovación en la novela de Hispanoamérica», in *Coloquio sobre la novela hispanoamericana.* México: Fondo de Cultura Económica, 1967, pp. 113-34.

LUBBOCK, PERCY: *The Craft of Fiction.* London: Jonathan Cape, 1921.

LUCAS, FRANK LAURENCE: *Literature and Psychology.* Ann Arbor: University of Michigan Press, 1957.

LUKÁCS, GYÖRGY: *Ensayos sobre el realismo.* Buenos Aires: Siglo Veinte, 1965.

— *Estética.* Barcelona: Grijalbo, 1966.

— *La teoría de la novela.* Buenos Aires: Siglo Veinte, 1966.

MAGIS, CARLOS H.: «Novela, realidad y malos entendidos». *Revista de la Universidad de México*, XXV, No. 6 (febrero, 1971), 10-17.

MALLEA, EDUARDO: *La bahía de silencio.* 4th ed. Buenos Aires: Sudamericana, 1960.

— *Cuentos para una inglesa desesperada,* in *Obras completas.* Buenos Aires: Emecé, 1961.

— *Historia de una pasión argentina.* 4th ed. Buenos Aires: Espasa-Calpe, 1945.

— *Poderío de la novela.* Buenos Aires: Aguilar, 1965.

— *Todo verdor perecerá.* Ed. D. L. Shaw. Oxford: Pergamon, 1968.

MANN, THOMAS: *Death in Venice, Tristan, Tonio Kröger.* Harmondsworth, Middlesex: Penguin, 1955.

MARTEL, JULIÁN [JOSÉ MARÍA MIRÓ]: *La bolsa.* 2nd ed. Buenos Aires: Estrada, 1955.

MARTIN, F. R.: «Pascal and Miguel de Unamuno». *Modern Language Review*, XXXIX, No. 2 (April, 1944), 138-45.

MELFI DEMARCO, DOMINGO: «Panorama literario chileno: la novela y el cuento». *Atenea*, XI (octubre, 1929), 287-96.

MENDILOW, A. A.: *Time and the Novel.* New York: Humanities Press, 1952.

MICHAUD, GUY: *L'Oeuvre de Pascal.* Paris: Hachette, 1950.

MICHAUD, GUY, et PHILLIPE VAN TIEGHEM: *Le Romantisme.* Paris: Hachette, 1952.

MISTRAL, GABRIELA [LUCILA GODOY ALCAYAGA]: «Recado sobre tres novelistas chilenos». *Las Ultimas Noticias,* XXXVI (28 de octubre, 1950), 3-4.

MONGUIÓ, LUIS: «Reflexiones sobre un aspecto de la novela hispanoamericana actual», in *La novela iberoamericana.* Albuquerque: University of New Mexico Press, 1952, pp. 91-104.

MONTESINOS, JOSÉ F.: «Modernismo, esperpentismo o las dos evasiones». *Revista de Occidente,* Nos. 44-45 (noviembre-diciembre, 1966), 146-65.

MOORE, HENRY T.: *Twentieth Century German Literature.* New York: Basic Books, 1967.

MORDELL, ALBERT: *The Erotic Motive in Literature.* Rev. ed. New York: Collier, 1962.

MORETIC, YERKO, and CARLOS ORELLANA: *El nuevo cuento realista chileno.* Santiago: Universitaria, 1962.

MUIR, EDWIN: *Structure of the Novel.* London: Hogarth Press, 1928.

NERVO, AMADO: *Sus mejores poemas.* Selección de Eduardo Barrios and Roberto Meza Fuentes. Santiago: Nascimento, [192?].

NIETZSCHE, FRIEDRICH: *Sämtliche Werke [Complete Works].* München: Hanser, 1960.

— *Werke in drei Banden [Work in Three Parts].* München: Hanser, 1965.

NOAILLES, ANNA ELIZABETH (DE BRANCOVAN): *Le Visage émerveillé.* Paris: Calmann-Lévy, 1904.

La novela iberoamericana. Memoria del Quinto Congreso del Instituto Internacional de Literatura Iberoamericana. Ed. Arturo Torres-Ríoseco. Albuquerque: University of New Mexico Press, 1952.

ONETTI, JUAN CARLOS: *Cuentos completos.* Buenos Aires: Centro Editor de América Latina, 1967.

— *El pozo.* 3rd ed. Montevideo: Arca, 1965.

ORREGO LUCO, LUIS: *Casa grande.* 2nd ed. Santiago: Zig-Zag, 1961.

ORTEGA Y GASSET, JOSÉ: «Ideas sobre la novela», in *Obras completas,* III, 387-90. Madrid: Revista de Occidente, 1962.

PASCAL, BLAISE: *Pensées.* Brunschvicq ed. Paris: Garnier, 1958.

PÉREZ DE AYALA, RAMÓN: *Principios y finales de la novela.* Madrid: Taurus, 1958.

— *Tinieblas en las cumbres.* Madrid: Castalia, 1971.

The Philosophy of Nietzsche. New York: Modern Library, 1937.

The Philosophy of Schopenhauer. Ed. Irwin Edman. New York: Modern Library, 1956.

Poems of Góngora. Ed. R. O. Jones. Cambridge: Cambridge U. P., 1966.

Poetas modernistas hispanoamericanos. Ed. Carlos García Prada. Madrid: Ed. Cultura Hispánica, 1956.

The Poetry of France. Ed. Alan M. Boase. London: Methuen, 1952.

The Portable Nietzsche. Ed., trans. Walter Kaufmann. New York: Viking Press, 1954.

PORTUONDO, JOSÉ ANTONIO: «El rasgo predominante en la novela hispanoamericana», in *La novela iberoamericana.* Albuquerque: University of New Mexico Press, 1952, pp. 79-87.

PRADO, PEDRO: *Alsino.* 5th ed. Santiago: Nascimento, 1951.

— *Flores de Cardo,* in *El llamado del mundo...* Santiago: Universitaria, 1971.

PRAZ, MARIO: *The Neurotic in Literature.* Cambridge: Cambridge U. P., 1965.

— *The Romantic Agony.* 2nd ed. London: Oxford U. P., 1951.

Prose for Borges. Ed. Charles Newman and Mary Kinzie. Evanston: Northwestern U. P., 1972.

RAMEAU, JEAN: *La Rose de Grenade.* Paris: Paul Offendorf, 1894.

Relations of Literary Studies. Ed. James Thorpe. New York: *PMLA,* 1967.

RICHARDS I. A.: *Practical Criticism: A Study of Literary Judgment.* 2nd ed. London: Kegan Paul, Trench, Trubner, 1924.

RIVERA, JOSÉ EUSTASIO: *La vorágine.* 9th ed. Buenos Aires: Losada, 1967.

ROBBE-GRILLET, ALAIN: *For a New Novel: Essays on Fiction.* Trans. Richard Howard. New York: Grove Press, 1965.

RODÓ, JOSÉ ENRIQUE: *Ariel.* Ed. Gordon Brotherston. Cambridge: Cambridge U. P., 1967.

RODRÍGUEZ FERNÁNDEZ, MARIO: *El modernismo en Chile y en Hispanoamérica.* Santiago: Instituto de Literatura Chilena, 1967.

RODRÍGUEZ MONEGAL, EMIR: «Juan Carlos Onetti y la novela rioplatense». *Número,* Nos. 13-14 (marzo-junio, 1951), 175-88.

ROGERS, ROBERT: *The Double in Literature.* Detroit: Wayne State U. P., 1970.

ROGGIANO, ALFREDO A.: «El modernismo y la novela en la América Hispana», in *La novela iberoamericana.* Albuquerque: University of New Mexico Press, 1952, pp. 27-45.

ROSENBLATT, LOUISE: *Literature as Exploration.* New York: Appleton, 1948.

ROSS, STEPHEN D.: *Literature and Philosophy: An Analysis of the Philosophical Novel.* New York: Appleton-Century-Crofts, 1969.

SÁBATO, ERNESTO: *El escritor y sus fantasmas.* 3rd ed. Buenos Aires: Aguilar, 1967.

— *Sobre héroes y tumbas.* 4th ed. Buenos Aires: Sudamericana, 1965.

— *El túnel.* Buenos Aires: Sudamericana, 1969.

SAINT-PIERRE, BERNARDIN DE: *Paul et Virginie.* Paris: Nelson, n. d.

SÁNCHEZ, LUIS ALBERTO: *Proceso y contenido de la novela hispanoamericana.* Madrid: Gredos, 1953.

SARTRE, JEAN-PAUL: «A propos de *Le Bruit et la fureur;* la temporalité chez Faulkner». *Situations I* (1947), 70-81.

— «Qu'est-ce que la littérature?». *Les Temps Modernes,* II (février-juillet, 1947), 770-885.

SCHWARTZ, KESSEL: *A New History of Spanish American Fiction.* 2 vols. Coral Gables, Florida: University of Miami Press, 1972.

SCHOPENHAUER, ARTHUR: *Essays and Aphorisms.* Sel., trans., intro. R. J. Hollingdale. Harmondsworth, Middlesex: Penguin, 1970.

SCHULMAN, IVÁN, *et al.: Coloquio sobre la novela hispanoamericana.* México: Fondo de Cultura Económica, 1967.

SHAW, DONALD L.: «Baroja y Mallea: Algunos puntos de contacto». *Actas del Tercer Congreso Internacional de Hispanistas.* México: Colegio de México, 1970, 847-52.

— *A Literary History of Spain: The Nineteenth Century.* London: Ernest Benn, 1972.

— «*Modernismo:* A Contribution to the Debate». *Bulletin of Hispanic Studies,* XLIV, No. 3 (July, 1967), 195-202.

— «Towards the Understanding of Spanish Romanticism». *Modern Language Review,* Vol. 58 (1963), 190-95.

SILVA CASTRO, RAÚL: *Los cuentistas chilenos.* Santiago: Zig-Zag, n. d.

SMITH, VERITY: *Ramón del Valle-Inclán.* New York: Twayne, 1973.

SOBEJANO, GONZALO: *Nietzsche en España.* Madrid: Gredos, 1967.

SOR JUANA INÉS DE LA CRUZ: *Obras escogidas.* 8th ed. Buenos Aires: Espasa-Calpe, 1951.

Spanish Lyrics of the Golden Age. Ed. P. D. Tetterborn. London: Bell, 1952.

STENDHAL [MARIE-HENRI BEYLE]: *De l'Amour.* Paris: Garnier, 1959.

— *La Chartreuse de Parme.* Paris: Ed. du Seuil, 1969.

— *Lucien Leuwen.* Paris: Fernand Hazan, 1950.

— *Le Rouge et le noir.* Paris: Livre de Poche, 1958.

STEVENSON, ROBERT LOUIS: *The Strange Case of Dr. Jekyll and Mr. Hyde.* New York: Airmont, 1964.

TORRE, GUILLERMO DE: *Doctrina y estética literaria.* Madrid: Guadarrama, 1970.

TORRES BODET, JAIME: *La educación sentimental.* Madrid: Espasa-Calpe, [1929].

UNAMUNO Y JUGO, MIGUEL DE: *Del sentimiento trágico de la vida.* 9th ed. Buenos Aires: Espasa-Calpe, 1950.

— *En torno al casticismo,* in *Obras completas,* Vol. III, pp. 155-303. Madrid: Afrodisio Aguado, 1958.

— *Tres novelas ejemplares y un prólogo.* 9th ed. Madrid: Espasa-Calpe, 1958.

URBISTONDO, VICENTE: *El naturalismo en la novela chilena.* Santiago: Ed. Andrés Bello, 1966.

VALLE-INCLÁN, RAMÓN DEL: *Sonata de primavera y Sonata de estío.* 2nd ed. Buenos Aires: Espasa-Calpe, 1945.

— *Sonata de otoño y Sonata de invierno.* Buenos Aires: Losada, 1938.

VARGAS LLOSA, MARIO: *La ciudad y los perros.* Barcelona: Seix Barral, 1962.

VERDUGO, IBER H.: «Perspectivas de la actual novela hispanoamericana». *Mundo Nuevo* (octubre, 1968), 82-83.

WAIN, JOHN: *Sprightly Running.* London: Macmillan, 1962.

WALKER, JOHN: «*Coloquio sobre la novela hispanoamericana,* por Iván Schulman et al.». *Erasmus,* Vol. 22, No. 6 (March, 1970), 301-06.

— «*A New History of Spanish American Fiction,* by Kessel Schwartz». *Queen's Quarterly,* LXXX, No. 2 (1973), 306-08.

WELLEK, RENÉ, and AUSTIN WARREN: *Theory of Literature.* New York: Harcourt, Brace, 1949.

— *Teoría literaria.* Versión española de José María Gimeno. Madrid: Gredos, 1966.

YÁÑEZ, AGUSTÍN: *Al filo del agua.* 10th ed. México: Porrúa, 1969.

ZIOLKOWSKI, THEODORE: *The Novels of Herman Hesse: A Study in Theme and Structure.* Princeton: Princeton U. P., 1965.

ZUM FELDE, ALBERTO: *Indice crítico de la literatura hispanoamericana. La narrativa.* Tomo II. México: Guaranía, 1959.

INDEX

Rogers, Robert, 167 n, 184.
Roggiano, Alfredo A., 184.
Rojas, Manuel, 4, 18.
Ronsard, Pierre de, 143.
Rosas, Juan Manuel, 86.
Rosenblatt, Louise, 57, 184.
Ross, Stephen D., 184.
Rossel, Milton, 1, 3, 21 n, 74, 83, 91, 128 n, 151 n, 161, 174 n, 175, 177.
Rousseau, Jean-Jacques, 10, 11.
Ruiz Vernacci, Enrique, 91 n, 152, 152 n, 153, 163, 178.
Rulfo, Juan, 173.

Sábato, Ernesto, 85, 166 n, 170, 170 n, 184.
St Augustine of Hippo, 43, 45.
St Francis of Assisi, 24, 45, 172, 182.
St John of the Cross, 45, 121, 135, 142 n.
St Paul, 43.
Saint-Pierre, Bernardin de, 184.
Saint-Simon, Comte de, 12.
St Teresa of Avila, 45, 121, 125, 137, 153.
St Thomas Aquinas, 45.
Sánchez, Luis Alberto, 78, 184.
Sánchez, Porfirio, 178.
Santiván, Fernando, 37, 74, 78, 83, 149 n, 178.
Sarduy, Severo, 163.
Sarmiento, Domingo Faustino, 86, 90 n.
Sartre, Jean-Paul, 44 n, 55 n, 63, 104 n, 184.
Schiller, Friedrich, 11, 23.
Schopenhauer, Arthur, 11, 20 n, 22, 23, 24-31, 32, 36, 43, 44, 49, 50, 51, 52, 57, 60, 61, 64, 66, 112, 167 n, 184.
Schorer, Mark, 172.
Schulman, Iván, 165 n, 166, 184.
Schwartz, Kessel, 184.
Sepúlveda Layton, Carlos, 175.
Shaw, Donald L., 16 n, 48 n, 49 n, 53 n, 69, 165 n, 184.
Shaw, George Bernard, 14.
Silva, José Asunción, 96, 108, 137.
Silva Castro, Raúl, 1, 3, 68 n, 74, 79, 81 n, 83, 84, 91, 126, 130, 134 n, 161, 178, 184.
Smith, Verity, 184.
Sobejano, Gonzalo, 35 n, 49 n, 184.
Sócrates, 36 n.
Sor Juana Inés de la Cruz, 39, 156 n, 184.
Souvirón, José María, 175.
Spell, Jefferson Rea, 1, 4 n, 74, 79, 131 n, 153, 178.
Spencer, Herbert, 12, 169.

Spinoza, Baruch, 36.
Stendhal [Marie-Henri Beyle], 36 n, 73, 85, 86, 174, 184.
Stephens, Doris T., 178.
Stevenson, Robert Louis, 167.
Swedenborg, Emanuel, 159.

Tetterborn, P. D., 142 n, 184.
Thorpe, James, 183.
Torre, Guillermo de, 55, 185.
Torres Bodet, Jaime, 11 n, 185.
Torres-Ríoseco, Arturo, 1, 3, 3 n, 4, 10 n, 11 n, 15 n, 54, 84, 91, 126, 126 n, 132, 132 n, 153, 161, 171, 178, 183.

Unamuno y Jugo, Miguel de, 7 n, 48, 48 n, 50, 51, 52, 54, 55, 56, 92, 95 n, 167, 185.
Urbistondo, Vicente, 185.

Valéry, Paul, 167 n.
Valle-Inclán, Ramón del, 126 n, 131 n, 153, 156, 162 n, 185.
Vargas Llosa, Mario, 163, 169, 185.
Vasconcelos, José, 7.
Vázquez-Bigi, Angel Manuel, 1, 1 n, 3, 3 n, 4, 5, 11 n, 21, 22 n, 23 n, 27, 32, 45 n, 49, 49 n, 74, 84, 85, 89 n, 91, 129 n, 161, 161 n, 178.
Vega, Manuel, 154 n.
Verdugo, Iber H., 172 n, 185.
Vicuña McKenna, Benjamín, 90 n.
Vidal, Hernán, 165, 166, 178.
Vigny, Alfred Victor de, 126.
Virgil, 90.

Wagner, Richard, 28, 159.
Wain, John, 185.
Walker, John, 178, 179.
Warren, Austin, 64 n, 185.
Wellek, René, 64 n, 185.
Wellman, Donna Sue, 178.
Wilde, Oscar, 14, 79.
Winckelmann, Johann Joachim, 34 n.
Woolf, Virginia, 163, 164.
Wordsworth, William, 58, 143.

Yáñez, Agustín, 166 n, 167, 185.

Ziolkowski, Theodore, 185.
Zamacois, Eduardo, 15 n.
Zola, Emile, 12, 36, 80, 169.
Zum Felde, Alberto, 78, 185.